Social Policy in China

Social Policy in China
From State-Led to Market-Led Economy

EDITED BY
Weizhen Dong

Rock's Mills Press
Oakville, Ontario
2019

Published by
Rock's Mills Press
www.rocksmillspress.com

Copyright © 2019 by Weizhen Dong
All rights reserved.

For information regarding this book, please contact Rock's Mills Press at customer.service@rocksmillspress.com.

ISBN-13: 978-1-77244-165-9 (paperback)

Contents

Preface
Understanding China through Its Social Policy ... v
WEIZHEN DONG

Chapter 1
Family Planning Policy in China ... 1
XIAOCHUN QIAO

Chapter 2
Population Mobility and Migration Policy ... 21
CHANGXING ZHAO AND WEIZHEN DONG

Chapter 3
Hukou System and Rural Migrant Workers' Assimilation ... 44
WEIZHEN DONG AND CHANGXING ZHAO

Chapter 4
Migrant Workers' Healthcare Access and Policy Implications ... 68
WEIZHEN DONG

Chapter 5
Aging-Related Welfare Policies in China ... 80
BAOZHEN LUO AND HEYING ZHAN

Chapter 6
Aging and Elder Care in Shanghai ... 98
XIN YANG AND WEIZHEN DONG

Chapter 7
Housing Policy: A Comparative Study of Shanghai and St. Petersburg ... 109
XIAOWEN LU

Chapter 8
Employment and Income Policy ... 124
WEIZHEN DONG AND XIN LE

Chapter 9
Education Policy in China ... 146
WEIZHEN DONG, LICHUN QIN, AND ZHENNAN WANG

Chapter 10
Healthcare Policy in Urban China ... 170
WEIZHEN DONG, CHUN CHEN, AND LI SHEN

Chapter 11
Healthcare Policy in Rural China ... 188
WEIZHEN DONG, QICHENG JIANG, SHANFA YANG, LIDAN WANG,
AND ZEHAN PAN

Chapter 12
Healthcare Policy and Reforms in Hong Kong ... 211
ALEX JINGWEI HE

About the Contributors ... 225

Preface
Understanding China through Its Social Policy

I have had the idea for this book for some time. It was triggered by the misperceptions about China I heard when living in Asia, Europe, and North America. During my many years of international experiences, I learned about different countries' socioeconomic issues. I found that knowing about a country's social policies could help us to understand its general socioeconomic reality and developmental trajectory, since social policies often have redistributive functions that help to protect vulnerable social groups. Therefore, social policies must reflect the core social values of the nation where these policies are formulated and implemented. Social policy is the best introduction to a country's basic social principles and the question of who is "in" and who is "out" in the country's development and transformation. My advantages in working on such a book are that I am familiar with most of the social policies in question, and that I have an excellent professional network. I was able to identify potential contributors for the book, and knew that these scholars could provide excellent work for this endeavor.

This book is for those who are keen to understand China—students, scholars, entrepreneurs, government officials, businessmen, or an individual with a curious mind. I hope this volume can serve as a bridge between our readers and China. Our readers will find that although China is old—a country with thousands of years of history and cultural heritage—China is also actually quite young: the People's Republic of China is just approaching its seventieth anniversary. In the past 69 years, there are lessons to be learned, there are successes to be celebrated, and there are also a lot of "growing pains". At a time when China is becoming more visible in world affairs, this book serves the purpose of addressing global curiosity about China, answering questions such as: What kind of socioeconomic system does China have? What are the main social welfare benefits the Chinese people enjoy? What are the main social issues facing China and the Chinese people? Is China a communist country? The current climate makes understanding among different countries and peoples more important than ever before.

The contributors of this book are social policy scholars from Canada, China, and the United States. Working on the project was relatively straightforward, since all authors have studied the policies and had lived experiences. We are fully aware, however, that studying social policy is like aiming at a moving target. Even while working on the manuscript, most of the chapters had to be updated due to new policy changes.

China has undergone major social and economic transitions since the establishment of the People's Republic in 1949, when Mao Zedong's Communist Party transformed China from a semi-feudal and semi-colonial country to an independent socialist nation. The core value of the new People's Republic was socialist egalitarianism. The revolutionary transformation, through its social policies, was implemented shortly after Mao's Communist Party seized power. The new government transferred ownership of the means of production in the country to the state or to the collective public. The dramatic social change broke down traditional class barriers and promoted new social norms—for example, that manufacturing workers and agricultural laborers were to be highly respected and admired, and that equal value and equal pay for different occupations and professions were to be honored. Although China had very limited resources and few trained managerial personnel, the government's policies ensured citizens' access to housing, education, healthcare and childcare with no or minor costs. The main accomplishments of the Chinese government, besides economic development, include the rapid improvement of the population's health status, with the near-doubling of the population's life expectancy and the elimination of major infectious diseases, as well as the establishment of a multi-tier public healthcare network, and a sharply reduced illiteracy rate.

China's economic reforms, begun in late 1978, changed major social policies that resulted in a dramatic social and economic transition from a state-led planned economy to a market-led economy. This transition was nothing short of astonishing. From the end of full and lifetime employment to the relaxation of rural-urban and other cross-regional migration, from the end of government-provided or minor-cost rental housing to fees for education and other services, the transition affected all aspects of citizens' lives—positively or negatively.

Economic reform in China started with the privatization of land and the implementation of the household responsibility system, along with the emergence of village and township enterprises in rural China. The immediate result of rural economic reform was a growing number of surplus labourers. Thus, relaxation of restrictions on population mobility became necessary. Massive numbers of young and untrained villagers began to move into cities and towns to seek employment. Providing this population with decent housing, healthcare, appropriate jobs, education for their children, and a sense of belonging was quite challenging, especially when the size of the population is in the hundreds of millions. In reality, the proper assimilation of migrant workers is still an ongoing process.

Each country goes through its own stages of development; China is no exception. China's social policy evolution reveals its societal transformation. If the redistributive policies were not designed with the poor and vulnerable in mind and without social justice consideration, they could institutionalize social inequality and legitimize social segregation. China's new policy initiatives since the beginning of the economic reforms marked a dramatic shift toward marketization and privatization. Thus, development in China in recent decades is not limited just to the country's economy; it has fundamentally changed the country's core social value system. Different administrations implementing new policies to meet societal demands is normal practice; however, major policy turns in China brought hardship to some social groups. For example, once the policy of full and lifetime employment ended and the power to hire and fire was given to individual work-units, a massive layoff of middle-aged workers, especially women, occurred. Those who had been earning basic wages for their entire lives now had to concern themselves with the cost of their children's education, healthcare expenses, and planning for retirement—all of which had been previously guaranteed by the government. The government's withdrawal from its social welfare commitments and the rapid widening of income gaps have been most harmful to social values.

China implemented full and lifetime employment policies with egalitarian income distribution in the early days of the People's Republic. After three decades, the country changed to a market-oriented employment and income distribution policy in the name of economic reform. The consequence of the relaxation of restrictions on hiring and firing and the deregulation of income distribution is income inequality. China is now among the countries with the largest income gap between rich and poor in the world. In the transitional era, China faces a dilemma: growth-driven policies push for marketization and tolerate unfair competition, while interest groups—political and market elites—form alliances to harvest the fruits of the nation's economic development for themselves.

Population has been China's major concern in its social and economic development. Furthermore, population pressures often dictated social policies. Therefore, it is vitally crucial for one to make sense of the challenges China faces because of the size of its population. Family planning policy has been among the most important of all social policies in China. Its "one-child policy" may be understood in the context of the country's limited resources and rapid population growth in the early decades of the new China. As a socialist nation, it also faced external obstacles, particularly during the Cold War era. Family planning policy in China has gone through quite a number of twists and turns in its evolution. For example, the implementation of the one-child policy reduced population growth, but many are now concerned with the population aging; thus, the recent "two-child policy". This policy change is partly based on traditional Chinese eldercare ideology and also as a potential answer to the problems posed by an aging society.

The resource limitations during the early years of the People's Republic led the Chinese government to set up a household registration system to distribute goods, housing, and assign jobs. China went through waves of restrictions and relaxation of restrictions on population movements at different stages of the country's development. Specifically, it transitioned from allowing almost no migration to nationwide open migration, which resulted in the rapid urbanization of the rural population in recent decades. China's household registration or *Hukou* system played a vital role in social resource distribution during the early years of the new but poor socialist nation. Since it is still an important system that determines one's access to education, healthcare and other social benefits, the *Hukou* system plays an important part in rural migrant workers' assimilation in urban China, or is a key barrier to assimilation. Migrant workers' vulnerability in their urban life calls for a better and more people-centered approach to the wellbeing of those new city dwellers. In fact China is in need of a citizenship-based universal social security system instead of the current scenario in which different social groups are entitled or not entitled to certain social welfare benefits.

Healthcare policy reforms have been a constant in China in recent decades.

However, the policy changes have not gone smoothly. Urban residents used to receive access to healthcare for free or at a minor cost, and medical charges were limited to the cost of medicine with government-regulated below-cost prices. Healthcare reforms started with the government (1) introducing market forces into the realm of medical care, (2) withdrawing its financial backing of the medical care delivery system, and (3) sharing medical care costs with individual citizens through various healthcare insurance packages for different population groups. Thus, different healthcare coverage for different socioeconomic groups is still a troubling reality.

China provided housing to urban residents in the same way the Union of Soviet Socialist Republics (USSR) did during the socialist era. Full employment made the provision of housing through the workplace feasible. Once the market reforms privatized and commoditized residential housing, most of the housing in China became privately owned or market rentals. This major policy change resulted in both gains and losses for citizens, and many experienced the "growing pains" of the transition. This can be said of education policy and healthcare policy reforms as well.

Education policy in China has been reformed a number of times, and has evolved from a state-sponsored educational system with minor or no tuition to high costs for schooling, from a policy of education for all to the emergence of numerous expensive elite schools. The growth of China's education sector has been quite impressive in the past few decades. That growth can be measured both in terms of quantity and quality, from pre-school to post-secondary institutions. Meanwhile, China accepts a large number of foreign students into its educational programs, and many Chinese students also go overseas to study each year. Such exchanges provide China's educational system with both challenges and opportunities.

Aging has become a pressing social issue, in both urban centers and rural villages. When the first generation of parents affected by the one-child policy became senior citizens, the traditional arrangement of family members caring for their elders became untenable. Who should care for the elderly is now an urgent question looking for an answer. It is particularly critical in rural China. Rural households may still have multiple children but rural-urban migration left only the old, sick and the very young at home. Out-migration broke the traditional self-reliant household structure, while no sufficient social services are available to fill the void. Developing new social infrastructure for meeting the growing eldercare demands and other needed services for seniors in both urban and rural areas is a pressing task.

Hong Kong was returned to China's rule twenty-odd years ago, on July 1, 1997; however, its previous system and social policies remain intact. This book's inclusion of a chapter on healthcare policy in Hong Kong aims to show how China's "one country, two systems" policy has been put in practice. It is nonetheless still unclear whether this practice has placated those who identify with the city or created a major challenge to national unity.

As in many other countries, social conflicts in China include the contradictions between the haves and the have-nots, the powerful and powerless, as well as regional disparities. Social policies can address these issues through effective redistribution of income and resources, and a strong universal social security system. Reducing social inequality and inequity can ensure the country's peaceful development. How to achieve growth with justice is a serious task facing the Chinese government. President Xi declared at the 19th Congress of the Communist Party of China in October 2017 that the main social issues facing the Chinese are the imbalance of development and insufficient material goods for the people, and that China has entered into a new era. This signals that the government's new focus for the next five years will be the improvement of the quality of life of its citizens. It is expected that some social policies will be further reformed. One hopes that policymakers will consider social values, public interests, and social equity in future social policy modifications, and that oriental wisdom will lead to peace and prosperity in the new century—for the people of China and beyond.

China is often referred to as "communist China", particularly in the western media and among western politicians. It is partly due to the fact that the ruling party of China is named the Communist Party, and partly due to people's limited knowledge of China and its governing party. It is true that China was a socialist nation during Mao's administration, which did intend to eventually make China a communist paradise; however, the material wealth to implement a full-fledged needs-based distribution system was missing. Therefore, it was never a communist country. In a poor country with a large population, Mao's government created a system that made sure most people would be provided with at least adequate quantities of food and other necessities. The household registration system and food rationing arrangement emerged as a national coping strategy, when the government was fundamentally believed to care for the masses and the members of the Communist Party were proletarians whose mission was to "serve the people".

However, post-Mao China took a very different turn, one that departed from its founding fathers' socialist principles. Market forces have entered all spheres of Chinese life—fortunately or unfortunately, depending on one's position in the society. China's market transformation to some was a sunrise, but to others a sunset: some became rich and powerful, and some lost ground. A series of social policies determined who gained and who lost in the transition. Even the Communist Party of China's membership eligibility has been changed since November 2002, when the General Secretary of the Chinese Communist Party called on his party to accept capitalists as well. Thus, since economic growth became the main goal of the regime four decades ago, China and its ruling party have deviated from communism and socialism. China is now on the path of "socialism with Chinese characteristics". Is it a redefined version of "socialism", a pragmatic socialism, or non-socialism? People familiar with China's main social policies will be able to draw their own conclusion.

The absence of government redistributive policy directives causes many social problems. In a country where the variances in regional development and wealth distribution are so great, well-formulated policies and central government funding can make a difference in social justice. In fact, it is not the absolute wealth but the distribution of wealth in a country that determines the wellbeing of its citizens. Nowadays widespread social inequality can be observed through Chinese news items and television reality shows. On the housing front, home renovation shows reveal how many households are living in unhealthy, inadequate, or substandard homes (e.g., *Mengxiang Gaizhao Jia, Xingfu Gaizhao Jia*). In terms of regional disparity, some shows exposed the rural poor's hardships and their struggles in every aspect of life raw and bare (e.g., *Women Zai Xingdong, Ran Shijie Tingjian*). The sustainability and quality of *Xiwang Xiaoxue* (Hope Primary Schools)—a charity program for children's education in poverty-stricken areas—is a concern. Young adults who cannot afford a university education due to financial difficulties are a familiar story as well. Migrant workers' access to social benefits has been a decades-long unresolved issue. Pension income disparity has also been a controversial area: retirees who worked as public servants, worked in government-affiliated institutions, and worked in enterprises receive very different amounts of pension income.

Knowing that socioeconomic inequality among social groups in a country is evident and persistent, and that most of it was caused by the authorities' actions or inactions, we therefore know what kind of society it is, no matter what or how it is being labeled. Indeed, there is no better way of understanding a country than learning its main social policies.

This book project coincided with China's Belt and Road initiative. This initiative is a development strategy and framework that focuses on connectivity and cooperation among countries in Eurasia, Africa, and beyond. The very meaning of this initiative is to connect peoples and unite nations for the common goal of economic growth, pursuing sustainable development, and improving the quality of peoples' lives. As the managing director of the International Monetary Fund, Christine Lagarde, has said, this initiative "is about connecting cultures, communities, economies, and people. It is about rejuvenating ancient trade routes and building new ones. It is also about adding new economic flavors by creating infrastructure projects that are based on 21st-century expertise and governance standards" (2017). UN Secretary-General Antonio Guterres says the Belt and Road initiative is making economic globalization more balanced, inclusive and harmonious. And the initiative is in line with the United Nations' 2030 Agenda for Sustainable Development (Wang, 2017). The Belt and Road initiative vows to bring together nations and improve the infrastructure and overall quality of life in relevant countries, especially developing countries. Meanwhile, mutual understanding between China and the participating countries will be the key to success. I hope this book can contribute to this important cause as well.

Weizhen Dong
Waterloo, Ontario, Canada

REFERENCES

Lagarde, Christine (2017, May 14). Belt and Road Initiative: Proven Policies and New Economic Links. Speech at the Belt and Road Forum, Beijing. https://www.imf.org/en/News/Articles/2017/05/14/sp051417-belt-and-road-initiative-proven-policies-and-new-economic-links.

Wang, Xinxin (2017, May 13). UN secretary-general: Belt and Road improves globalization. Speech at the Belt and Road Forum, Beijing. https://news.cgtn.com/news/3d457a4d32677a4d/share_p.html

Chapter 1
Family Planning Policy in China

Xiaochun Qiao

ABSTRACT
The objective of this chapter is not only to portray but also to explore the causes of the long-term fertility transition in China. The data used for the earlier period are from the One Per Thousand National Fertility Survey in 1982 and the National Fertility and Contraceptive Survey in 1988. Both were retrospective surveys, in which the respondent women were asked to recall their childbearing experiences. The data used for the later period are mostly from China's censuses. Unfortunately, data collected after 1990 were severely underreported. In order to obtain acceptable total fertility rates (TFR), we estimated TFR from government-reported crude birth rates (CBR) after 1990. In this article we focus on the causes and effects of family planning policies in relation to the fertility transition, and consider how the policies shifted and how the modified policy caused the change in fertility.

1. INTRODUCTION
China is not only the largest country in the world but also a country whose fertility has experienced tremendous transitions since the 1950s. The family planning policy in China was formally and universally implemented in the early 1970s. The policy was adjusted several times, from two-child to one-child, to one-and-a-half-child, to two-child for one member of a couple from a one-child family, and then finally back to two-child again. The objective of this chapter is to examine changes in family planning policy, with a focus on the reasons why the policy changed and what was achieved. First, the early phases of China's population policies will be introduced. Second, the start of formal family planning policy and its changes or modifications will be discussed. Finally, the new policies of 2013 and 2015 and their results will be analyzed.

2. EARLY POPULATION POLICY (1949–1972)
In pre-revolutionary China, population was characterized by a high crude birth rate (CBR), a high crude death rate (CDR), and a low natural increase rate (NIR). Between 1840 and 1949, the population grew from 412 million to 542 million, the rate of increase averaging only 2.6 per thousand for the 109 intervening years. It was estimated that the birth rate in 1936 was as high as 38.9 per thousand, but as the death rate was also very high—27.6 per thousand—the net increase rate stood at no more than 11.3 per thousand.

After the new China was founded in 1949, the country's economy recovered rapidly and living conditions were improved enormously. Under such circumstances, policies pursued by the state encouraged and favored a higher number of births. For example, state-owned-sector employees were given an extra allotment for the birth of every new baby after 1949. Promotional sayings, such as "Families could not afford many children in the old society and only the new society can guarantee the livelihood of families with many children", encouraged the concept of "many children" within the new social order. From 1949 to 1957, the birth rate remained at a level of 30 or more per thousand, the same as in old China. However, the death rate started declining in that period. For the first time in China's history the death rate dropped to 10.8 per thousand in 1957, from 20 per thousand in 1949. As a result, the speed of China's population increase accelerated considerably, averaging as much as 20 per thousand annually, and the net increase in population was enormous, amounting to over 10 million a year. The total fertility rate (TFR) on average was 6 children per woman during this time (see Table 1).

Table 1. Total Population, CBR, CDR, NIR, and TFR, 1949–1972

Year	Total Population (millions)	CBR (%)	CDR (%)	NIR (%)	TFR
1949	541.7	36.0	20.0	16.0	6.14
1950	552.0	37.0	18.0	19.0	5.81
1951	563.0	37.8	17.8	20.0	5.70
1952	574.8	37.0	17.0	20.0	6.47
1953	588.0	37.0	14.0	23.0	6.05
1954	602.7	38.0	13.2	24.8	6.28
1955	614.6	32.6	12.3	20.3	6.26
1956	628.3	31.9	11.4	20.5	5.85
1957	645.6	34.0	10.8	23.2	6.41
1958	660.0	29.2	12.0	17.2	5.68
1959	672.1	24.8	14.6	10.2	4.30
1960	662.1	20.9	25.4	-4.6	4.02
1961	658.6	18.0	14.2	3.8	3.29
1962	673.0	37.0	10.0	27.0	6.02
1963	691.7	43.4	10.0	33.3	7.50
1964	705.0	39.1	11.5	27.6	6.18
1965	725.4	37.0	9.5	28.4	6.08
1966	745.4	35.1	8.8	26.2	6.26
1967	763.7	34.0.	8.4	25.5	5.31
1968	785.3	35.6	8.2	27.4	6.45
1969	806.7	34.1	8.0	26.1	5.72
1970	830.0	33.4	7.6	25.8	5.81
1971	852.3	30.7	7.3	23.3	5.44
1972	871.8	29.8	7.6	22.2	4.98

Source: CBR, CDR and NIR from National Statistical Bureau, *China Statistical Yearbook*; TFR from Yao and Yin, *Basic Data of China's Population*, Data Usser Service, Population Press, 1994

Adopting the Soviet Union's socialist state model, China implemented a planned economic system in which all enterprises belonged to the state, especially in the urban areas, which meant that the government assumed responsibility for providing necessities, including food, clothes, housing, jobs, healthcare, pensions, etc. The government planned not only material production, but also arrangements for the livelihood of its citizens.

With rapid population increase, population pressure on government resources became increasingly evident in terms of improvement of people's living standards, education, housing, and medical care. Meanwhile, some educated women realized that the frequent pregnancies caused health problems, which seriously impacted their lives. Thus there was a growing demand for birth control among the general public, especially among women.

In 1953, the Government Administration Council, predecessor of the State Council, directed the Ministry of Health to assist the public with contraceptive measures. At the same time, it revised the relevant regulations to relax restrictions on induced abortion. In 1954, some women wrote to the government stating their unwillingness to have so many children and expressing the hope that the government would provide guidance on methods of contraception. Responding to such demands, government convened a forum on birth control in December 1954, at which it declared that the government endorsed birth control and that birth control should be promoted and not opposed. In 1956, the Ministry of Health launched an extensive campaign providing general information on contraception. In September, Premier Zhou Enlai pointed out in his "Report on the Proposals for the Second Five-Year Plan": "We agree that a due measure of birth control is desirable, and the Ministry of Health should, in cooperation with the other relevant institutions, carry out intelligent propaganda and adopt effective measures towards this end." In 1956, Chairman Mao Zedong mentioned that family planning should be promoted, particularly in densely populated regions. In 1957, he proposed that "there should also be a ten-year program for family planning" and "complete realization of family planning in the future" (Mao, 2001).

Under such circumstances, Professor Ma Yinchu, an economist, demographer and the President of Peking University at the time, realized that it was the right time for him to speak his mind on population control at a meeting of the People's Congress, after which he published an essay called "New Population Theory" in the *People's Daily* in 1957. He analyzed the various conflicts between excessive population increase and the acceleration of capital accumulation, the raising of productivity, the improvement of living standards, and the development of science, and advocated "improving the quality of the population and controlling its size" (Ma, 1957).

However, impacted by changes in the political climate, "Leftist" population theory gained predominance, and Professor Ma Yinchu was criticized publicly by the government in 1958. The idea that "the more people the better" resumed its priority. It was explicitly emphasized that there could be no population problems in socialist countries like China and Soviet Union. The government claimed that population problems only existed in capitalist countries, so that China did not have to fear rapid population growth, but should prepare favorable conditions for it. It was asserted that more people would provide greater human resources for economic development and accumulate more wealth, making it possible to develop the socialist economy at greater speed. As Karl Marx opposed Thomas Malthus, who had called for controlling population, all propositions concerning control of population growth were equated with Malthusianism and attributed to protesters against Marxism. Anyone who mentioned birth control ran the risk of being labeled Malthusian. Under such circumstances, not only Professor Ma Yinchu but also some other scholars were subjected to criticism. As the professional discussion become political, no scholar dared to touch the topic of population, which became taboo in China.

The "Great Leap Forward" (*Da Yue Jin*) movement started in 1958, with the aim of catching up with advanced economies such as the United Kingdom and United States. In addition, the withdrawal of experts from the Soviet Union and a three-year-long series of natural disasters suddenly caused a huge decrease in the food supply. There were serious crop failures and a great number of people starved to death. This caused a sharp decline in the birth rate and a great increase of death rate, bringing the rate of natural increase down to negative levels (see Figure 1).

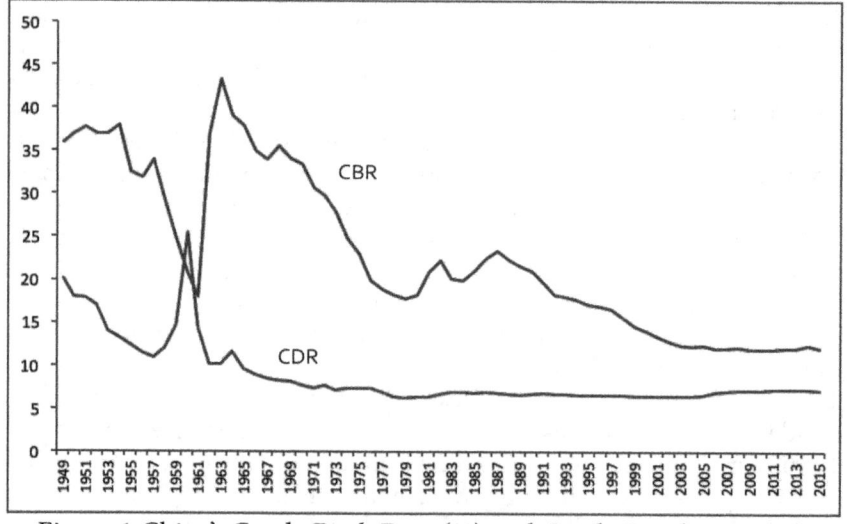

Figure 1 China's Crude Birth Rate (%) and Crude Death Rate (%), 1949 to 2015

Source: CBR, CDR and NIR come from National Statistical Bureau, *China Statistical Yearbook*, TFR before 1993 is from Yao and Yin, *Basic Data of China's Population*, Data User Service, Population Press, 1994; TFR after 1993 is estimated by the author.

By 1962, China's economy had recovered, and population growth rebounded. In 1964, the natural increase rate reached its peak, 33.3 per thousand, and TFR increased to 7.5 children per woman. It followed that the population pressure and problems again became more severe. In 1964, the state set up a special agency to take charge of matters pertaining to family planning: the family planning office of the State Council, along with its corresponding offices in each province, city and autonomous region. This laid the organizational basis for implementation of family planning in earnest and the control of population growth throughout China. Family planning at that time was mostly focused on urban and some relatively wealthier rural areas. But when the Cultural Revolution began in 1966, the work of the state family planning agencies came to a standstill, and China's population figures again soared.

The years from 1966 to 1971 were a period of sustained high birth rates and natural increase rates. This period's net annual increases in population were the highest in China's history. The government faced the challenge of a severe shortage of housing, grain and daily necessities, lack of spaces in kindergartens and schools, as well as a shortage of jobs (Qiao, 2016).

In summary, due to lack of population control and high population increase rates, China experienced two baby-boom waves since 1949. The first baby-boom caused an increase in population of 104 million from 1950 to 1958, a jump of 19.2 percent; while the second baby-boom led to an increase in population of 157 million, or 23.3 percent, from 1962 to 1970.

In 1971, the State Council declared that family planning measures should be strengthened, and in 1972, it further stressed that implementation of family planning would align the rate of population increase with national economic development.

3. THE INITIAL PERIOD OF FAMILY PLANNING (1973–1979)

The State Council set up a National Family Planning Leading Group in 1973. This marks a milestone in family planning in China. It was the first time that family planning was implemented nationwide, including both urban and rural areas. It was also the first time that family planning formally became a part of a national economic plan. Chairman Mao Zedong once more emphasized in 1974 that "population growth must be controlled". In the same year, the State Council's leading group for family planning, together with the ministry concerned, issued a circular to the effect that contraceptives were to be supplied free of charge. The universal family planning program started in 1973. Population policy at that time could be summed up as follows: "On the basis of vigorously developing production and raising the living standards of the people, the goal of the population policy is to develop universal medical and health care services, to strengthen mother-and-child care, to encourage late marriage and late child-bearing, to lower the death rate and, above all, to bring the birth rate under control. At the same time, however, all necessary treatment will be given to those suffering from infertility." Such a statement said nothing about the exact number of births which should be targeted even though late marriage, delayed child-bearing and fewer births were encouraged (Qiao, 2016).

In fact, the policy embodied the principle of combining state direction with voluntary action by the masses. On the one hand, the state formulated and implemented unified regulations to bring population growth within the orbit of state planning and to co-ordinate it with material production. It energetically supported family planning by providing financial aid, scientific techniques, medical personnel and materials. On the other hand, the general public was called on to discuss and revise the targets in the population plan, in order to link their own interests with those of the state and to pave the way for the realization of the state's population plans.

This practice avoided coercion and compulsion and the initiative of the masses was aroused. The requirements for family planning were summed up by the slogan: "Late, Long, and Few". "Late" meant that young people were required and expected to respond to the state's call and of their own accord delay their marriage date, that is, to practice late marriage. Although the state did not set any age standards for late marriage, stipulations were made in many localities. The lowest age of marriage was 20 for men and 18 for women based on the Marriage Law promulgated in the early 1950s. This also implied another requirement, that the married couple postpone child-bearing as long as possible. "Long" meant that the interval between births should be stretched out, preferably to about four years between the first child and the second. "Few" meant, quite simply, a smaller number of births. The government recommended "two children would be most suitable" during the initial phase of the family planning policy, and later (from 1978 to 1979) "at most two, best only one".

Under state guidance, various contraception methods were recommended and information was made available to encourage married couples to have fewer children. The number of people practicing birth control through contraception gradually increased from 13.05 million in 1971, to 21.28 million in 1974, and to 23.59 million in 1977.

In 1978, the First Session of the Fifth National People's Congress ratified the new Constitution in which it was explicitly stipulated that "The state advocates and encourages family planning" (Yang, 2001). This was the first time since the founding of the New China that family planning was affirmed constitutionally and became one of the fundamental duties of all citizens.

In this period, however, measures aiming at achieving the target of "two children per family" were limited almost exclusively to ideological education and promotion. Although the Constitution contained provisions on practicing family planning, no specific laws and regulations pertaining to population matters had yet been formulated. Thus, the realization of population targets depended almost entirely on government propaganda, mobilization, education, guidance, persuasion, explanation, and assistance, as well as on the people's cooperation, rather than on coercion.

Even though family planning had been promoted by the national government, there was still a lack of theoretical support for why a socialist country, like China, was acting legitimately in controlling population. In contrast, socialist economic theory, mainly derived from the Soviet Union and Marxist principles, clearly indicated that overpopulation only existed in capitalist countries, while the population law that applied to socialist countries was the law of continuous increase. In that case, family planning policy in China violated socialist theory, and was an offence against Marxist principles. Another obstacle was that in his book *Capital*, Marx strongly opposed the ideas of Malthus, who proposed birth control. As a Marxist, how could one stand against the ideas of Marx himself?

Thus, the Chinese government was eager to find a theory that would show that birth control was appropriate for socialist countries and consistent with Marxism. Under such circumstances, the government proposed to set up an institute for population research. The first Institute of Population Research was set up at Renmin (People's) University of China in January 1974. The original task for the Institute was to provide theoretical support for the family planning program. Obstacles to population research existing since Professor Ma Yinchu's times were removed, and population research became widespread in China. Support for facilitating demographic training and research from the United Nations Fund for Population Activities (UNFPA) in the 1980s and 1990s also stimulated the development of population studies in China, and more population institutes have been set up since then.

Searching through the works of Karl Marx and Friedrich Engels, Chinese scholars finally found some evidence to provide support for the implementation of family planning in China. Marx held that social production embodies both the production of material goods and production of human beings themselves. Both forms of production have existed side-by-side, relying on and constraining each other, ever since the dawn of human society. Furthermore, material production is closely and intrinsically linked with the production of human beings themselves. The population, as a body of producers, must increase at a rate commensurate with the increase in means of material production and maintain a proper ratio in relation to the latter, if social production as a whole and the national economy are to develop at a reasonable pace (Liu, 1985).

After the political obstacle was removed, propaganda and implementation of family planning policy became more efficient, which led to very effective results in reduced fertility. TFR dropped from 5.44 in 1971 to 2.24 in 1980, one of the fastest declines anywhere in the world (Qiao, 1995). Apart from the effectiveness of propaganda, the two-child policy, more flexible and reasonable, was easily accepted by most families, including families in rural areas. The planned economic system also provided a convenient tool for restricting the increase in births, especially through the system of collective economy in rural areas.

Table 2. CBR, CDR, NIR, and TFR, 1971–2000

Year	CBR	CDR	NIR	TFR
1971	30.65	7.32	23.33	5.44
1972	29.77	7.61	22.16	4.98
1973	27.93	7.04	20.89	4.54
1974	24.82	7.34	17.48	4.17
1975	23.01	7.32	15.69	3.57
1976	19.91	7.25	12.66	3.24
1977	18.93	6.87	12.06	2.84
1978	18.25	6.25	12.00	2.72
1979	17.82	6.21	11.61	2.75
1980	18.21	6.34	11.87	2.24

Year	CBR	CDR	NIR	TFR
1981	20.91	6.36	14.55	2.63
1982	22.28	6.60	15.68	2.87
1983	20.19	6.90	13.29	2.42
1984	19.90	6.82	13.08	2.35
1985	21.04	6.78	14.26	2.20
1986	22.43	6.86	15.57	2.42
1987	23.33	6.72	16.61	2.59
1988	22.37	6.64	15.73	2.52
1989	21.58	6.54	15.04	2.35
1990	21.06	6.67	14.39	2.31
1991	19.68	6.70	12.98	2.16
1992	18.24	6.64	11.60	2.00
1993	18.09	6.64	11.45	1.98
1994	17.70	6.49	11.21	1.94
1995	17.12	6.57	10.55	1.87
1996	16.98	6.56	10.42	1.86
1997	16.57	6.51	10.06	1.82
1998	15.64	6.50	9.14	1.76
1999	14.64	6.46	8.18	1.75
2000	14.03	6.45	7.58	1.76

Source: CBR, CDR and NIR from National Statistical Bureau, *China Statistical Yearbook*, TFR before 1993 is from Yao and Yin, *Basic Data of China's Population*, Data User Service, Population Press, 1994, and TFR after 1993 is estimated by the author.

4. ONE-CHILD POLICY (1980–1984)

China began its policy of "economic reform and opening up" in 1978. Vice Premier Deng Xiaoping proposed in 1979 a target for the reform: GDP per capita should reach 1,000 USD by the end of the century (GDP per capita was only 226 USD in China in 1978). The target linked the increase in the size of the national economy with population. In order to reach this goal, not only should GDP be increased but also the population should be brought under control. Accordingly, the target for total population proposed by the government was 1.2 billion by the end of the 20th century (Chang, 1992). However, no one knew how many children a family should have, on average, to hold total population to 1.2 billion. As most demographers addressed the subject from the perspective of political economy, they were less likely to be familiar with demographic techniques and statistics, and lacked the technical skills to make the appropriate calculations.

Nevertheless, because of success in the implementation of the family planning policy in the initial period, the idea of a more restricted requirement, the one-child policy, was favored by some national leaders. This idea was supported by the work of some cybernetic scientists in 1979, who carried out a population projection and got the result that if each couple had 1.7 children on average from 1980 to 2000, the total population in China in 2000 would be 1.2 billion (Qiao, 1991).

At the third session of the Fifth National People's Congress in 1980, the State Council put forward a general call to implement a policy of "only one child per couple" through legislative, administrative, and economic measures. In early September 1980, Hua Guofeng, the Premier, announced to the National People's Congress that "after much research" the government had adopted a one-child policy and population target of 1.2 billion by the end of the year 2000. The one-child policy, applied to both rural and urban areas, was formally released through "An Open Letter" published in *Guang Ming Daily* by the central government on September 25, 1980. It said: "In order to hold China's population to 1.2 billion at the end of this century, the State Council has called to all people in China, advocating that one couple only has one child".

In 1981, the National Family Planning Commission was set up, thereby strengthening the organizational foundation for further implementation of the policy of planned control of population growth. At the fourth session of the fifth National People's Congress in 1981, the government report stated that "implementing family planning and strictly controlling population growth is a long-term strategic task." In 1982, the report at the 12th Conference of Central Party indicated that "within the [area of] economic and social development, population is still the most important issue, [and] implementing family planning program is a Principal National Policy." In order to provide legal grounding, the fifth session of the fifth National People's Congress passed a revised Constitution in 1982, adding some content relevant to family planning: "The State promotes family planning and adapts population increase to the plan for economic and social development.... Couples have the duty to implement family planning" (Yang, 2001c).

The initial steps in economic reform happened in rural areas, which shifted from a collective economy to a private economy in the early 1980s. Under the collective model, farmers in the same village worked together and received their earnings together as part of the same production team. Each farmer got his or her income based on a fair redistribution system within the team. Such a system offered means to manage the behavior of the people in a village. For example, it was easy to take measures if someone violated the family planning policy.

The new system was called a "family responsibility system". The land was distributed and privatized and an output quota was fixed for each family. Once families were given responsibility for their own farming, more children, especially male ones, were needed for family income-generation activities; therefore, rural residents' desire to have more children was reinforced. Apart from this, the decentralized new system reduced the ability to manage farmers' private affairs, including birth control. As a result, it made the implementation of the one-child policy more difficult.

In February 1982, the Central Committee and State Council issued a document entitled "Directive of Further Implementing Family Planning Work", which emphasized the universal application of the one-child policy in rural areas: "Someone who really has difficulties could be allowed to have the second child through approval and arranged plan; no one could be allowed to have the third one whatever happens" (Yang, 2001b). This document specified implementation details for the one-child policy. The directive contained a hint of impending urgency: some progress had been made since the central government issued the "Open Letter", but the "new situation" had made progress difficult (Central Committee and State Council, 1982).

In April 1982, the central government secretariat discussed the family planning program and complained that "not a few" localities were controlling population poorly; policies must under no circumstances be relaxed. As a result, policy enforcement became more severe in 1982–83. Subsequently, family planning operations—sterilization and induced abortions—increased sharply from 1978 to 1983. Even so, the data derived from the 1982 national population census showed that both the birth rate and TFR had increased. Specifically,

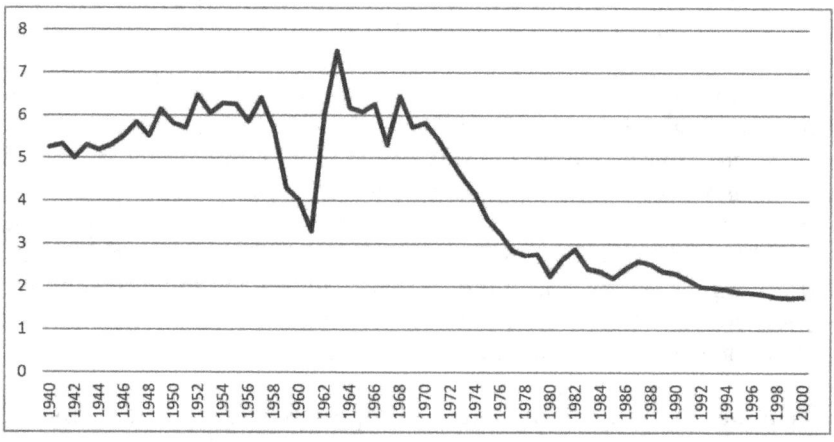

Figure 2. Total Fertility Rate, 1940 to 2010

Source: TFR before 1993 is from Yao and Yin, *Basic Data of China's Population*, Data User Service, Population Press, 1994, and the TFR after 1993 is estimated by the author.

TFR increased from 2.24 in 1980 to 2.87 in 1982 (see Table 2 and Figure 2). This meant that the goals of the one-child policy would not be realized, especially in rural areas where about 80 percent of the Chinese population resided at the time. Enforcing a rigorous one-child policy was quite difficult and seemed unsustainable. This led the central government to change the policy again (Yang, 2001d).

5. THE ONE-AND-HALF-CHILD POLICY (1985–2013)

It was difficult for the government to implement the one-child policy in rural areas, since there was a serious conflict between the strong desire by farmers to have more children and the government's policy. The central government proposed a policy adjustment: "The family planning policy in rural areas should be more lenient, to mitigate conflict between the people and government personnel" (Central Government, 1984). The government directed provincial governments to open "a small crack" in family planning policy in rural areas (Yang, 2001d). Due to diverse situations among the provinces, the central government allowed provincial governments to make their own decisions, based on the guidance provided by the national family planning policy.

The one-child policy was still universally applied to ethnic Han Chinese families in urban China. For ethnic Han in rural areas, five provinces consistently followed the one-child policy, eighteen provinces allowed families to have a second child if their first-born was a girl and there was a four- to five-year gap between the children, and five provinces allowed two children. For ethnic minority couples, most provinces allowed two children, some allowed three, and four provinces had no limit at all (Feng & Hao, 1992).

Until 1991, twenty-eight provinces, excluding Xinjiang and Tibet, issued provincial regulations for family planning based on the national policy and the socioeconomic situation of the provinces. The implementation of family planning was based on the regulations formulated by provincial governments, rather than the general policy issued by the central government. These regulations also included administrative policies on issues like the frequency of induced abortion, and encouraged the application of contraceptives if new birth was not approved. Fourteen provinces stipulated that women who had one child should have an IUD, and couples who had two children should be sterilized. Twenty-four provinces stipulated that remedial measures, such as stopping gestation and eliminating unplanned conceptions (Feng & Hao, 1992). Such measures were mostly carried out in rural areas where implementation of the family planning program was much more difficult. The use of contraception in rural and urban areas and among Han and ethnic minorities varied considerably.

After the blanket one-child policy was eliminated in most rural areas, the crude birth rate (CBR) increased significantly from 19.9 per thousand in 1984 to 23.3 per thousand in 1987, and the TFR increased from 2.2 in 1985 to 2.6 in 1987 (see table 2). Due to the rebound in fertility, the new policy was publicly and strongly criticized by the cybernetic scientists who had supported and proposed the one-child policy before 1980, some of whom had already become national leaders. This caused some disruption in implementing the new policy, and finally the central government openly confirmed that allowing couples in most rural areas to have more than one child was appropriate under the current situation (Qiao, 1991). TFR declined after 1987. According to the fourth population census data, the CBR and TFR in China in 1990 were 21.1 and 2.3 per thousand respectively (see Table 2 and Figure 2).

6. TRANSITION OF THE FAMILY PLANNING PROGRAM

The central government issued "Directives of Central Committee about Strengthening Family Planning Work and Rigorously Controlling Population Growth" on May 20, 1991. It emphasized the importance of leadership by various governments, which led to some tightening of family planning in certain provinces, such as Henan and Guangdong.

The central government held an annual Central Family Planning Working

Meeting following the annual meeting of the People's Congress in 1991. This meeting was attended by all the highest-ranking leaders from the central party committee and central governments at both the national and provincial levels, and emphasized the commitment of leaders at the highest levels to the family planning program.

The government again made a new ten-year birth control plan covering the years 1991 to 2000, and a new target for population control was set, that is, to have the annual population increase rate reduced to 12.5 per thousand within ten years, which meant the total population by the end of the century would be 1.294 billion (Chen & Zhao, n.d.). This seemed to confirm that the previous target of 1.2 billion would not be realized, and that China was unable to hold fertility to the very low levels planned in the early 1980s.

There were two features of the previous family planning program, the effort to control the number of births as well as administrative measures. Administrative enforcement of birth control affected the relationship between the government and the citizens. The new president of the National Family Planning Commission (NFPC), Madam Peng Peiyun, proposed that the family planning program should not only be "strengthened" but also "done well". "Strengthened" meant continuing to control the overall number, while "done well" meant taking measures appropriately, rather than harshly. It was the first time that the government proposed that the family planning program should be accepted by the people, rather than imposed by the government (Peng, 1992).

Since 1991, family planning programs have gone through further changes, although the change in the number of children per family was minor and applied to only some provinces. The NFPC held that those working in family planning should realize that it was inappropriate to merely control the number of births. Number-centered family planning should be transformed into human-centered family planning, and overt restrictions converted into indirect instruction in family planning. The NFPC stressed that "caring for and securing the rights and interests of rural people should be family planning's basic requirement in its development; ... it must prevent and correct any inappropriate action that are causing and have caused aversion" (Editorial, 1993).

The International Conference on Population and Development (ICPD) held in Cairo in September 1994 was a milestone in the history of population and development, as well as in the history of women's rights. At the conference, it was agreed that population is not just about counting people, but about making sure that every person counts. During the conference, ICPD delegates reached a consensus that the equality and empowerment of women was a global priority. The conference took the perspective that universal human rights, and of advocating a woman's ability to access reproductive health rights as the cornerstone of her empowerment, were both key to sustainable development (ICPD Action Program, September 1994, 1995).

After the ICPD, reproductive health rights were introduced into the family planning program in China, and improvement in reproductive health was considered a priority. In March 1995, the NFPC initiated a trial of the quality of service of family planning in six counties. It introduced various choices of contraceptives, high-quality reproductive care services, and a family planning program without quotas (ICPD Action Program, September 1994, 1995). The ICPD resulted in five changes in China's family planning program, including shifting from a focus on family planning to overall population issues, from management and administrative restrictions to services and capacity building, from birth control to reproductive health and quality of births, from punishment and collecting social compensation fees to benefit incentives, and from childbearing women to the general population and vulnerable populations. Furthermore, the NFPC proposed family planning program reform and changes in conceptions and means of family planning (Yang, 2001e).

During this period, nationwide birth rates declined by a remarkable degree. The NFPC published adjusted fertility rates based on the 1992 National Fertility Survey showing a TFR of 1.7 in 1992, which indicated that China's fertility had dropped to below replacement level. Based on the One-Percent National Population Survey conducted by the National Statistical Bureau, the directly estimated TFR in 1995 was only 1.46. The adjusted and published CBR in 1995 was 17.12 per thousand, and the corresponding TFR was 1.87. Furthermore, the TFR directly calculated from the 2000 and 2010 national censuses was as low as 1.22 and 1.18 respectively (NBS, n.d.). However, there was a heated debate on the real level of TFR, since both researchers and the government believed that underreporting occurred in all directly estimated TFR from various national surveys and censuses after 1990. Even though since 1991 there have been officially published data, which adjusted CBR upward, there are still no generally accepted fertility data for China (Qiao, 2010).

Everyone believed that the fertility in China had already dropped to a very low level, even in the absence of accurate fertility data. In 2000, the central government issued a document entitled "Stabilizing Low Fertility". It was the first time that the government signalled that lowering fertility was no longer the goal of the nation's family planning efforts.

Subsequently, the National Family Planning Commission (NFPC) changed its name to the National Population and Family Planning Commission (NPFPC) in 2003. The goals of the commission have shifted from controlling the size of the population to resolving overall population issues. In 2006, the central government issued another document entitled "Resolution on Strengthening Population and Family Planning Work and Integrally Resolving Population Issues". Since then, China's population and family planning program have faced two tasks: stabilizing low fertility and tackling issues concerning overall population.

7. FIRST STEP TOWARD RELEASING THE TWO-CHILD POLICY (2014–2015)

Since 1973, family planning policies had been adjusted several times—from allowing couples to have two children at the beginning of the program, to the one-child policy beginning in 1980, to the policy allowing rural couples to have a second child if their first child was a girl, the so-called one-and-half-child policy, in 1984. After that, the fertility policy did not change until 2013. However, there has been a prolonged debate on the family planning policy among scholars and concerned individuals in China in recent years. From 2000 onward, the government expected to stabilize low fertility, whereas more and more researchers and the general public hoped to end the one-child policy and move to a two-child policy (Qiao, 2015b).

The reasons for relaxing the family planning policy were obvious. One is that most low-fertility countries in Europe confront serious population and socioeconomic problems caused by very low fertility, and have adopted policies for stimulating an increase in fertility. Some Asian countries, originally intending to limit their populations, changed their initial policies to ones encouraging increases in fertility in the 1990s (for example, Japan and South Korea) (Qiao, 2015c). The debate centered on whether China would face the same problems as Europe, Japan and South Korea in the future and whether China should shift from a more restrictive family-planning policy to moderate or uncontrolled policies (Qiao, 2015b). However, based on the experiences of low fertility countries, increasing fertility is almost impossible, so China should be aware that in matters of fertility lower is not always better, and that family planning programs must end before the number of children per couple drops too low.

Chinese scholars made numerous efforts to convince the government to change the family planning policy over many years, but action only began in 2010 when the TFR reported in the 2010 census was shown to be low (Qiao, 2014b). Despite pressure from the public to release the new two-child policy, it worried about a large population increase once the family planning policy was relaxed. Whether the policy could be changed depended on the number of births.

At a working meeting in February 2011, the NPFPC announced that the government planned to launch a pilot project for a two-child policy in five provinces. However, it was not implemented and no one knew why the government changed its mind.

The 18th Conference of the Central Party held at the end of 2012 decided to combine the NPFPC and Ministry of Health (MOH) into a new agency: the National Health and Family Planning Commission (NHFPC). As demands for relaxing the family planning policy had gathered momentum, the new agency had to reconsider adjustment of its policy. Instead of a two-child policy, the NHFPC shifted its focus to a more conservative policy, allowing couples to have a second child if one member of the couple is from one-child family. The government asked researchers to conduct a study on this policy choice. The research indicated that there would be 33 million women who qualified under this policy, of whom 10 million to 12 million wanted to have a second child, meaning the highest number of births should be 26 million a year. There would be 10 million additional births compared with the previous year (16 million) if the new policy was put into effect, and the highest TFR should be 2.4 (Qiao, 2015d). As this result seemed acceptable, the third session of the 18th Conference finally announced a new family planning policy on November 15, 2013, stating that a couple, if one of them is from a one-child family, is allowed to have a second child.

Even though the central government had already issued the new policy, putting it into practice required additional administrative work. First, the provincial governments were asked to estimate how many couples were eligible under the new policy, how many of them wanted a second child, and when they were going to have that second child. Second, the provincial governments had to submit an application to the NHFPC for approval. Third, the provincial Population and Family Planning Regulation should be revised to conform to the new policy, which should be passed by the People's Congress of the province. As a result, different provinces started implementing the new policy at different times. Zhejiang Province was the first to start implementing the new policy, on January 17, 2014. By 2015, 29 provinces had started to carry out the new policy, all except Tibet and Xinjiang (Qiao, 2015a).

In order to estimate how many additional new babies would be born due to the new policy, I calculated the number of couples where one member came from a one-child family,[1] the number of couples who had only one child, and the number of couples, in rural areas, who only had one male child, based on data from the national birth desire survey conducted in 2013 and data from the 2010 census.

My work shows that 11 percent of couples satisfied the first condition, 8.26 percent met the first two conditions, and 5.25 percent met all three conditions (s.e. = 0.0885%). Based on those results, I estimated that the total number of married women aged 15–44 was 212.9 million, and that the total number of them meeting the requirements of the new fertility policy was 11.18 million at the end of 2013 (Qiao, 2014a).

Family planning policies in different areas, especially for urban and rural areas, are quite different. Areas with more restricted policies may derive greater benefit from the new policy if they are home to more couples who are eligible under the new policy; this would include urban areas and areas that have not yet modified the one-child policy.

A recent birth desire survey shows that, among eligible couples, 50.4 percent want a second child, 32.4 percent did not want a second child, and 17.2 percent are undecided. Taking 50.4 percent as the lower limit and 67.6 percent (50.4% + 17.2%) as the higher limit, we can estimate that the number of couples aged 15 to 44 who can and want to have a second child ranges from 5.633 million to 7.336 million, which would also be the total additional number of births (Qiao, 2014a).

This data also shows that 22.4 percent of married couples who can have a second child under the new policy plan to have the second child in the next year, 10.6 percent were planning to have their new baby the year after next, 5.7 percent to have the new baby in three years, and the rest had not decided yet. If we assume that the time frames for undecided couples are the same as for those who have decided, 57.9 percent of couples planned to have their second child next year, and 27.4 percent planned to do so the year after next and 14.7 percent three years from now. The corresponding number of additional births under the new policy in the next three years should be around 3.262 to 4.375 million, 1.543 to 2.07 million, and 0.828 to 1.111 million. Based on national

---

1. Under the one child policy, if both of the parents are single children, they are allowed to have two children.

statistics, the average number of annual births was around 16 million from 2010 to 2012; adding the new births produced by the new policy, the total number of births would increase to 19.26 to 20.38 million.

However, the reality was far different. There were cumulatively only 1.07 million couples who met the requirement of the new policy applying for having a second child by the end of 2014; that number reached 1.45 million in May 2015. The total number of births were 16.40 million, 16.87 million, and 16.50 million respectively. It was very clear that the new policy was given a cold shoulder.

Under such circumstances, most scholars made strong appeals to extend the two-child policy to all couples immediately. However, the NHFPC did not acknowledge that the new policy had met with an unenthusiastic reception, but insisted that the result of the implementation of the new policy met their expectation, and that a broader two-child policy could not be released immediately (Qiao, 2015b).

8. THE TWO-CHILD POLICY (2016–)

While there were heated debates over whether the two-child policy should be released in China, a paper based on a study conducted in 2011 supported the government's position. Published in the *Journal of Population Research* in early 2014, this paper set out the reason why the government did nothing in 2011 after announcing the release of a new family planning policy (Zhai, 2014). In 2010, the NPFPC asked a Chinese scholar to conduct a research on how many new babies could be born and how high the TFR would be if the two-child policy were adopted in 2011. This scholar found that, with the release of the two-child policy in 2011, the total number of families (or couples) qualifying for the policy was 152 million, and the number of births could be as high as 50 million per year and TFR could reach 4.5 (Zhai, 2014). The total number of births was actually around 16 million a year from 2010 to 2012; the highest number of births in Chinese history, 28 million per year, occurred in 1970 when TFR was 5.8. Due to the frightening projection, the NPFPC stopped considering release of its two-child policy in 2011 (Qiao, 2014b).

I conducted and published my own research result (Qiao, 2014b) in November 2014, which countered the other scholar's findings. In regard to the two-child policy, I found that the number of women qualifying for the two-child policy was 96.5 million, rather than 152 million; the highest number of births should be 22.7 million a year, rather than 50 million; and the highest TFR should be 2.26, rather than 4.5 (Qiao, 2014b). The shortcoming of the previous research was that the author included all couples who had already had one child as qualifying for a second child, and did not eliminate those couples who had already been allowed to have a second child, especially couples in rural areas whose first child was a girl.

As the number of births due to the new policy was much fewer than expected—or perhaps the government realized that the study they had relied upon was wrong—the two-child policy was finally issued on October 29, 2015, allowing all couples to have two children without any conditions. The policy came into effect on January 1, 2016 after the National Population and Family

Planning Law was revised and approved by the People's Congress (Standing Committee of People's Congress, 2015).

National Statistical Bureau data show that there were 17.86 million babies born in China in 2016, 1.31 million more than in 2015 when there were 16.55 million births, but that in 2017 the number fell by 0.63 million, to 17.23 million births.

We cannot attribute all the increase to the two-child policy as it only took effect on January 1; a bigger factor may be the conditional two-child policy issued at the end of 2013. In any case, the number of births is still too low. It would be very unfortunate if reality shows that the desire of Chinese for more children has declined to a very low level, and the country might be unable to raise fertility to replacement levels.

The family planning policy is still in effect, controlling the number of third children. However, the decrease in fertility could not be reversed even if the policy were totally removed in the future.

9. DISCUSSION

There have been two important events that changed China dramatically in the last forty years, economic reform and family planning. The former increased living standards and strengthened the country's development, while the latter changed the family structure and age structure of the population, leading to changes in kinship and individual relationships. China may benefit from economic development yet bear the burden of the changes in population composition in the years ahead.

The fertility decline in China may be driven by both internal and external factors. The internal factor involved personal choices about the number of children parents wanted that were caused by socioeconomic development and cultural change, while the external factor was the national family planning policy. There are some debates about which factor played the leading role in the fertility decline. Even though scholars have different views, it must be acknowledged that the family planning policy has had a very important effect on Chinese society, especially in the early periods.

Family planning is commonplace throughout the world, especially in most developing countries. However, once administrative intervention was introduced into the program, the nature of family planning changed, so that it became China-specific. If we come to the conclusion that the family planning program was successful in China, it was only successful in terms of reducing the number of births. Even though lowering China's rate of population increase brought some positive changes in socioeconomic development, the negative consequences are enormous, such as the rapid aging of the overall population, distorted sex ratios, disability caused by inadequate family planning operations, the fact that many families lost their only child and are now childless, and lack of family care for the elderly.

As a matter of fact, the family planning policy is the product of the planned economy. The population crisis of the 1960s and 1970s was mainly due to the shortage of economic resources rather than the population; that is, the supply of goods, as the responsibility of the government, was unable to meet the needs of the population. As it was claimed that socialist institutions were better than capitalist institutions, economic backwardness could not be due to the institutions and was attributed instead to the high rate of population increase. Population was used as an excuse for slower development. There is in fact no clear evidence about how much family planning policy has contributed to the development of modern China.

10. CONCLUSION
Recalling the history of family planning policy, we can identify some of the failures in terms of policy making and implementation.

1. The government should not have linked economic development with population size at the beginning of economic reform, something which resulted in the setting of a population target of 1.2 billion by the end of the 20th century. This was the direct cause of the one-child policy, which totally changed the nature of the family planning program in the 1980s.

2. The family planning program in the 1970s relied on advocacy by the government with couples making their own childbirth decisions. However, administrative intervention changed the nature of family planning; enforced sterilization, induced abortion, and the violations of human rights were overwhelming during the 1980s and 1990s.

3. The government did not make timely adjustments to the one-child policy. The policy ran for more than 35 years, from 1980 to 2015. In fact, it should have ended just after TFR reached replacement levels in the early 1990s.

4. There was no reliable fertility data after 1990. Almost all directly calculated fertility rates from national surveys or censuses after 1990 were too low. No one, including the government, knew the real fertility situation. This usually led to overestimates of fertility levels, and made it difficult to set effective policy.

5. The one-child policy should have been changed in the 1990s. Even though the government started research on adjusting family planning policy in 1998, that research unfortunately became the grounds for issuing the policy of "stabilizing low fertility" in 2000, which left the one-child policy unchanged.

6. The two-child policy should have been released in 2011 (Qiao, 2015d). However, due to a wrong estimate of the effects of a two-child policy, the government did not do so, but issued a partial or conditional two-child policy at the end of 2013, allowing couples to have second child if one of them was from a one-child family.

7. The consequences of wrong policymaking are dramatic. Based on the 2010 census, the number of childbearing women age 30–34, 35–39, 40–44, and 45–49 were 47.64 million, 57.63 million, 61.15 million, and 51.82 million respectively. As the two-child policy was released four to five years late, women aged 45 to 49 had passed out of their childbearing years and women aged 40 to 44 were approaching that point. The number of affected women was more than 110 million. Even though women aged 30 to 39 still have the ability to have a second child, they are subject to high-risk deliveries as well as high maternal death and birth defect rates. The failure of policymaking led to very serious consequences.

Family planning policy in China is coming to an end. However, the costs and the impacts of the policy will never end. If the government was focused on resolving population pressure before, moving forward it will have to focus on resolving the many problems caused by its family planning policy.

REFERENCES

Central Committee and State Council. (1982, February 9). Directive of further implementing family planning work (No. 11 Document of Central Government).

Central Government. (1984, April 13). Document No. 7.

Chang, C. (1992). *Contemporary Family Planning Affairs in China*. Contemporary China Press.

Chen, S. & Zhao, X. (n.d.). Population statistics and planning. *China Population Press*, 313.

Editorial (1993, April 19). Comments. *China Population Daily*. This official newspaper is authorized by the State Family Planning Commission.

Feng, G., & Hao, L. (1992). Overview of 28 provincial family planning regulation. *Population Research* (4): 45–49.

ICPD (Action program, September 1994). (1995). Population and development documents. *China Population Press*, 171-280.

Liu, Z. (1985). *Course of Population Theory*. Renmin University Press.

Ma, Y. (1957, July 5). New population theory. *People's Daily*.

Mao, Z. (1957, February 27). On the correct handling of contradictions among the people, address at the 11th enlarged meeting of the Supreme State Conference.

Mao, Z. (2001). Event highlights of China's population and family planning. *China Population Press*.

NBS. (n.d.). Data of China population census, 2000 and 2010. China Statistical Press.

Peng, P. (1992, March 27). Report of national family planning working meeting.

Qiao, X. (1991). Considerations on the history, contemporary and future of the family planning in China, challenge and countermeasure of China's population. *China Population Press*, 221–233.

Qiao, X. (1995). Comparison of population development between China and Japan: process, consequence, and countermeasures of fertility decline. *Chinese Population Science* (2): 35.

Qiao, X. (2010). Whether the sixth census could get the accurate fertility? *Population and Development* (2).

Qiao, X. (2014a). What will bring when carrying out the new policy. *Population and Family Planning* (3): 18–22.

Qiao, X. (2014b). How high would the fertility be reached if releasing the two-child policy? Discussion with Prof. Zhai Zhenwu. *Population and Development* (6): 2–15.

Qiao, X. (2015a). Can new fertility policy turn the low fertility up in China? Paper Presented at the Annual Meeting of Population Association of America.

Qiao, X. (2015b). Choice of the future fertility policy based on the policy of two child for one of couples from one child family. *Chinese Population Sciences* (2): 26–33.

Qiao, X. (2015c). The necessity of adjustment of fertility policy in China, from the process of removing fertility policy in South Korea. *Journal of Southeast University* (4): 21–27.

Qiao, X. (2015d). Two-child policy for one of couple from one-child family. *A Failure Policy* (6), 2–6.

Qiao, X. (2016). One-child policy: A historical failure. *Academic Bimestrie*, No. 1, 52–61.

Standing Committee of People's Congress. (2015, December 27). Resolution of amending the population and family planning law.

Yang, K. (2001a). Event highlights of China's population and family planning. *China Population Press*, 62.

Yang, K. (2001b). Event highlights of China's population and family planning. *China Population Press*, 96.

Yang, K. (2001c). Event highlights of China's population and family planning. *China Population Press*, 104.

Yang, K. (2001d). Event highlights of China's population and family planning. *China Population Press*, 117.

Yang, K. (2001e). Event highlights of China's population and family planning. *China Population Press*, 343.

Yao, X. & Yin, H. (1994). Basic data of China's population, Data User Service. Population Press.

Zhai, Z. (2014). Analysis on the consequences of currently releasing two-child policy. *Journal of Population Research* (2): 2–17.

Chapter 2
Population Mobility and Migration Policy

Weizhen Dong, Changxing Zhao

ABSTRACT
Population mobility in China has gone through some very different stages in the past several decades: from freedom of population movement to somewhat controlled movement; from nearly no migration before 1980 except urban to rural migration to open migration since the economic and societal transformation began in the 1980s. The restriction of migration was mostly due to the country's limited resources in its early years, but it did cause a rural-urban divide, which has had long-term social economic consequences.

Economic reform emancipated rural surplus labour, as well as relaxed population movement. Although migrants still face inequality in accessing public services and social programs in their new location, they are free to move and can settle down wherever they like. As a result, rural-urban migration in China urbanized a high percentage of its rural residents. Since the relaxation of restrictions on migration, more than 300 million rural villagers have moved to various cities and towns. In 1980, 19.5 percent of China's population was urban; by the end of 2016, that proportion reached 57.35 percent.

Large-scale migration has been a great challenge to China as a whole. Moreover, China has also opened its doors to international migration since the government's "open door policy" took effect.

1. INTRODUCTION
Since the founding of the People's Republic of China in 1949, the government's policy concerning population mobility has been changed several times. It shifted from allowing free migration at the beginning of the 1950s, to restraining the rural labour force from migrating to cities (except for established employment or school enrollment) in 1955, to the introduction of the urban and rural dual household registration system in 1958, which fully controlled rural-urban migration. Since the mid- to late 1980s, free-flowing migration has been allowed under some control. In the 1990s, with the establishment of China's socialist market economy system, urban areas began to see a massive influx of migrants, which was described as the "overflow of migrant labourers". The policy during that period was mainly strict management. After 2000, the Chinese government strengthened the macro-control of rural-urban migration, while the social policy changed from strict management to offering basic public services to this population in the cities.

In this chapter, "floating population" refers to those who have moved out of their permanent residence location and have lived in the new location for less than six months, and "mobile employment" refers to those who work in jobs with short-term contracts, and who have to move from one city to another to remain employed.

2. TRANSIENT FREEDOM OF MOVEMENT (1949 TO EARLY 1950s)
Free migration generally refers to citizens' right to freely move and settle within a country and to go abroad or emigrate. This right was endowed and safeguarded by China's constitution and laws. Article V in *the Common Program of Chinese People's Political Consultative Conference* passed on September 29, 1949 stipulates that "The people have the freedom to migrate". In 1954, Article 90 in the *Constitution of the People's Republic of China* further reaffirmed and refined this provision: "The citizens of the People's Republic of China have the freedom of residence and migration".

Article I of *Provisional Regulations of Management of Urban Household* issued by the Ministry of Public Security in 1951 dealt with the protection of people's freedom of movement (Population Research Institute of CASS, 1986). This was reflected in the implementation of the policy, for example in Article V: When the household has changed, the householder shall, in accordance with the provisions, carry out the necessary procedures with local public security bureau that holds the household register. When people move out of a district, they shall make a prior declaration of migration and cancellation of household registration as well as obtaining a migration certificate from the local public security bureau. When people move in, they shall make a residence registration with the local police station within three days of arrival at the new residence. Those with a migration certificate shall present it; those without a migration certificate shall submit other appropriate documents (Population Research Institute of CASS, 1986).

There were no additional requirements for reporting or approval, nor any mention of the urban or rural status of the migrants, or impositions of any particular restrictions. In short, until early 1955, migration was not restricted in China.

3. STRICT RESTRICTION OF RURAL MIGRATION TO CITIES (MID- TO LATE 1950s TO EARLY 1980s)
From the late 1950s to the early 1980s, Chinese government policy tightly restricted population migration, with the chief focus on controlling movement of the rural population to urban areas. The restrictive measure employed by the government was the household registration system, which was the basis of the nation's food supply system.

3.1. Launching of restrictive policies
The mid-1950s witnessed high unemployment, and also the in-flow of a large number of rural residents into the cities. To solve this problem, the CCP Central Committee and the State Council promulgated numerous documents restricting peasant migration.

On April 17, 1953, the State Council announced the *Instructions on the Discouragement of the Rural Residents Blindly Moving into Cities*, and noted that "urban construction has just begun", "the demand for labour was limited", and members of the "rural population blindly moving into the cities" were creating an "increase of unemployment ... and other difficulties; while in rural areas, the reduced labour force had a serious effect on the spring farming, resulting in the loss of agricultural production". The countermeasure was not only to "persuade" but also to "stop" such migration, including "prohibiting issuing reference letters", "mobilizing migrated populations to return home", and "prohibiting recruitment of rural workers without authorization".

In March 1954, the Ministry of the Interior and the Ministry of Labour issued an article titled *Instructions on the Continuous Discouragement of Rural residents from Blindly Flowing into the Cities*. In March 1955, the Ministry of Interior and the Ministry of Public Security restricted free movement of rural labour into the city: rural labourers without proof of employment from urban workplaces or admission by urban schools were prevented from migrating (Wang, 2013).

In 1956, China established the rural collective economic system, but rural residents in some areas lacked enthusiasm for the new socialist system, and natural disasters occurred frequently during that period in some areas; hence, heightened levels of rural-urban migration. The autumn of 1956 witnessed large-scale migration by rural residents, demobilized soldiers, and villagers in the provinces of Anhui, Henan, Hebei, and Jiangsu. The population generally moved toward big cities and key centres of industry. Though the cities tried to accommodate the influx, capacity was limited; large numbers of people could not be accommodated, but the flow of population continued (Wang, 2013).

The CCP Central Committee further strengthened restrictions on rural population migration. From June 1955 to December 1957, the State Council issued or approved and forwarded a series of notices, instructions and reports successively, which were as follows:

(1) *Instructions on the Establishment of Regular Household Registration System* (The State Council, 1955).

(2) *Instructions on the Prevention of Blind Outflow of Rural Populations* (The State Council, 1956).

(3) *Supplementary Instructions on the Prevention of Blind Outflow of Rural Populations* (The State Council, 1957).

(4) *Report on the Outflow Situation of Rural residents in Disaster-Stricken Areas and Disposal Methods* (Ministry of the Interior, 1957).

(5) *Report on the Outflow Situation of Rural Residents in Disaster-Stricken Areas and Disposal Methods Approved and Forwarded by the Ministry of the Interior* (Ministry of the Interio,1957).

(6) *Report on the Implementation of Prevention of the Blind Inflow of Rural Residents into Cities and the Reduction and Solutions for the Problems Faced by the Urban Population Work* (The Ministry of Public Security, 1957).

(7) *Report on the Implementation of Prevention of the Blind Inflow of Rural Residents into Cities and the Reduction and Solutions for the Problems Faced by the Urban Population Work Approved and Forwarded by the Department of Public Security Department* (The State Council, 1957).

(8) *Notice on the Prevention of Blind Inflow of Rural Residents into Cities* (The State Council, 1957).

(9) *Instructions on the Suppression of Blind Outflow of Rural Residents* (CCP Central Committee and the State Council, 1957).

In particular, the above-mentioned joint documents by the CCP Central Committee and the State Council included specific restrictive measures, among them the formation of a specialized agency led by the Civil Affairs Department, with participation by other departments such as the police, railways, transportation, commerce, food, and supervision, with overall responsibility for the suppression of "blind" migration.

In addition to the formation of specialized agencies, it was also required that rural officials strengthen the ideological education of the masses, so as to prevent the outflow. The railway and transport sector was directed to carefully check tickets on the main railway and transport lines to prevent the flow of rural migrants into the cities. The Civil Affairs Departments were to repatriate country dwellers back to their homes, and forbid them from begging on the streets. The Ministry of Public Security would impose strict household management, forbidding rural residents who had moved to cities from obtaining urban resident status through the cities' household registration system. The Food Department was not to supply food for people without urban household registration. Urban workplaces were not allowed to enroll workers and temporary workers without authorization.

According to the *Instructions on the Prevention of Blind Outflow of Rural Populations*, those who had already left the countryside were treated according to their specific circumstances:

1. Those with relatives and friends to live with, or who could find a way to make a living, would be allowed to stay in the cities.
2. Those who could be settled in the suburban rural areas near the cities should be moved there. Especially in those areas with fewer people but more space, they could be settled in the countryside to engage in the reclamation of land for production purposes.
3. People with no relatives or friends to live with and no viable way of making a living shall contact their home governments. The government of their place of origin would arrange to send them home. After returning home, the local government would help them find a way to make a living.
4. When workplaces in the city needed additional labourers, they were directed to plan in advance, and conduct a coordinated allocation of rural surplus labour through the labour department instead of through private recruitment.

The massive rural-urban migration then was an enormous pressure on the cities' governments on various fronts; including employment, housing, food supply, and other services and arrangements. The strategy adopted was combining possible resettlement with go-back-to-home persuasion. It was a relatively moderate approach. Almost at the same time, however, a strict migration system was established. From 1958 to 1976, the government implemented a firm policy that restricted migration.

3.2. Long-term Restrictions on Migration
The turning point in the migration system's transition from "free" to "completely restricted" did not happen till 1958, with the launch of the *Household*

Registration System. Article 10 of this policy stipulated that if a citizen wanted to migrate out from the household registry jurisdictional area, the individual himself or herself or the head of the household must register with the local household registration authority prior to the move, so that migration certificates could be obtained, and the original household registration cancelled. Citizens wishing to migrate from rural to urban areas had to provide proof of employment in the city, an admission letter from a school, or a migration approval certification from the urban household registration authority (Population Research Institute of CASS, 1986).

Careful scrutiny of this provision will show that unrestricted freedom to migrate was limited to migration from urban to rural areas, while an approval system was established for migration from rural areas to urban areas. For adults, only those who were employed or attending schools above the level of technical secondary schools could proceed with the migration procedures.

The reasons for the government's introduction of this restrictive system were as follows (Ministry of Public Security, 1986):

1. The flow of population into the cities resulted in difficult situations in various aspects of urban life, including transportation, housing, food supply, employment, and schooling.
2. The massive out-migration of members of the rural labour force affected agricultural production.
3. Large-scale migration interfered with the state's policy of integrated planning for the urban and rural labour forces.
4. After moving into the cities, migrants from the countryside could not find jobs, and their lives became more difficult; hence, the urban social order would be affected.

In August 1964, the State Council approved the *Regulation of the Handling of Hukou Migration by the Ministry of Public Security (Draft)*, clarifying the principles for the handling of Hukou migration. Migration from the countryside to cities and towns, and from towns to cities, remained tightly controlled. In addition, restrictions were placed on migration from small cities to big cities, and from other cities to Beijing and Shanghai. This regulation did not restrict "migration from the mainland densely populated areas to the remote sparsely populated areas". The focus was on control of the urban population, especially the population growth of big and middle-sized cities.

Another noteworthy migration phenomenon occurred from the mid-1960s to the late 1970s. Through the introduction of a policy for urban-educated youth to move to the countryside and mountainous areas, China witnessed a huge wave of counter-urbanization. After the "Down to the Countryside" policy was implemented at the beginning of 1968, the number of educated young people relocated to rural China by 1978 totaled 16.23 million, equivalent to about 13 percent of the urban working age population, and representing members of more than one-third of all urban households. Young people aside, a considerable number of urban workers and ranking officials also moved to the countryside, voluntarily or otherwise. During this decade, the total number of urban residents relocated to rural areas reached about 30 million (Lu, 2004).

3.3 Food Rationing's Effect on Migration

The State Council issued the *Interim Measures for the Rationing of Food in Cities and Towns* in 1955, clarifying the relationship between food supply and residency status. Article VIII stipulated that city and town residents who had experienced changes such as marriage, birth, death, separation and cohabitation shall, after updating their household registration information, arrange for the increase, reduction and transfer of food supply quantity accordingly. Article IX stipulated that town residents who migrate should obtain a food supply transfer certificate from their local government, and the certificate would enable them to access food through their destination authority (State Council Legislative Affairs Bureau, 1996).

The shortage of food for the non-agricultural population was the reason for controlling the migration of rural population to urban areas. Control of the food supply and the established food distribution system within the household registration system effectively limited the free movement of the population (Wang, 2013). Tying food supply to household registration was a significant constraint on the population's movement. During the implementation of the system (from the mid-1950s to mid-1980s), the restraint that food coupons imposed upon people's consumption made sure that all residents got enough food to survive. The food distribution system effectively prevented unnecessary loss of life and suffering.

Meanwhile, the strict household registration system and the food supply system limited the migration of rural residents to urban areas during the period, but did not fundamentally inhibit the spontaneous flow of population from densely populated areas to those remote sparsely populated areas.

3.4. Urban-Rural Migration of Educated Youth

From 1967 to 1976, a total of 1.617 million urban people, about one-tenth of the urban population, migrated into rural areas or the country's border areas. For instance, from 1966 to 1979, the far northeast province of Heilongjiang accommodated an average annual inflow of nearly 200,000 migrants, including a high percentage of major Chinese cities' middle-school graduates who were mobilized by the state to work there. During the period from 1966 to 1976, Inner Mongolia Autonomous Region saw an inflow of 246,000 urban residents (Lu, 2002). Several other provinces' rural areas also accepted urban youth, such as the provinces of Anhui, Jiangxi, Jiangsu and Yunnan. However, most of these migrants returned to their city of origin by late 1970s.

4. RELAXATION OF RESTRICTIONS AND OPEN MIGRATION (END OF 1970s ONWARD)

From the late 1970s onward, although the country continued its restrictive policies on the migration of rural population into the cities, some restrictions have been relaxed. Since the mid-1980s, the policy of free mobility has been in place, but strict management of the "floating population" was put in place by means of the temporary residence permit system. After 2005, the government gradually relieved the migration restriction for big and middle-sized cities, and emphasized the provision of basic public services for migrants through reform of the household registration system.

4.1. END OF THE 1970S: RELAXED RESTRICTIONS

In November 1977, the State Council approved the *Regulation of Handling of Hukou Migration by the Ministry of Public Security*, which allowed the reunion of immediate family members and married couples (The State Council, 1997). This policy allows the migration of agricultural residents who have marital relationships or parent-child relationships with urban workers and residents who cannot live independently; educated urban youth who were sent to the countryside during the previous years were also allowed to move back to cities if they were ill, had disabilities or special circumstances in their families, and if they could not take care of themselves. This means those urban residents' spouses, parents, and children who were able to work in rural areas and take care of themselves were excluded. However, it allowed "agricultural people to be given non-agricultural resident status", which was a somewhat relaxed position under the strict regime.

In January 1980, *Notice on the Gradual Resolving of Married Couples Who Had Been Living in Two Regions for a Long Period of Time* was issued by the Organization Department of the CCP Central Committee, the Ministry of Civil Affairs, the Ministry of Public Security, and the State Labour Bureau. The notice required that the relevant departments should, depending on workplace needs, gradually resolve the practical difficulty of couples living apart for long periods of time, solving such problems while adhering to the principle of the proper control of the urban population, the total number of workers, and the sales volume of commodity grain (The Organization Department of the CCP Central Committee, the Ministry of Civil Affairs, the Ministry of Public Security, and the State Labour Bureau, 1980). The main focus of this policy was non-agricultural resident couples both members of which were working; but if one member was a rural resident, they were also included in the target demographic, although not all of their family members could be relocated into cities or towns at once. This policy opened the way to change some of these workers' family members househould registration status from "agricultural" to "non-agricultural".

In March 1988, the *Notice on the Gradual Resolving of Married Couples Who Had been Living in Two Regions for a Long Period of Time* was issued by the Ministry of Labour and Human Resources, the Ministry of Public Security, and the Ministry of Commerce. It stressed that older employees' reunification with their spouses would be based on the principle of moving from big cities to smaller ones, and from inland cities to more remote ones. If older employees left their current posts, the workplaces and human resources department would help them move to where their spouse was and find a new workplace close by. It is important to note that this policy assumed that non-agricultural population growth was under control. Implementation of this policy was based on the principle that each year the number of employees' rural families migrating to cities and towns and those transferring to non-agricultural status should not exceed two per thousand of the total non-agricultural population.

Each region was to relocate older employees' spouses and minor children from the countryside and give them non-agricultural status so as to gradually resolve the family separation issue (the Ministry of Labour and Human Resources, the Ministry of Public Security and the Ministry of Commerce, 1988). It is evident that the policy was carried out on the basis of limited numbers of approvals, and the government did not completely give up efforts to control the growth of the non-agricultural population.

4.2. Mid-1980s: Temporary Resident Permit System

Since the mid-1980s, China's urban economic development has accelerated, attracting a large number of rural surplus labourers to the cities. The Chinese government did not impose any restrictions on this migration but instead encouraged it. However, obstacles still existed for transferring migrant workers' household registrations, especially those of rural migrant workers. In order to control information for migrant workers without a permanent resident household registration in the city, the temporary residence permit system was launched in the mid-1980s, and was placed in the charge of the public security bureau of the city.

In 1984, the State Council issued the *Notice on Rural Residents' Settlement in Cities and Towns*. According to this policy, workers with a rural household registration were allowed to move their households from their native home to the town of business and work engagement if they have been working or doing business there, own a home, have the ability to do business, or have a stable job. They would be counted in the statistics as being among the non-agricultural population. This was an important shift in migration policy and the household registration system with considerable economic and social significance, and it demonstrated that the government had changed its position to one of allowing and even encouraging rural residents who work or do business in a town or city to be given a non-agricultural status (Wang, 2013).

In 1985, *Interim Provisions on Management of Urban Transient Population by the Ministry of Public Security* required that people above the age of 16 with an intended temporary residency period of more than three months shall apply for a Temporary Residence Permit (State Council Legislative Affairs Bureau, 1986). Because of the high mobility of workers, although many applied for the permit, most failed to obtain it.

In fact, migration barriers and restrictions at this time were greatly reduced. The purpose of strengthening the registration and administration of urban temporary populations was to control crime and locate criminals. The purpose of the temporary residence permit management system for the migrants was mainly to strengthen urban social order and public security.

4.3. 1990s to 2000: Macro-control of Rural-Urban Migration

Since 1992, China has started to speed up the implementation of the market economy system and make adjustments to the economic structure of agriculture. The economy entered a rapid growth period, and the non-agricultural employment policy of rural migrants changed from limited migration to an orderly macro-controlled migration. The trans-regional population mobility and employment system (or employment-card control and management) was implemented, and small towns' residential household registration systems were reformed.

On November 3, 1993, the Ministry of Labour proposed to establish a nationwide basic system, market information system, and service network for trans-regional labour force migration, so that the main cities that receive migrants will manage and support the new population of rural labourers well.

On November 17, 1994, the Ministry of Labour issued the *Interim Provisions on the Management of Rural Labourers' Inter-Provincial Mobile Employment*, which required that the rural workers recruited by trans-provincial workplaces must apply for migrant worker employment registration cards and migrant worker employment certificates. The combination of these two documents, namely, the Mobile Employment Permit, served as a valid document to authorize *mobile* employment. This was the first standardized program for trans-regional mobile employment of the rural labour force, with employment card management as the core; meanwhile, it was also the first significant change since the strict policy on rural-urban migration through the household registration system that had been put in place in 1958 (Zhang, 2010).

In September 1995, the central social security comprehensive management committee issued advice on *Strengthening of Floating Population Management*. The meeting formulated the guiding ideology, main tasks and key measures of floating population management, and clarified that whether the Temporary Residence Permit and Employment Permit were in an individual's possession would be regarded as the important basis for custody and repatriation. Thus, China's floating population regulation policies were gradually standardized and institutionalized.

On May 20, 1997, the Ministry of Public Security issued the *Pilot Program on the Reform of the Household Registration System of Small Towns*, and proposed the appropriate reform of the household registration management system: "The rural population working and living in small towns and meeting certain conditions are allowed to apply for permanent residence in the small towns, so as to promote short-distance and orderly migration of rural surplus labour to small towns", but "the mechanical growth of population in the middle and big cities, especially Beijing, Tianjin and Shanghai, etc., shall continue to be strictly controlled". And it highlighted the fact that "the persons settled in small towns can have the same treatment as the native local residents. The local people's governments and relevant departments and units shall treat them equally in regard to their education, employment, grain and oil supply, social security, etc."

In November 25, 1997, the General Office of the State Council forwarded the *Advice on the Further Improvement of Organization of Orderly Mobility by Migrant Workers* by the Labour Department, highlighting the need to earnestly "organize the orderly flow of migrant workers" and directing that the local governments and relevant departments shall "make overall planning and reasonable arrangements and strengthen macro-control of urban and rural labour employment ... to guide and organize the flow of migrant workers as demanded" and "encourage and attract migrant workers to return to home villages to start business, promote the transformation of migrant workers' income to direct investment and the peripheral transfer of rural surplus labourers".

In general, the policies of rural labour mobility gradually changed during this period, which played an important role in the eventual establishment of a integrated rural and urban labour market. However, as the economic system of the entire country was still in transition, the relevant labour policies were not perfect. For instance, in the late 1990s, due to limited accommodation in urban areas, the state-owned enterprises' reforms caused a sharp increase in the numbers of laid-off and unemployed workers, and urban employment pressure surged. Therefore, the government also formulated a number of policies and regulations that discriminated against migrant workers, creating some obstacles for rural residents to migrate to the cities (Zhang, 2010).

4.4. 21st Century: Orderly Flow of Population

Since 2000, the policy orientation in regard to rural residents migrating to the cities has been shifted to ensure migrant workers' access to urban services, and various restrictive policies and regulations have been eliminated to create a fair environment for their employment and realize the "fair and orderly flow" of rural labour forces to the cities.

In June 2000, the CCP Central Committee and the State Council issued the *Opinions on Promoting the Healthy Development of Small Towns*, which proposed that from year 2000, rural residents with legal permanent residence and a stable job or source of income in small and middle-sized towns could be granted urban household registration status, and receive the same treatment as urban residents in terms of children's schooling, joining the army, obtaining employment, etc. No discriminatory policies would be implemented and no extra fees or other charges would be levied on the rural residents settled in small towns. The *Opinion*'s provisions indicate that Chinese population mobility policy has entered a new phase.

On March 30, 2001, the Ministry of Public Security issued *Advice on the Promotion of Small-Town Household Registration System Reform*, which noted that people with legal permanent residence status, a stable job or source of income in small towns, and whose immediate relatives lived with them could apply for permanent residence in towns if they wished.

On June 20, 2003, the State Council issued the *Administrative Measures for the Rescue of Vagrants and Beggars in Cities without Living Conditions* while abolishing the *Detainment and Repatriation Measures for Urban Vagrants and Beggars* issued by the State Council in May 1982. The new approach proposed the principle of voluntary relief, and abolished compulsory means. For vagrants and beggars, the role of government changed from management to that of service provider. In fact, not only for vagrants and beggars, but for all migrants, the government has begun to shift its role and function, with an increasing emphasis on provision of public services.

In 2005, the Ministry of Public Security started to further reform the household registration system. It proposed to eliminate the distinction between agricultural and non-agricultural in household residential registration, and explored the establishment of an integrated rural and urban household registration management system; meanwhile, the government gradually lifted restrictions on migrants' household registrations in medium-sized and large cities.

On March 27, 2006, the State Council issued the *Opinions on Solving the Problem of Migrant Workers*, and proposed the basic principles of "fair treatment and enhanced services" to address the problem of social security for migrant workers, and to effectively provide public services for migrant workers as well as safeguarding their interests. This was the most detailed elaboration yet of the rights and interests of migrant workers since the founding of New China.

On July 30, 2014, the State Council issued *Advice on Further Promotion of Household Registration System Reform*, providing for reasonable direction of the orderly transfer of rural residents to urban areas, and the urbanization of rural migrants. The major changes were as follows:

1. Further adjustment of household residence migration policies. Restrictions on relocation to towns and small cities were completely removed, restrictions on settling in medium-sized cities were gradually eliminated, and conditions for relocation into large cities were to be decided on reasonable grounds, while the populations of the very largest cities were still strictly controlled.

2. An integrated rural and urban household registration system was established. This ended the dual system of household registration after 50 years. Systems of education, healthcare, employment, social security, housing, land and population statistics appropriate to a unified urban and rural household registration system were to be established.

3. The residence permit system was established. If citizens left their permanently registered residence and lived in cities in other districts for more than six months, they were to apply for a residence permit in their new place of residence. Basic public services provision mechanisms tied to years of residence were established. Residence permit holders enjoy the same rights to access employment, basic public education, basic health services, family planning services, public cultural services, and licenses and certification registration as the local registered population; and over time, they gradually gain equal entitlement to employment support, housing security, pensions, social welfare, and social assistance, while their children will eventually be eligible to take college entrance exams locally.

4. Coverage of basic public services was expanded. The right to education for the migrant agricultural population and other residents and their children in cities was guaranteed. The employment and unemployment registration management system, unified urban and rural medical assistance system, and basic pension system for urban and rural residents were to be improved over time, as was the social assistance system in order to protect basic housing provision for rural migrants.

5. Financial guarantees for basic public services were strengthened. Financial transfer mechanisms tied to urbanization of rural migrants were established. The central and local departments were to undertake and share the corresponding financial responsibilities in accordance with the division of administrative authority.

On October 30, 2014, National Health and Family Planning Committee, Central Committee for Comprehensive Management of Public Security, State Council Rural Migrant Workers Affairs Steering Group Office, the Ministry of Civil Affairs, and the Ministry of Finance jointly issued *Guidance on Improving Basic Public Healthcare and Family Planning Services for Rural Migrants*, which clarified the following points:

1. Based on rural migrants' place of residence, efforts to equalize their public healthcare and family planning services should be included among the responsibilities of the grassroots-level centers for comprehensive management of public security, centers for comprehensive services for rural migrant workers, service centers for floating populations, and community healthcare and family planning service centers.

2. Floating populations would be included in the target demographics of the community healthcare and family planning service system, providing basic public healthcare and family planning services to them.

3. A mechanism would be established corresponding to the unified urban-rural household registration system to fully carry out 11 types of basic public healthcare programs, with priority given to six types of basic public healthcare services, namely, children's preventive vaccination, prevention and control of infectious diseases, maternal and childcare services, family planning, and healthcare education. Meanwhile, patients with severe mental disorders should be the responsibility of the authorities at their place of residence.

4. An information sharing system for migrants should be established and enhanced. Building on the comprehensive information platforms for community public services, further enhancement should be made to information sharing about basic public healthcare services and migrants' family planning services.

5. Non-government organizations should be mobilized to create new service modes. Collaborations should be sought with mass organizations and other social organizations such as the Family Planning Committee to assist in managing migrant populations.

In order to guarantee migrants' equal access to national basic healthcare and family planning services, to offer accurate and effective healthcare education to the population, and to improve their healthcare awareness level, on June 7, 2016, the General Office of the National Health and Family Planning Commission issued the *Action Plan for Health Education and Health Promotion for Migrants (2016–2020)*. The main objectives included in the Action Plan were to encourage the development of a favorable policy environment, increase the accessibility of healthcare and family planning services, promote basic public health and family planning policies, raise the healthcare awareness of migrants, provide accurate health education for migrants (including the new generation of migrants in which rural workers were the majority, as well as migrant women and school-age children), build spaces dedicated to the improvement of migrants' health, create healthy families, and engage in outreach activities to promote the improvement of migrants' health.

5. OVERVIEW

5.1. Main Stages of Population Mobility Policy in China

In the early 1950s, a free migration system was essentially in place; there were few or no restrictions on migration of the rural population to towns for employment or to join relatives and friends.

After 1955, massive migration of rural labourers into the cities led to tension due to shortages of employment and household goods in the cities. The policy restricting free migration to cities and towns of rural labourers was initially instituted in March 1955, and the *Household Registration Ordinance*, providing for a high degree of control, was set out in 1958. There were only a limited number of channels for migration to urban areas, such as planned recruitment, junior college and special secondary school admissions, and promotion to officer rank after serving in the army.

From the late 1960s to middle 1970s, a reverse migration took place when millions of urban youth were mobilized to work in rural areas and the state border regions by the government. The obvious reason behind this mass urban-rural migration was employment pressure in urban China. There had been a large population increase since 1950, but China lacked infrastructure. Providing employment, education, and other services in urban China was enormously difficult.

Since the late 1970s, restrictions on couple-reunion migration and migration by immediate family members have been gradually eased. In the mid-1980s, the migration of rural labourers to work in industry in the cities began; "agricultural people who were given non-agricultural status" gradually became the main component of small towns' population. The temporary residence permit system began to be implemented in 1985.

In the 1990s, with the gradual establishment of market economy, the flow of population was carried out in a standardized manner under macro-control. The government introduced a combined migration certificate and temporary resident card management system for migrant workers.

After 2000, the policy restrictions on migrant rural workers were reduced. Rural residents were allowed to move to the cities, the mobility of the rural population was regulated, and employment services were offered. The new policies focused on the orderly transfer of the surplus rural labour force, while more emphasis was placed on equity and assimilation issues, and reforms highlighted the offering of comprehensive support and the institutional assurance (Wang, 2013).

5.2. Scale of Migration

Population mobility in China has generally manifested itself as movement between urban and rural areas. The most common migration pattern was from rural to urban areas, except between the late 1960s and the mid-1970s when the reverse migration took place. According to the statistics from China's National Bureau of Statistics (see Figure 1 and Table 1), during the 66 years from 1949 to 2015, China's total population increased by 832.95 million people; the urban population increased by 713.51 million, and the rural population increased by 119.44 million.

Table 1. Urban Population and Urbanization Rate, 1949–2015 (millions)

Indicators	1949	1955	1960	1965	1970	1975	1980
Total population	541.67	614.65	662.07	725.38	829.92	924.20	987.05
Urban population	57.65	82.85	130.73	130.45	144.24	160.30	191.40
Rural population	484.02	531.80	531.34	594.93	685.68	763.90	795.65
Urbanization rate %	10.64	13.48	19.75	17.98	17.38	17.34	19.39
Indicators	1985	1990	1995	2000	2005	2010	2015
Total population	1058.51	1143.33	1211.21	1267.43	1307.56	1340.91	1374.62
Urban population	250.94	301.95	351.74	459.06	562.12	669.78	771.16
Rural population	807.57	841.38	859.47	808.37	745.44	671.13	603.46
Urbanization rate %	23.71	26.41	29.04	36.22	42.99	49.95	56.1

Data Source: National Bureau of Statistics (1949–2016). http://data.stats.gov.cn/easyquery.htm?cn=C01.

In the 66 years after the founding of socialist China, China's urbanization rate increased from 10.64 percent to 56.1 percent (see Figure 2). In particular, after the urbanization rate exceeded 30 percent in 1996, the next 18 years witnessed an accelerated urbanization process with the average annual increase in the urbanization rate standing at 1.35 percentage points, and the annual increase in the total urban population exceeding 20 million. Thus, it can be seen that the scale of population mobility experienced by China over these two decades is truly unprecedented.

Figure 2 shows that China's urban population accounted for 57.35 percent of the total national population by 2016. In year 2017, China's total population reached 1.39008 billion (urban population: 813.47 million, rural population:

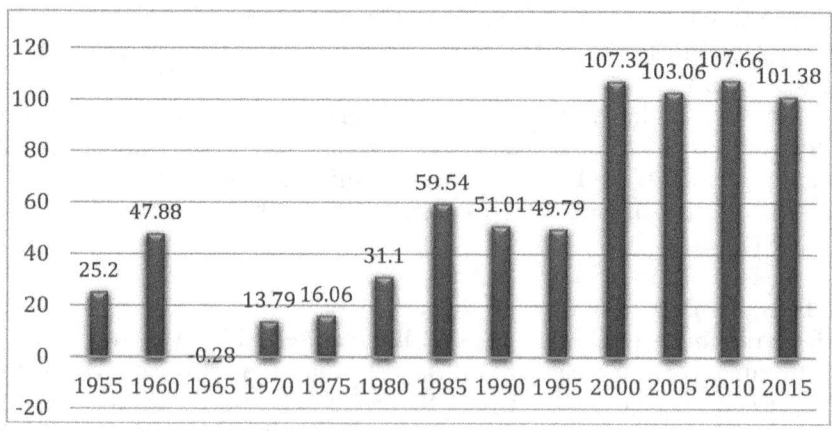

Figure 1 Additions to Total Urban Population in Five-Year Blocks (1955–2015)

Data Source: National Bureau of Statistics (1956-2016);
http://data.stats.gov.cn/easyquery.htm?cn=C01

576.61 million), and the urbanization rate reached 58.52 percent. If China's urbanization rate were to reach or exceed 80 percent in the next few decades, and assuming that China's total population remains unchanged, then a few more hundreds of millions of people will added to its urban areas in the foreseeable future.

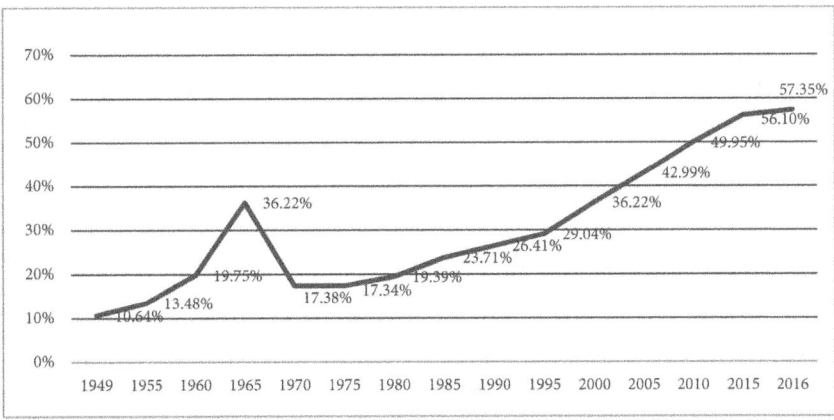

Figure 2. Urbanization in China (1949–2016)

Data Source: National Bureau of Statistics (1950-2017)
http://data.stats.gov.cn/easyquery.htm?cn=C01

5.3. CHALLENGES

5.3.1. Government's management capability

China has experienced a rural-urban migration involving hundreds of millions of people in recent decades. This caused severe challenges during a period of rapid economic development. Since the late 1970s, China has been trying to maintain a balance among reform, development, and stability. But from the late 1970s onward, it gradually relaxed restrictions on movement of the rural population into the cities, hence the surging growth of the urban population. The entry of a large number of migrants into the cities inevitably had varying degrees of impact on the cities' employment, environment, public security, order, and resources. By year 2017, 286.5 million rural migrants were living in the cities (see Figure 3), where they had to be provided with jobs, housing, and schools for their children, and also the overall stability and social order of the cities had to be maintained, which in itself was a test of the government's resolve and ability to cope with such challenges.

5.3.2. Provision of basic social public services

Since the 1980s, free movement of the population has been essentially realized, but the temporary residence permit system introduced in the mid-1980s imposed strict management on migrants. The government's attitude towards migrants changed from strict management to offering public services to them in the new century. *Advice on Further Promotion of the Household Registration*

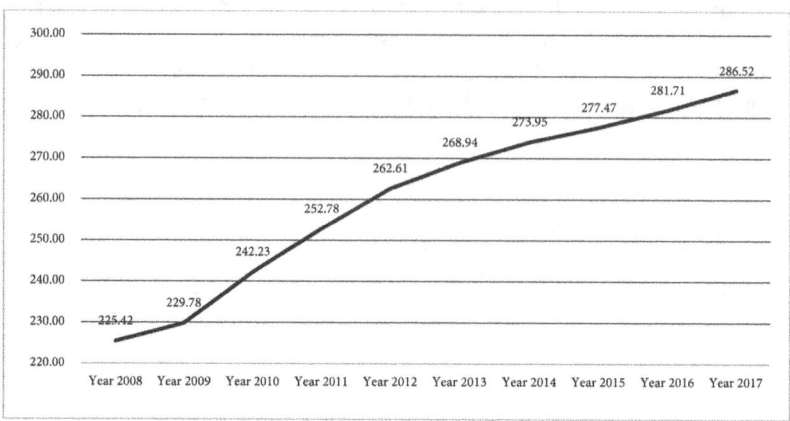

Figure 3: Migrant Workers in China 2008–2017 (million)

Data Source: National Bureau of Statistics 2009-2018

System Reform, issued in 2014, proposed more explicitly the expansion of public services and improvement of various social security mechanisms. Because China's total population is so large, the entry of hundreds of millions of rural migrants into the cities would pose tremendous challenges for urban public services.

Due to the restrictions of the household registration system, there is one population group in China that is only "semi-urbanized". They are living in a city or town but their residential status continues to be rural. Therefore, there is a difference between the registered urban population rate and the actual rate of urbanization. In 2016, the urbanization rate, counting all city dwellers, was 57.35 percent, while based on the household registration system the urbanization rate was only about 41.2 percent (The State Council, 2014). The difference between the two figures was mostly due to rural-urban migrant workers who have moved to the cities but have not yet obtained official urban status. This group faces special difficulties as new urban dwellers.

The salient features of this population are that they have jobs in the city, while their household registration is rural; they contribute their hard labour for the city's development, while their families are in the countryside; they earn income in the city, while the accumulation of their wealth and property is in their home villages; they are living in the city, while their roots are in rural areas. Such differences not only require further acceleration of reforms of the household registration system, but also indicate that basic public services in urban areas are not equally accessible by migrant workers.

According to the National Bureau of Statistics (2018), there were a total of 286.5 million rural-urban migrant workers in 2017 (see Table 3 and Figure 3). At present, many of these migrant workers still cannot fully access the same public services and social welfare programs that registered urban residents enjoy, and there is still much room for improvement in terms of housing security, public transportation, children's education, social insurance, and social assistance.

Table 3. Recent Data on Migrant Workers (2008–2017) (million)

Indicators	2008	2009	2010	2011	2012
Total migrant workers	225.42	229.78	242.23	252.78	262.61
Migrate out of province	140.41	145.33	153.35	158.63	163.36
Left alone	111.82	115.67	122.64	125.84	129.61
With whole family	28.59	29.66	30.71	32.79	33.75
Migrate within province	85.01	84.45	88.88	94.15	99.25

Indicators	2013	2014	2015	2016	2017
Total migrant workers	268.94	273.95	277.47	281.71	286.52
Migrate out of province	166.10	168.21	168.84	169.34	171.85
Left alone	130.85	132.43	-	-	-
With whole family	35.25	35.78	-	-	-
Migrate within province	102.84	105.74	108.63	112.37	114.67

Data Source: National Bureau of Statistics: 2017 national monitoring survey of migrant workers, http://www.stats.gov.cn/tjsj/zxfb/201804/t20180427_1596389.html

5.3.3. Financial pressure of the urbanization cost on rural migrants

In July 2013, the Chinese Academy of Social Sciences released *Urban Blue Book*, which noted that the per capita public cost of rural migrants' urbanization in China's eastern, central and western regions was ¥176,000, ¥104,000 and ¥106,000 respectively, and that the national average was ¥131,000 per person. From the perspective of government costs, by 2025, the problem of urbanization of the agricultural population will be basically solved. The national average annual consumption will exceed 14 million, an increase of 11 million, that is, the problem of about 25 million people will be solved every year. If it was calculated as a one-time public investment of ¥26,000 per capita, the annual expenditure of government financial resources is about ¥650 billion, accounting for 5.5% of the national public income in 2012 (Pan and Wei, 2013). Moreover, such financial funds should be included in the budget for continuous payment in the next few decades, which will be a challenge to the central and local governments financially.

5.4. INTERNATIONAL MIGRATION

China had almost no international population mobility in the first three decades after the establishment of the People's Republic. Once the Chinese government relaxed its domestic migration policy and allowed open migration between rural and urban and between regions, it also opened its doors to the outside world. Although immigration has been controlled, there are now over 600,000 foreigners who have become long-term residents in China. There is also a large number of international students enrolled in various schools in China.

Immigration in China was regulated by the Law of Administration of Entrance and Exit of Foreigners (1985). There has been a 35-fold increase in the number of foreign entries into China since then, including rising numbers of tourists, students, and business travelers. By year 2010, when the national census recorded foreign residents for the first time, there were approximately 594,000 immigrants living in China; the top countries of origin were the Republic of Korea, the United States, Japan, Burma, and Vietnam. In recent years, China also saw numbers of illegal immigrants number grow, particularly in the province of Guangdong (Haugen, 2015).

China has also been accepting refugees. By the end of 2015, China harbored 301,622 refugees from countries such as Vietnam, Somalia, Nigeria, Iraq, and Liberia, as well as from other regions. In September 1982, China acceded to the 1951 Refugee Convention and 1967 Protocol. Between 1978 and 1979, 260,000 Indochinese refugees settled in China; between 1981 and 1982, China provided resettlement opportunities for 2,500 Lao and some Cambodian refugees from camps in Thailand. In July 2013, China issued its new Exit-Entry Administration Law, which includes provisions for refugee/asylum-seekers' documentation details (UNHCR, 2015).

Meanwhile, as a result of the economic reforms, China reduced barriers for people to leave the country. In fact more than five million Chinese citizens have emigrated to other countries in recent decades. From 1980 to 1995, about 600,000 Chinese emigrated overseas, of which the highest proportion went to the United States, followed by Canada (Zhuang, 1997). A high percentage of these emigrants are highly educated professionals. The open-door policy presented an opportunity for Chinese youth to study overseas beginning in the 1980s; this continues to be a popular choice in the 21st century. Since the 1990s, professional-class immigration also has gained attention and momentum, as well as investment-class immigration among the wealthy (Xiang, 2016).

5.5. THE GOVERNMENT'S VISION OF URBANIZATION AND MIGRATION

On March 5, 2017, Premier Li Keqiang delivered his Report on the Work of the Government at the Fifth Session of the 12th National People's Congress of China. In it, he stresses that "Urbanization is the path we need to take to develop a modern China". Specifically, he elaborated on the following major steps to be taken in 2017:

1. *Grant urban residency to more people who are living in urban areas but with rural household registration.* Premier Li points out that the Chinese government "will deepen the reform of the household registration system and relax the restrictions on urban residency eligibility"; work swiftly to ensure that permanent urban residents currently without urban residency status are issued with residence cards, which will enable them to enjoy, as provided for by law, the right to access compulsory education, employment, medical care, and other basic public services; and promote the development of small towns and small- and-medium-sized cities in the central and western regions "to help more rural migrant workers find employment or start businesses in urban areas closer to home so that they do not have to choose between earning money and taking care of their families".

2. *Promote the construction of government-subsidized housing in urban ar-*

eas as well as the healthy development of the real estate market. In 2017, six million housing units were to be built in rundown urban areas. People displaced by the rebuilding of such areas would receive monetary compensation rather than housing. Other steps included taking into consideration people's demand for buying homes or improving their housing conditions; improving tax and credit policies to support personal housing consumption and adopting different policies in different cities as appropriate to the local situation, in order to cut housing inventory and promote stability in the housing market; and enabling non-registered urban residents to access public rental housing.

3. *Improve educational opportunities for rural-urban migrants.* Premier Li stressed that the government "will continue to help see the increased enrollment of students from poor rural areas into key universities, and improve and implement policies enabling children who live with their migrant worker parents to go to secondary school or take college entrance exams in their city of residence". Meanwhile, in order to help migrant workers to improve their skills, they will be provided with over 21 million training opportunities.

6. CONCLUSION

Population mobility policies in China dictated its population's migration and urbanization process. From the early years of no restrictions to restricted household registration, from loosely controlled migration to open rural-urban migration, China was one of the few countries in the world that provided a food security program (or ration system) based on residence location. Once resources were no longer scarce, especially food, the migration door was cracked open and, later, it was widely open to all.

Large-scale migration in China has been mainly rural to urban in nature. Currently, there are over 300 million new urban dwellers living in China's towns and cities. This poses a great challenge to all sectors of China, from urban planning to education, from public health to employment and transportation. Meanwhile, the old-fashioned household registration system became a barrier to the migrants' accessing social programs and public services. The reform of the household registration system, however, was delayed; and that delay caused many unnecessary difficulties in migrants' lives.

The progress of urbanization in China has been slow, except during recent years. As the world's most populous nation, China finds managing its population a difficult task. The Chinese government made efforts to explain its policies effectively during each of the transitional periods, something which gained citizens' cooperation in most cases. The government's recent policy directives have made promises to migrants and future migrants that issues of housing, employment, training, and household registration will be soon resolved. The Chinese government will also take care of their children's education, including compulsory education and higher education.

7. RELEVANT POLICY DOCUMENTS

1951-07-16. Ministry of Public Security. "Provisional Regulations on the Administration of Urban Household Registration." http://www.chinalawedu.com/falvfagui/fg22598/71149.shtml.

1953-04-17. Government Administrative Council. "Instructions on Discouraging [People] from Blindly Moving into the Cities." http://www.fsou.com/html/text/chl/1602/160268.html.

1955-08-25. "The State Council's Order on the Interim Measures for the Ration Supply of Grain in Towns and Cities." http://www.lawxp.com/statute/s1009605.html.

1958-01-09. Standing Committee of the National People's Congress People's Congress. "Regulations of the People's Republic of China on Residence Registration." http://www.npc.gov.cn/wxzl/gongbao/2000-12/10/content_5004332.htm.

1977-11-01. The State Council approved the "Ministry of Public Security's Provisions on How to Handle the Reallocation of Registered Permanent Residence." http://www.pkulaw.cn/fulltext_form.aspx?Gid=162946.

1980-01-21. The Organization Department of the Central Government, the Ministry of Civil Affairs, the Ministry of Public Security, and the State Administration of Labor. "Circular on Gradually Solving the Problem of Long-Term Separation of a Married Couple Due to their Employment Location." http://www.law-lib.com/law/law_view.asp?id=44104.

1984-10-13. "Circular of the State Council on the Issue of Farmers Registering Their Residence Status after Moving to the Market Towns." http://www.gov.cn/zhengce/content/2016-10/20/content_5122291.htm.

1985-07-13. "Interim Provisions of the Ministry of Public Security on the Administration of Temporary Urban Residents." http://www.rmlt.com.cn/2014/0731/300535.shtml.

1986-12-03. "Detailed Rules for the Implementation of the Law on the Administration of the Entry and Exit of Citizens of The People's Republic Of China." Approved by the State Council, Issued on December 26, 1986 by the Ministry of Public Security, the Ministry of Foreign Affairs and the Ministry of Communications. http://www.fmprc.gov.cn/chn/gxh/tyb//bszn/dafw/t9782.htm.

1986-12-03. "Exit and Entry Administration Law of the People's Republic of China." Approved by the State Council, issued by the Ministry of Public Security, Ministry of Foreign Affairs on December 27, 1986; revision approved by the State Council on July 13, 1994; issued on July 15, 1994 by the Ministry of Public Security, Ministry of Foreign Affairs. http://www.fmprc.gov.cn/chn/gxh/tyb//bszn/dafw/t9778.htm.

1988-03-03. Ministry of Labor and Human Resources, Ministry of Public Security and Ministry of Commerce. "Notice on the Resolving of Relevant Problems of Senior Workers' Long-term Separation from Their Spouses Due to Employment Location. http://www.lawxp.com/statute/s575678.html.

1994-11-17. "Notice of the Ministry of Labor on the Dissemination of the Interim Provisions on the Administration of the Employment of Rural Labor Force." http://china.findlaw.cn/fagui/p_1/206985.html.

1995-09-19. General Office of the State Council and the General Office of the China People's Congress' Central Committee. "Opinions on Strengthening the Management of Floating Population." http://www.110.com/fagui/law_3658.html.

1997-05-20. Ministry of Public Security. "The Pilot Scheme for The Reform of the Household Registration System in Small Towns." http://www.law-lib.com/law/law_view.asp?id=13344.

1997-11-25. "The General Office of the State Council Approved and Disseminated the Ministry of Labor and Other Departments' Circular on Further Improving the Work of Organizing the Orderly Flow of Migrant Workers." http://www.chinalawedu.com/falvfagui/fg23051/853.shtml.

2000-06-13. "Some Opinions of the Central Committee of the Communist Party of China and the State Council on Promoting the Healthy Development of Small Towns." http://www.gmw.cn/01gmrb/2000-07/05/GB/07%5E18472%5E0%5EGMA1-008.htm.

2001-03-30. "Notice of the State Council Approving the Ministry of Public Security Opinions on the Small Towns' Household Registration Management System Reform." http://fgk.chinalaw.gov.cn/article/fgxwj/200103/20010300277424.shtml.

2003-06-20. State Council. "Measures for the Relief Management for Vagrants and Beggars with No Income from the City." http://www.mca.gov.cn/article/zwgk/fvfg/shflhshsw/200711/20071110003390.shtml.

2003-12-01. "Provisions of The Ministry of Foreign Affairs on Further Simplifying the Formalities for the Entry of Foreign Professionals in China." http://www.fmprc.gov.cn/chn/gxh/tyb//bszn/dafw/t9785.htm.

2004-08-15. "Measures for the Administration of Application and Approval of Permanent Residence of Foreigners in China." Approved by the State Council on December 13, 2003. Ministry of Public Security, Ministry of Foreign Affairs Issued the Seventy-Fourth Orders on August 15, 2004. http://www.fmprc.gov.cn/chn/gxh/tyb//bszn/dafw/t267618.htm.

2006-03-27. State Council. "Some Opinions on Solving the Problems of Migrant Workers." http://www.gov.cn/zhuanti/2015-06/13/content_2878968.htm.

2006-05-12. People's Republic of China Passport Act. "Order of the President of the People's Republic of China" (Hu Jingtao). http://www.fmprc.gov.cn/chn/gxh/tyb//bszn/dafw/t251906.htm.

2012-06-30. National People's Congress, 2012. "Exit and Entry Administration Law of the People's Republic of China." Adopted at the 27th meeting of the Standing Committee of the Eleventh National People's Congress of the People's Republic of China, Beijing, China. http://www.fmprc.gov.cn/chn/gxh/tyb//bszn/dafw/t9778.htm.

2013-07-01. "Exit and Entry Administration Law of the People's Republic of China." Adopted at the 27th meeting of the Standing Committee of the Eleventh National People's Congress on June 30, 2012. http://cs.mfa.gov.cn/zlbg/flfg/crjxg/t1054650.shtml.

2014-07-30. State Council. "Opinions on Further Promoting the Reform of the Household Registration System." http://www.gov.cn/zhengce/content/2014-07/30/content_8944.htm.

2014-10-14. Office of Migrant Workers' Issues Leading Group, State Council. "Circular of the State Council on the Outline of the Opinions on Further Improving the Work Regarding Providing Services for Migrant Workers." http://www.mohrss.gov.cn/gkml/xxgk/201410/t20141015_141984.html.

2014-11-24. National Health and Family Planning Commission, the Comprehensive Management Office of the Central Government, Migrant Workers Office of the State Council, the Ministry of Civil Affairs, the Ministry of Finance. "Guiding Opinions on Providing Essential Public Health and Family Planning Services Well for The Floating Population." http://www.moh.gov.cn/ldrks/s3577/201411/053b067aa3c84bbd9b87bf51da0c1199.shtml.

2016-06-07. State Health and Family Planning Commission General Office, 2016. "On the Dissemination of the Plan for the Floating Population's Health Education and Promotional Actions (2016-2020)." http://www.nhfpc.gov.cn/ldrks/s3577/201606/cf593583b37241a58068e0aa0b86d-2de.shtml.

REFERENCES

Haugen, Heidi Østbø (2015, March 4). Destination China: The Country Adjusts to its New Migration Reality. *Migration Information Source*. http://www.migrationpolicy.org/article/destination-china-country-adjusts-its-new-migration-reality.

Lin, Huochan (2016, April 26). There is a 16.2 percent gap between our country's urban long-term residents and registered urban population. *Economics Daily*. http://www.gov.cn/zhengce/2014-03/16/content_2640075.htm.

Lu, Xueyi (2004). *Social Mobility of Contemporary China*. Social Sciences Academic Press.

Lu, Yu (2002). *Fifty Years of Demography in New China*. China Population Publishing House.

Ministry of Human Resources and Social Security of China (2017). The total number of migrant workers continues its steady increase in 2016. http://www.mohrss.gov.cn/nmggzs/NMGG-ZSgongzuodongtai/201702/t20170227_266967.html.

Ministry of Labor and Human Resources, Ministry of Public Security and Ministry of Commerce (1988). Notice on the Resolving of Relevant Problems of Long-term Separated Living at Two Places of Couple of Senior Workers. http://www.lawxp.com/statute/s575678.html.

Ministry of Public Security (1986). Instruction of Ordinance for Household Registration of People's Republic of China (Draft) (1958). *China Demographic Yearbook (1958)*. China Social Sciences Press.

National Bureau of Statistics (2016). *Statistical Yearbook 1950–2016*. China Statistics Press, 1950–2016.

National Bureau of Statistics (2016). 2015 National Monitoring Survey of Migrant Workers. http://www.stats.gov.cn/tjsj/zxfb/201604/t20160428_1349713.html.

National Bureau of Statistics (2017). 2016 Statistical Report. http://www.stats.gov.cn/tjsj/

sjjd/201702/t20170228_1467357.html.

Organization Department of the CPC Central Committee, the Ministry of Civil Affairs, the Ministry of Public Security, and the State Labor Bureau (1980). Notice on the Gradual Resolving the Issue of Married Couple's Long-term Separation due to Work in Different Locations. http://www.law-lib.com/law/law_view.asp?id=44104.

Pan, Jiahua and Wei Houkai (2013). *Annual Report on Urban Development of China No. 6*. Social Sciences Academic Press.

Population Research Institute of CASS (1986). *China Demographic Yearbook (1985)*. China Social Sciences Press.

State Council Legislative Affairs Bureau (1986). *Compilation of Regulations of the People's Republic of China No. 85*. Law Press.

State Council Legislative Affairs Bureau (1996). *Compilation of Existing Laws and Administrative Regulations of the People's Republic of China (1949–1994) No.1*. China Legal Publishing House.

State Council (2014). National New Urbanization Plan (2014-2020). http://www.gov.cn/zhengce/2014-03/16/content_2640075.htm.

Xiang, Biao (2016). "Emigration Trends and Policies in China: Movement of the Wealthy and Highly Skilled", Transatlantic Council on Migration Report, February 2016. Migration Policy Institute. http://www.migrationpolicy.org/research/emigration-trends-and-policies-china-movement-wealthy-and-highly-skilled.

UNHCR (United Nations High Commissioner for Refugees) (2015). The People's of Republic of China Fact Sheet. http://www.unhcr.org/5000187d9.html.

Wang, Yuesheng (2013). On Changes of China's Contemporary Population Migration Policy—Based on the 1950-1990s Era. *Journal of the Renmin University of China* (5): 103–111.

Zhang, Huiqing (2010). Rural–Urban Migration Policy Review since 1990s. *Frontier* (17): 111–114.

Zhuang, Guotu (1997). Some thoughts on Chinese international migration in the past 20 years. *Overseas Chinese History Studies*, Issue 2, 1997.

Chapter 3
Hukou System and Rural Migrant Workers' Assimilation

Weizhen Dong, Changxing Zhao

ABSTRACT

China restricted population mobility under the control of its Hukou system (household registration system) for more than two decades, particularly during the years when the country had limited supplies of food and other resources. The economic reforms that started 40 years ago led to relaxed migration restrictions; thus, a massive supply of surplus rural labour, regional development imbalances and income disparities resulted in a large-scale movement of rural residents to urban areas. By the end of 2016, there were 282 million rural-urban migrant workers in China (Huang, 2017). This population became a great factor in advancing China's urbanization.

However, these rural migrants and their families have not been as completely urbanized in the cities as their city native counterparts, particularly in accessing essential social benefits and public services such as housing, education and healthcare. Their assimilation into the cities is vital for China's overall development. Only when the country can remove barriers to migrant workers' access to social benefits and public services will these new urban dwellers be fully assimilated into the cities. The obvious barrier is the Hukou system and its effect on nearly all aspects of the social welfare and social security system.

1. INTRODUCTION

Rural-urban migrant workers constitute the main segment of the migrant population in urban China. Since the 1980s, China has gradually loosened policies restricting the migration of the rural population. As a result, some surplus rural laborers began to enter the cities to seek employment opportunities. Economic reform in the urban sectors provided rural migrants with greater access to the urban labour market from the 1990s onward, when rural-urban migration accelerated. Due to the Hukou regulations, rural migrant workers could seldom change their residential status from rural to urban, and therefore, even when they were working and living in the cities, they remained "rural migrant workers", a term meaning rural villagers who work in cities (Li, 2003). After approximately 20 years, the number of rural migrant workers grew to 282 million in 2016, and it continues to grow.

China has entered a new phase of urbanization, which includes industrialization, the advent of the information economy, and agricultural modernization; coordinated development of population, economy, resources and environment; coordinated and integrated development of different sizes of cities and towns; centralizing of population, "citizenization" of rural migrants and providing and developing appropriate public services for them; and promoting integrated urban and rural development (Ge, 2013). It is also a human-centered phase of urbanization. Rural migrant workers and their families are the main concern of this wave of urbanization.

This chapter analyzes the existing barriers the migrant workers face in accessing social benefits and essential public services. It discusses the difficult reality and explores how to promote the citizenization of rural migrant workers. Finally, it proposes ways in which migrant workers can gradually assimilate into the cities, and urges the policymakers to remove institutional barriers for rural migrant workers. Once all of the public programs and services that urban natives enjoy are offered to migrant workers, China will enter a new phase of urbanization and renewed socioeconomic development.

2. RURAL MIGRANT WORKERS AND THEIR CHALLENGES

2.1. THE LABELING OF THE GROUP

The term "rural migrant worker" in Chinese literally means "farmer workers" or "peasant workers", and was originated by sociologist Yulin Zhang of the Chinese Academy of Social Sciences (CASS) in a work that appeared in 1984 in the Academy's Sociology Studies News Report (State Council Research Institute, 2016). The term specifies the group's household registration category as rural residents who are working in the city. In national demographic data, the term migrant workers refers to those whose household registration is still in rural areas, but who are engaged in non-agricultural work in the region or in another urban area for six months and above (NBS, 2017).

This group has acquired a few "nicknames" that have passed into popular use. One is "mangliu" or "blindly-flowing population": this refers to the mass movement of rural villagers into the cities, especially at the end of 1980s and the beginning of 1990s. Second, "dagong zai", or "selling-labour-for-money young men", a term imported from Hong Kong, where many residents thought that foreign migrant workers could only be engaged in hard, low-skill-level, poorly paid jobs. Third, "jingcheng wugong renyuan", or "rural to urban migrant workers", which is an official definition in China that refers to those who work in the cities with rural household registration status (Lu, 2007).

Scholars called for the renaming of this group, since a discriminatory or disparaging label carries social implications. Members of this group are often not paid as well, fail to receive adequate social welfare benefits, and even find that basic rights are often violated in the community (Lei and Lei, 2012). However, changing the label does not bring about meaningful change in the group's social status and living conditions if there is no corresponding change in their pay levels and access to social benefits and public services.

2.2. REGIONAL DISTRIBUTION AND NUMBER OF RURAL-URBAN MIGRANT WORKERS

The total number of rural migrant workers continues to grow. According to recent data from the National Statistics Bureau, the total number of Chinese rural migrant workers increased from 229.78 million in 2009 to nearly 286.52 million in 2017 (see Figure 1). Rural migrant workers accounted for more than 20 percent of the total population of China in 2017, and the total number of rural migrant workers is expected to continue to grow in the next few years (National Statistics Bureau, 2018).

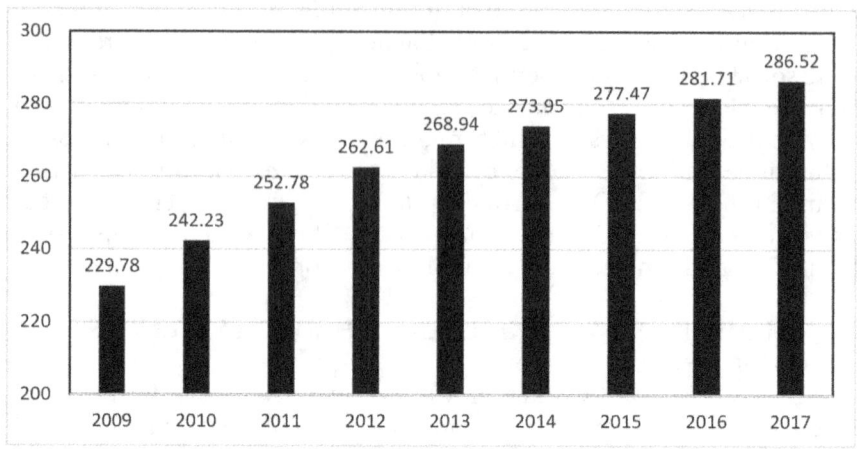

Figure 1. Total Number Of Rural Migrant Workers (2009–2017, million)

Data source: National Statistics Bureau's annual *National Rural Migrant Workers Monitoring and Survey*

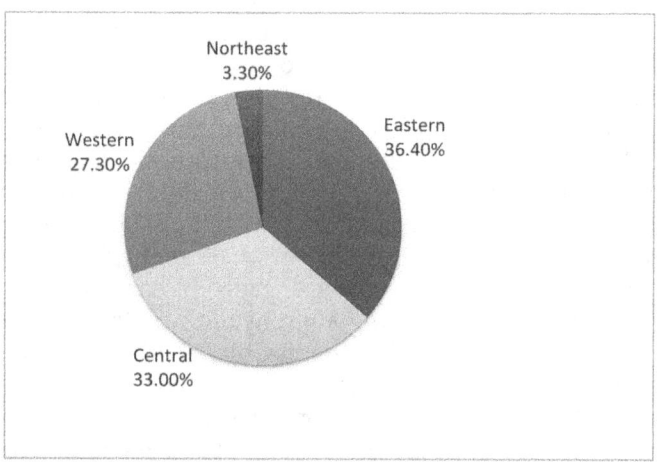

Figure 2. Regional Distribution of Migrant Workers (2017)
Data source: National Statistics Bureau,
National Rural Migrant Workers Monitoring and Survey (2017)

The distribution of migrant workers in China is shown in Figure 2. Eastern China has the highest number of migrant workers, since it is the wealthiest region of the country, while northeast China has the lowest number of migrant workers due to its relatively fewer resources and opportunities.

2.3. Relevant Government Policies about Rural Migrant Workers

Once the number of migrant workers increased to a critical mass, the social issues surrounding this population became apparent. Their employment, their income, their healthcare, their children's education, their housing, their social benefits entitlements all became hot topics. Relevant government departments issued policies and regulations for addressing these pressing issues. Following are some of them:

- Opinions on Further Strengthening Compulsory Education for Rural Migrant Workers' Children (Ministry Of Education, 2003)
- Measures for the Rural Migrant Workers to Participate in the Basic Pension Plan (State Council, 2006)
- State Council Opinions on Solving the Problems Concerning the Rural Migrant Workers (State Council, 2006)
- Notice of the General Office of the State Council on Effectively Carrying Out the Tasks Concerning Rural Migrant Workers (2008)
- Notice of the Ministry of Education on Effectively Carrying Out Vocational Education and Other Training Programs for Returning-to-Home-Village Rural Migrant Workers (2009)
- Opinions of the Ministry of Civil Affairs on Promoting the Assimilation of Rural Migrant Workers into Urban Communities (2012)
- Opinions of the State Council On Further Improving the Work Of Providing Services for Rural Migrant Workers (2014)
- Notice of the Printing and Distributing of the Interim Measures for the Convergence of Urban and Rural Pension Insurance Systems (Ministry of Finance And Ministry Of Human Resources And Social Security, 2014)
- Opinions of the General Office of the State Council on the Support of Migrant Workers Returning to their Hometowns for Starting Businesses (2015)
- Notice of the State Administration for Industry and Commerce on Further Improving the Work of Migrant Workers (2015)
- On Further Strengthening Cultural Services for Migrant Workers (Ministry of Culture, Office of the State Council, Leading Group of Migrant Workers, National Federation of Trade Unions, 2016)
- Opinions of the General Office of the State Council on the Comprehensive Management of the Wages of Migrant Workers in Arrears (2016)

These policy statements are generally well-thought-out and written with the interests of rural migrant workers and their families in mind. However, most of them were issued later than they should have been, and some of them did not address fundamental issues. In short, rural migrant workers in China still face great challenges in their daily life.

2.4. Inequality and institutional barriers

Rural migrants energized urban development in China. However, rural migrants now face challenges in the cities they reside (Dong, 2015). Due to migrant workers' rural residential registration, they face difficulties in accessing local (city) social benefits and social services. The Hukou system was initially set up by the state as a means of distributing social welfare and services, such as food, housing, healthcare, and education, as well as arranging for employment, in an era of limited resources. In today's China, the distribution of social welfare benefits is mostly still based on the decades-old household registration system, which automatically blocked access for rural migrant workers and their families.

Unfortunately, the essential functioning of the Hukou system as an entry point for access to various social benefits and public services has never changed. As Table 1 shows, migrants' social security program enrollment rates in 2015 were very low (National Bureau of Statistics, 2016).

Table 1. Migrant Workers' Social Security Program Enrollment, 2015

Social Security Program	Enrollment (Million)	Migrant Workers (%)
Pension	55.85	20.13
Medical Insurance	51.66	18.62
Unemployment Insurance	42.19	15.21
Work-related Injury Insurance	74.89	26.99

Data source: National Bureau of Statistics, *National Rural Migrant Workers Monitoring and Survey Report*, 2016.

2.4.1. Educational access barriers

Rural migrant workers' access to vocational education as well as their children's access to compulsory education are both disadvantaged compared to the access enjoyed by urban "natives".

With limited education, upon entering cities rural migrant workers can only undertake "dirty, heavy, tiring, and dangerous" work with low incomes. In order to change that situation, rural migrant workers must improve their vocational skills. However, there is no suitable vocational educational program for rural migrant workers, something that slows down their individual human capital development as well as their socioeconomic assimilation into cities.

Until recent years, the most difficult situation facing rural migrants often involved their children's education. Initially, migrant workers' children had limited access to public education in cities due to their Hukou status. Some migrants saw a business opportunity in opening schools targeting these children, since their numbers were large, and migrant workers' children's schools run by migrants emerged. They charged high fees but did not provide high quality education.

As for compulsory education, problems mainly lie in the high dropout rate, difficulties in admission, and lack of participation in examinations by rural migrant workers' children who live in cities. According to official statistics, there were 19.8 million migrant children under 14 years of age, of whom 74 percent (or 14.6 million) are registered as rural residents, and more than 8 million of whom fall within the age range for compulsory education. Of these, 9.3 percent of migrants' children were not attending school: 6.85 percent of them had never attended any school, and 2.45 percent of them had dropped out (Research Group under State of Council, 2006). According to the sample data in the 2010 national census, it can be inferred that the number of migrants' children under age 17 in rural and urban areas totaled 35.81 million, of whom children registered as rural residents accounted for 80.35 percent of that total (28.77 million) (National Women's Federation Research Group, 2013).

For preschool education, which is not included in the compulsory educational system, rural migrant workers have to choose kindergartens that are affordable in cost, which usually translate into substandard in conditions and remote in location. Otherwise, they could only leave their children at home. By comparison, in the compulsory education stage, most migrants' children can attend public schools thanks to the improved policies in recent years, although some of them still have to go to private schools or the schools for migrants' children.

After receiving compulsory education, migrants' children who choose to attend senior high school and college in the cities in which they reside may still face many difficulties, such as college and university entrance examinations, participation in which is restricted by Hukou registration location. Although the central government has called for lower-level governments to accommodate migrant children's needs, some localities are unable to meet the demand (Ministry of Education, 2012). In short, rural migrants' children face educational disadvantages compared to urban citizens' children.

2.4.2. Medical care service access barriers
Without urban Hukou, rural migrant workers and their children cannot enjoy full and equal access to public health services, including children's healthcare, pregnant women's healthcare, epidemic prevention and treatment, vaccination, etc. Children entering cities with their migrant parents are not fully included in the urban family planning service system, and their disease prevention and monitoring are not covered. This means migrant workers' children may not receive adequate immunization and related healthcare, and are therefore more likely to suffer from certain immunological diseases in comparison with urban children. Rural migrant workers have low awareness of personal occupational health issues and little knowledge about occupational hazards. Meanwhile, rural migrant workers live in densely populated areas with bad living conditions and high flow rates, where infectious diseases are common (Ling, 2000; Dong, 2015).

The level and quality of the medical care provided to rural migrant workers is also inferior. As a result of their working environments and labour conditions, migrant workers suffer a higher rate of occupational diseases and work-related injuries when compared to urban employees, but medical insurance and capacity for treatment are far from satisfactory. Most rural migrant workers find it so difficult and expensive to see a doctor that they seldom go to hospitals or medical centers (Dong, 2015). The latest data shows that migrant workers' medical care insurance enrollment rate is only 18.62 percent, which implies medical care access among rural migrant workers remains a major concern.

2.4.3. Pension access

China offers different pension systems for rural and urban residents. In urban areas, the basic pension service for urban employees and the public institution retirement system predominate, but in rural areas the family-oriented new-mode rural social pension system is most commonly found. According to existing policies, when working in the cities, rural migrant workers should enjoy the same pension benefits as urban employees, but in reality the opposite occurs. At present, the regional planning of the pension insurance fund is at odds with the instability and high flow rate of rural migrant workers' employment. The current pension transfer and connection system is imperfect, and regional divides are severe. Therefore, when rural migrant workers change their working location, their pensions cannot be freely transferred or connected. This results in reduced participation by both rural migrant workers and their employers in the pension insurance schemes, with many rural migrant workers even canceling their pension.

Because many migrant workers are in short-term contract jobs and pension plans were not made to be portable, a trend of pension plan cancellation by rural migrant workers has emerged in some areas of China, especially where rural migrant workers were concentrated, like Guangdong Province. From 2002 to 2007, nearly 10 million rural migrant workers quit their pension plans, and pension cancellation grew by an annual rate of 17 percent.

In 2007, a total of 4.94 million rural migrant workers joined the basic pension plan in Shenzhen City, but 830,000 of them withdrew from their pension plans at the end of the year. Meanwhile, only 9,672 migrant workers successfully transferred their pension plans to their new workplaces. This means for every 10,000 rural migrant workers who joined a pension plan, 1,680 (16.8 percent) withdrew and only a tiny fraction were able to transfer their pension plans to other workplaces (Zheng, 2008).

In order to further maintain the basic rights and interests of rural migrant workers, the human resources and social security department released *Regulations on Rural Migrant Workers' Participation in Basic Pension System* in 2009. This was aimed at reducing the payment ratios of rural migrant workers, specifying pension transfer procedures and treatment after full payment, and encouraging employers and rural migrant workers to actively pay into the basic pension system. In spite of this new regulation, rural migrant workers' basic pension participation rate across the country in 2014 rose by only 0.5 percent when compared to the previous year, with overall pension participation levels as low as 16.7 percent (National Statistics Bureau, 2015); by 2015, it reached 20.13 percent (see Table 1).

2.4.4. Work-related injury insurance

Rural migrant workers' work environment, including poor working conditions, intense labor, and high risks, all result in a higher physical injury rate than that of other urban employees. However, few employers provide labor contracts to rural migrant workers providing for payments for work-related injury claims. In 2014, only 26.2 percent of migrant workers were insured for work-related injury (National Statistics Bureau, 2015).

In case of a work-related injury accident, rural migrant workers usually must pay out-of-pocket for costs that are supposed to be covered by insurance. Some hazardous industries can cause occupation-related diseases, which can result in long-term medical expenditures that are not covered by work-related injury insurance. Among the tens of thousands of work injury cases across the country every year, as many as 40 percent involve rural migrant workers, but only 5 percent receive compensation and remedy (Xiong, 2015).

For example, from the 1950s through 2011, the total nationwide number of occupational disease cases reached 779,849, of which 702,942 (90.13 percent) were cases of pneumoconiosis, which is the most prevalent severe occupational disease in China. The fatality rate of this disease is as high as 22 percent. At least 6 million rural migrant workers currently suffer from pneumoconiosis and need treatment. However, only between 10 percent and 20 percent of pneumoconiosis patients were diagnosed as having occupational disease and have registered at disease control centers (Pan, 2013).

Without a labor contract or work-related injury insurance, pneumoconiosis patients have difficulty obtaining occupational health compensation and other rights and benefits. One example is Haichao Zhang, a 28-year-old rural migrant worker in Xinmi City, Henan Province. He was diagnosed with pneumoconiosis in several hospitals in Zhengzhou and Beijing in 2009. However, the Occupational Disease Prevention and Treatment Hospital of Zhengzhou diagnosed him with phase 0+ tuberculosis. After being rejected by several hospitals, Zhang risked his life to receive a thoracotomy and proved that he was suffering from pneumoconiosis instead of tuberculosis (Lu and Wei, 2009). Haichao Zhang's case clearly highlights rural migrant workers' difficulties in accessing occupational disease diagnoses and relevant benefits.

2.4.5. Housing security
Rural migrant workers' housing security is not covered under the urban housing security system. It is not realistic for rural migrant workers to purchase apartments in the cities with their relatively low incomes. Therefore, most of them live in rural-urban fringe areas, "villages-in-the-city," dormitories or sheds. Rural migrant workers' housing expenditures accounted for 47.1 percent of their total essential living expenditures; 36.9 percent of migrant workers rented accommodation, 28.3 percent live in workplace dormitories, 17.2 percent live in sheds and operating sites, and only 1 percent were able to purchase an apartment in the cities where they work (National Statistics Bureau, 2015).

Although the central government has called for the construction of affordable housing in recent years, rural migrant workers still cannot enjoy such benefits due to the Hukou restrictions. Participation in the housing fund by migrant workers is the lowest of all six types of social insurance. In 2014, only 5.5 percent of rural-urban migrant workers paid into the housing provident fund (National Statistics Bureau, 2015). Part of the reason for such low participation is that one has to be enrolled in four other social security programs in order to be eligible, plus present proof of income, Hukou status, and a labour contract (Chen, 2016).

In May 2015, Puyang Municipal Government arranged for rural migrant workers to purchase housing in groups. The Puyang government's policy, *Ways of Encouraging Rural Migrant Workers to Purchase Housing in Cities and Promoting Housing Consumption*, was officially enacted on December 3, 2015. Rural residents would be offered a subsidy of ¥150/m² for their first-time purchase of newly built property, ¥100/m² for second-time home buyers who wish to improve their quality of housing, and ¥200/m² for the purchase of second-hand housing. In addition, the government also improved the efficiency of financial services for rural migrant workers purchasing housing in cities, raised the level of credit support for purchases of commodity housing, and implemented a minimum standard for the downpayment ratio and mortgage interest rate. The Financial Department of Puyang City offered ¥50 million to set up a housing security institution at the urban real estate management center in order to assist rural migrants to purchase housing in cities (Yong, 2015).

2.4.6. Employment and income security
Rural migrant workers' employment barriers include limited job opportunities. Compared to native urban residents, migrant workers receive lower incomes. In 2014, the average monthly income of rural migrant workers was ¥2,864, accounting for 61 percent, 60 percent, 80 percent and 94.5 percent respectively of the average monthly income of all employees in urban units, urban state-owned units, urban collective units, and urban private units. In 2015, the average monthly income of rural migrant workers was ¥3,072, accounting for 59 percent, 56 percent, 79 percent and 93 percent respectively of the average monthly income of all employees in urban units, urban state-owned units, urban collective units, and urban private units (National Statistics Bureau, 2015 and 2016). The monthly average income of migrant workers in 2016 was ¥3,275; although it had increased from the year prior, it was only about 59.4 percent of the average income of native urban employees. Only 36.2 percent of migrant workers signed labor contracts with their employers. Meanwhile, the average working time of rural migrant workers was 10.1 months per year, 25.2 days per month, and 8.7 hours per day (National Bureau of Statistics, 2016; Financial News, 2017).

Since most rural migrant workers have only received secondary school education (Mursal and Dong, 2018), lack of further education makes it nearly impossible to improve human capital. Their employment is limited to the bottom tier of the labor market, which not only affects their incomes, but also severely inhibits their assimilation into the cities.

3. DISCUSSION
3.1. Dual household registration system as a barrier to migrant workers' assimilation
China implemented the "urban-rural dual system" with the household registration system at its core in the late 1950s. It divides the Chinese population into an agricultural population and a non-agricultural population, or farmer and citizen, and strictly limits the agricultural population from migrating into the cities through household registration management. Apart from clarifying

identity and restricting migration, the effect of the urban-rural dual system is manifested in the resource allocation mode that differentiates between urban and rural areas (Qian, 2011). Some go as far as to argue that the state divides the population into an agricultural population and a non-agricultural population to limit its financial support in education, medical care service, employment, social security, and other resources (Li, 2014).

There is a consensus among the Chinese general public and in academia that the various economic, political, social, and institutional obstacles confronted by rural migrant workers during their process of citizenization has made them de facto second-class citizens (Liao and Wei, 2003). Rural migrant workers have encountered a wide range of problems such as institutional or policy-incurred social exclusion, insufficient individual human resources, and deficient social capital accumulation, during the process of their assimilation into the cities. Those obstacles have greatly inhibited their assimilation into the cities.

In March 2014, the *China Economic Weekly* and Institute for Urban and Environmental Studies of the Chinese Academy of Social Sciences jointly released the *Report on the Citizenization Progress of Chinese Migrated Rural Population (2012)*. According to this report, the composite index of Chinese rural migrant workers' citizenization in 2012 was 39.63 percent, almost the same as the previous year (Li, 2014). Studies show that the citizenization level of the new-generation rural migrant workers in China is 50.18 percent, which means half of the rural migrant workers are already citizenized. When the assimilation of rural migrant workers in cities is measured against five factors—living conditions, social relationship, economic life, psychological identification and political participation—their realization rates are 59.33 percent, 54.45 percent, 53.38 percent, 42.58 percent and 32.35 percent respectively (Li, 2013).

Liu et al. (2009) designed an index system composed of four factors, namely career, social status, individual qualification, and awareness and behavior, and reached a conclusion that the citizenization of the new-generation rural migrant workers was 45.53 percent, which is 3.5 percent higher than that of the first generation. Xu (2008) declared that the citizenization level of rural migrant workers in China was about 50 percent. Based on a nationwide survey, Zhang (2011) pointed out that the citizenization level of the new-generation rural migrant workers was already as high as 45 percent. After carrying out a measurement of the new-generation rural migrant workers' citizenization in Xi'an, Ren (2012) believed that less than half of the new-generation rural migrant workers in this city feel they have become citizenized.

3.2. EDUCATION AND TRAINING DETERMINE INCOME

Most of the rural migrant workers have a poor educational background, which is the fundamental factor that inhibits them from improving their income and integrating into cities. As Table 2 shows, over 60 percent of rural migrant workers have only gone as far as junior high school. Rural migrant workers with senior high school education or above from 2011 to 2015 account for 23 percent, 23.7 percent, 22.8 percent, 23.8 percent, and 25.2 percent of all migrant workers respectively (National Statistics Bureau, 2016). A comparison of rural migrant workers moving elsewhere for work with the total population of rural migrant workers shows that they have higher levels of education at various levels, including junior high school, senior high school, technical secondary school, college, and above. It proves that education plays an important role in allowing rural migrant workers to move to assume jobs in other places.

However, when compared with the nationwide education level, rural migrant workers lag far behind other groups in college attendance or higher levels of education. Due to limited data availability, comparisons were only made for the years 2010 and 2011. In 2010, 8.93 percent of all rural migrant workers in China attained an educational level of college or above, while only 7.0 percent of all rural migrant workers moving elsewhere for work attained this level of education (National Statistics Bureau, 2011 & 2012). Compared with urban citizens, rural migrant workers' education level was significantly lower.

Limited by their educational background, rural migrant workers mainly work in labor intensive industries, such as manufacturing, construction, transportation, retail, accommodation, catering, housekeeping, etc. In other words, they usually take the dirty, tiring, hard, and dangerous work in the cities, but work for lower pay. Their living conditions, consumption level and assimilation capability are greatly limited.

Table 2. Education Level of Migrant Workers (%)

Year	2010	2011	2012	2013	2014	2015	2016	2017
Education level	Nationwide census	Migrant Workers						
No education*	4.08	1.5	1.5	1.1	1.2	1.1	1.0	1.0
Primary school	26.78	14.4	14.3	14.8	15.4	14.0	13.2	13.0
Secondary school	38.79	61.1	60.5	60.3	60.6	59.7	59.4	58.6
High school or vocational school	14.03	17.7	18.0	16.5	16.1	16.9	17.0	17.1
College or above	8.93	5.3	5.7	7.3	6.7	8.3	9.4	10.3

* The proportion of illiterate people 15 years old or above.
Data source: Based on *2010: The Sixth Nationwide Census Data Bulletin (No. 1)* and the National Statistics Bureau's annual *Rural Migrant Workers Monitoring and Survey 2011-2018*.

The low education level of rural migrant workers directly determines or affects their employment, income level and assimilability in the cities they reside. Therefore, an increasing number of rural migrant workers are motivated to receive technical training, although the proportion is still quite low. Table 3 and Figure 3 show the occupational skill training among migrant workers in recent years. Although the proportion of occupationally trained rural migrant workers increased from 30.8 percent in 2012 to 34.8 percent in 2014, rural migrant workers without technical training remain in the majority (National Statistics Bureau, 2015). Meanwhile, young rural migrant workers are more inclined to take part in non-agricultural vocational training, and there are more young migrant workers than older rural migrant workers. The trend is clear: the younger rural migrant workers are, the less willing they are to receive agricultural skills training.

Table 3. Rural Migrant Workers Having Received Technical Skills Training (%)

Age	Received agricultural skills training			Received non-agricultural skills training			Received technical skills training		
	2012	2013	2014	2012	2013	2014	2012	2013	2014
20 or younger	4.0	5.0	6.0	22.3	29.9	31.4	24.0	31.0	32.6
21-30	6.2	5.5	6.0	31.6	34.6	37.0	34.0	35.9	38.3
31-40	11.0	9.1	8.8	26.7	31.8	34.0	32.0	34.1	36.1
41-50	14.9	12.7	12.6	23.1	27.8	29.9	30.5	32.1	33.7
Older than 50	14.5	12.4	12.7	16.9	21.2	24.0	25.5	25.9	28.8
Total	10.7	9.3	9.5	25.6	29.9	32.0	30.8	32.7	34.8

Data source: Based on the *2012–2014 National Rural Migrant Workers Monitoring and Survey Report* released by the National Statistics Bureau annually.

Skills matter. According to the information from large construction companies such as the Building Group of Qingdao and Qingdao First Construction Group, the salaries of short-term workers and general labourers were between ¥100 and ¥150 per day and between ¥3,000 and ¥4,000 per month. Salaries of carpenters and bricklayers with specialized skills ranged from ¥260 to ¥350 per day and between ¥7,000 and ¥8,000 per month (minimum) in 2013. The monthly income of migrant workers with excellent skills could exceed ¥10,000. For example, skilled workers such as scaffold workers, welders, electricians and elevator/crane operators earn as much as ¥300 to ¥500 per day, and ¥10,000 a month (Zhang, 2014).

Related studies show that, compared with unemployed workers, each additional year of education that urban workers receive increases their opportunity for entering public enterprises by 5.8 percent. However, each additional year of education received by rural migrant workers increases their opportu-

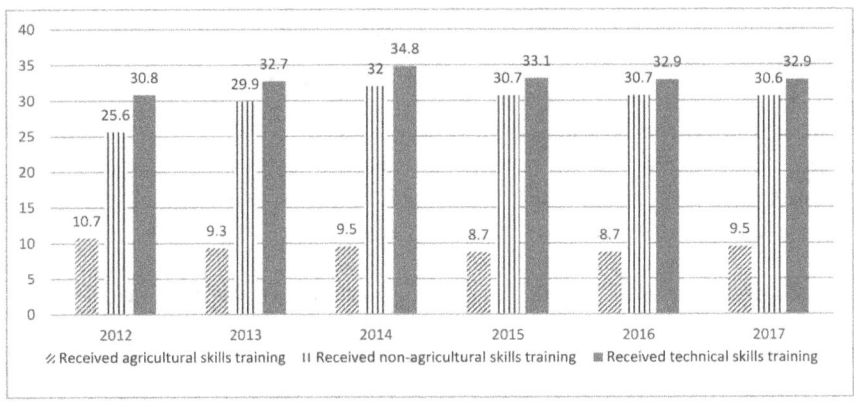

Figure 3. Rural Residents Having Received Skills Training, 2012 to 2017 (%)

nity for entering public enterprises by only 0.8 percent. Meanwhile, for every additional year of education urban workers receive, their opportunity for entering private or foreign-funded enterprises decreases by 4.7 percent, but for every additional year of education rural migrant workers receive, their opportunity for entering private or foreign-funded enterprises decreases by only 1.1 percent. As such, with the same level of education, rural migrant workers have fewer opportunities for entering the public sector than urban workers, and they are more likely to work in non-public sectors (Feng, 2010).

3.3. Social support for new urban dwellers is important

The lack of social support for rural migrant workers is mainly caused by the lack of traditional social networks as well as the absence of institutional and organizational support.

First, the traditional social network of rural migrant workers is an extension of trust-based kinship and regional connections. Rural migrant workers' trust-based personal relationships are their primary social relationships in the cities, and are mostly built upon kinship and hometown connections. This kind of deep kinship and geographical relationship helps rural migrant workers settle down in the cities and seek employment opportunities; however, it also blocks them from fully integrating into new urban social surroundings.

Second, rural migrant workers are not adequately supported by institutions and organizations (Wang, 2010), and the lack of related institutions and rural migrant worker organizations makes it difficult for rural migrant workers to fully assimilate into the cities. For instance, when encountering difficulties, rural migrant workers are more inclined to seek help from their countrymen, relatives or friends instead of from the institutions they associate with, labor unions, or social public welfare organizations (Zhao, 2014). Social benefits and public services are the most crucial social support provided by the government for all citizens to meet their living and development needs. For rural migrants in urban areas, the most important public services should include education, medical care, employment, and housing.

3.4. Points-system is not designed for migrant workers to obtain urban Hukou

Scholars have studied the main obstacles and solutions to rural migrant workers' assimilation into cities from a variety of perspectives: macro factors, such as income distribution, urbanization and industrialization, production factors accumulation and environmental bearing capacity; medium-level analysis, such as social security, public finance, employment stability, organized expression and population management; and micro-level analysis, namely, personal reasons for migration, such as social capital, human capital, social stratification, intergenerational differentiation, self-identification, etc.

The debate on how to grant some migrant workers urban household registration status has been on going among scholars as well as the concerned public. So far, "jifen luohu" or a points system for household registration has attracted the most interest. The system converts individual migrants' employment, accommodation, educational background, skill level, tax payments, and credit records, among other things, into points. Once they reach a specified number of points, the migrant would be eligible to change their household registration status (Peng et al., 2014; China Daily, 2015). Let us take a look at one city's points system as an example.

3.4.1. *The points system in Guangzhou*
General eligibility under Guangzhou City's points system involves a number of factors, including holding a Guangzhou residence permit for more than three years, being under the age of 45, purchasing local basic social insurance coverage continuously for more than four years, owning real estate in the city, meeting the city's family planning policy regulations, etc. (Unless otherwise specified, information for the following sections is from the Guangzhou government website: http://www.gz.gov.cn.)

Specifically, the points calculation scheme is as follows:

Education level:
Bachelor degree (60 points); college degree or higher (40 points); technical and vocational school or high school (20). [Note: Take only the highest score, not accumulated points. No score for high school or lower.]

Technical skill (highest score only):
Intermediate professional title (60 points); senior skilled worker, third-level institution technical staff (30 points); intermediate skilled workers, fourth-level institution technical staff (10 points).

Occupational qualifications or occupational specialty:
Occupational and technical licenses or types of work in line with the Guangzhou vocational qualifications and occupational specialty, based on Guangzhou points system's list of occupational qualifications (20 points).

Social services:
In the past five years, participated in blood donation (2 points each time) or volunteer work (2 points for every 50 hours). No more than 2 points for each year, and the cumulative maximum no more than 10 points in this category.

Tax:
In the previous three years, in accordance with the law of the city of Guangzhou, paid personal income tax, cumulative up to ¥100,000 or more (20 points).

Documents required for application: social insurance certificate and payment records, real estate license, family planning certificate, no criminal record certificate, ID card, diploma, certificate, professional/occupational qualification certificate, proof of work, etc.

Based on the point system, most migrant workers cannot reach the specified points level in the city of Guangzhou or elsewhere. Therefore, some say that the system "has nothing to do with rural migrant workers" (Wang, 2012; Huang, 2016). For example, as we noted earlier in this chapter, most migrant workers have only completed secondary school, so they would receive no points for education; most migrant workers are in low-income jobs, therefore earn no property ownership points; their jobs tend to be low grade and low skill, therefore they earn no technical qualification points; many of them have to work overtime, therefore have no time for volunteerism, and thus earn no points for social service; social insurance certificates and payment records are difficult for rural migrants to obtain, since the nature of their jobs tends to be precarious. Finally, it is not likely that an ordinary rural migrant worker would pay income tax over ¥100,000 in three years.

3.4.2. Recent modification of Guangzhou's points system

Guangzhou City government seems to be gradually lowering the points system's eligibility requirements. The most recent modifications of the criteria are as follows:

Age: 26–40 years old; if holds senior technician qualification, up to 45.

Skill: Has obtained level one (senior technician), level two (technician), or senior technician from license from Guangdong province or Guangzhou city's occupational skill identification center, no matter in which occupation.

Marriage/property ownership: Meet one of the following criteria: married, unmarried owns Guangzhou real estate (excluding Conghua, Zengcheng), or unmarried without property

Education: received high school or technical school education or above

Technicians, senior technicians have social insurance in Guangzhou for a number of years

Family planning: no childbirth without marriage, no over-policy-allowed-number of children, and no violation of family planning regulations.

Even with lowered education requirements, most rural migrants are still ineligible, since they only have secondary school education. The requirement to purchase personal social insurance for a number of years is also a barrier. Thus, changing rural migrants' household registration status for social services access through the points system is not realistic.

Meanwhile, small towns and small cities have relatively more achievable household registration criteria. This may lead more rural migrants to relocate their families in the near future. A recent study shows that rural migrants cannot return to their childhood village lives once they have lived in the city (Dong, 2016); if settling down in the city where they currently work seems too difficult, small towns and small cities near their home village will be their best alternative location.

4. POLICY RECOMMENDATION
4.1. Enhancing and securing rural migrant workers' basic livelihood services

It is necessary to promote equal employment for rural migrant workers and guarantee their rights to work compensation, breaks and holidays, and vocational training. Corresponding policies should be people-oriented to help rural migrant workers find jobs and increase income, gradually eliminate the current inequality and division in employment policies, and harmonize the employment policies in rural areas with those in urban areas. Vocational training for rural migrant workers should be established and improved. The government should consider the weak human capital of rural migrant workers, increase public expenditure on their vocational training, provide subsidies for them to participate in training, and promote participation in professional skills training generally. These factors can encourage the improvement and accumulation of human capital, as well as enhance competence in the employment market.

Rural migrant workers should be included in the urban pension system. The major reason for the low pension participation rate of rural migrant workers is uncertainty surrounding future revenues. The current pension system is not uniform across the country, so pensions cannot be transferred between different provinces. However, one prominent feature of rural migrant workers is high mobility. Therefore, rural migrant workers should be included in urban social insurance systems so that they may enjoy equal pension rights. It is necessary to form an unblocked pension transfer channel to remove uncertainty in pension income, and further realize nationwide pension collection and management. Last, rural migrant workers should be encouraged to take part in the pension system.

Having a place to live is the essential need of rural migrant workers. It is the responsibility of the government to ensure citizens' access to essential public services, including housing. Therefore, basic housing security should be provided to all, including rural migrant workers.

First of all, rural migrant workers should be included in the urban housing security system, especially affordable housing and public rental housing, so that they can enjoy equal housing security rights as urban citizens. Meanwhile, the government should reform the housing fund system by including rural migrant workers in the system, and all employers must pay into the housing fund for rural migrant workers. The government should provide proper rental subsidies for those rural migrant workers who have yet to solve their housing problems through the private market, as well as strictly control the rental market and improve the housing service level. At present, the central and local governments are actively attempting to support rural migrant workers to purchase housing in cities by reducing the downpayment ratio, providing preferential rates for mortgages, and offering housing purchasing subsidies.

Affordable housing and low rent apartment should be available for the low-income social groups.

4.2. Improving the quality of public welfare services
4.2.1. *Realizing education equality*

Education is the fundamental method of improving human capital, and also the most decisive factor for the lower classes and vulnerable groups to change their destiny and move forward.

1. It is necessary to strengthen fundamental education in rural areas, and gradually achieve equality between rural and urban education. Education funding and teaching conditions in rural villages should be improved. Teacher salaries should be improved to attract a more outstanding teaching force. The allocation of teaching resources should be slightly tilted toward rural areas. Tuition and fees for preschool and compulsory education in rural areas should be exempted.

2. A vocational skills education system should be built and improved in order to enhance rural migrant workers' practical skills, integrate teaching resources for vocational skills, and strengthen the development of skills and comprehensive abilities. Innovation can be made in training approaches, and the government can make use of social forces to encourage the development of vocational skills education (Jin, 2011).

3. Preschool education should be made compulsory as soon as possible, so that rural migrant workers can choose public kindergartens for their children. On the other hand, private kindergartens should be standardized to control quality.

4. The government should strive for equality in compulsory education when ensuring migrants' children's access to education.

Most rural migrant workers' children have access to public schools currently, but the results are still far from satisfactory. Rural migrant workers' children should be entitled to enjoy the same educational conditions, teaching resources, and quality of teachers as urban children. In order to achieve this goal, the government should offer additional financial support to schools receiving migrants' children. Targeted intervention or psychological counseling should also be offered to rural migrant workers' children to realize equality in their social environment.

4.2.2. *Migrant workers' access to public health service*

The core idea of "prevention first" should be insisted upon so that everyone has equal access to the public health service. Since the SARS outbreak in 2003, China has put a great deal of financial and material resources into public health to gradually improve the service system, further improve the public health guarantee capability, improve disease control, health monitoring and public health information systems, and upgrade the response system to public health emergency events.

However, the public health services that target the "floating population", especially the great numbers of rural migrant workers, continue to lag behind and require improvement in coordination between the government, public health departments, and communities. The government should first establish that rural migrant workers are an important target for public health intervention, increase financial support, and provide funds to be exclusively used for public health services targeted at rural migrant workers.

Public health service departments should regard "serving the public" as their responsibility, and provide better and more targeted public health services for rural migrant workers in certain areas, such as disease prevention and control, maternal and children's healthcare, as well as occupational health and environmental hygiene monitoring. This would drastically cut down costly public health accidents among rural migrant workers. Currently, communities are the direct providers of the public health service.

Appropriate public healthcare facilities need to be set up in communities and workplaces where rural migrant workers are concentrated, in order to provide maternal and children health service, health education, and disease monitoring and prevention for rural migrant workers and their family members in a more convenient way (Sun, 2012; Dong, 2015).

4.2.3. *Exploration of the mechanism connecting the urban and rural medical insurance systems*

"Too expensive to seek care and too difficult to seek care" has been a social issue for years and one that was never truly resolved. Migrant workers tend to be engaged in high-risk jobs with relatively low incomes, and they are more likely to suffer physical harm. Rural migrant workers are covered by the new rural cooperation medical care insurance in rural areas, but they cannot enjoy it while working long-term in the cities. They can also take part in the urban basic medical insurance, but only 17.6 percent of the migrant workers were enrolled in 2014 (National Bureau of Statistics, 2015).

Initially, therefore, it is necessary to encourage rural migrant workers to participate in basic medical insurance to reduce the risk of falling into poverty caused by illness. Rural migrant workers should be informed of the effects of medical insurance on individuals and their families. Secondly, the government must explore mechanisms that will connect urban basic medical insurance with new-mode rural cooperation medical insurance, and promote the establishment of new-mode rural cooperation among medical care service institutions in the cities. This would not only allow rural migrant workers in the new-mode rural cooperation system to visit a doctor more conveniently, but also allow rural migrant workers to be reimbursed for all sorts of medical care service charges (Yang, 2014). Finally, chronic illness healthcare coverage and reimbursement schemes should be further improved to enable rural migrant workers the ability to visit hospitals, as well as guarantee their healthcare rights.

4.3. Deepen the functional reform of the government

With rapid socioeconomic development and the promotion of urbanization, demand for essential public services is high and continues to grow. When integrating into cities, rural migrant workers' rights and interests are detrimentally affected due to the inequality in essential public services, which greatly restricts citizenization and assimilation. As the main supplier of public services, the government should enforce related reforms, strengthen the functions of essential public services, deepen reform of the household registration reform and public financial system, and increase public expenditure to meet social needs. This will allow the government to better meet the demands of both urban and rural residents for essential public services, and provide public guarantees for economic and social development as well as national modernization (Yan, 2014).

4.3.1. Strengthen the basic public service function of the government

With the growing demand for social and economic development in China, the government is changing from the traditional "administrator" role to a "service provider" role. This service-oriented government can enhance the awareness and capabilities of public services. The government is required to define its own orientation and roles, change traditional administration and management practices, and improve the awareness and capabilities of its staff, especially front-line civil servants. More concretely speaking, the functional departments closely related to rural migrant workers, such as the employment service, social security, basic education, public health service and family planning, should not create unreasonable obstacles for rural migrant workers in accessing services. Instead, these departments should actively seek to solve the problems encountered by rural migrant workers in city life, provide high-quality and efficient services where possible, improve rural migrant workers' living standards and quality of life, and promote equality in essential public services for rural migrant workers and urban residents.

4.3.2. Deepening household registration reform

The rural-urban dual household registration system is the institutional cause of inequality between urban and rural essential public services. In order to provide equal levels of essential public services in urban and rural areas, the household registration system must be reformed radically. In addition, it is necessary to set up a uniform urban-rural public services supply system.

The government should connect the financial transfer payment with rural migrant workers' citizenization and assimilation into cities, reasonably determine the citizenization cost shared by governments at different levels, and gradually improve state-level financial expenditures in essential public services such as compulsory education, basic pension and basic medical care service (Zhong, 2015) to improve the government's capability in supplying essential public services.

The reform of the household registration system is a key step in promoting rural migrant workers' assimilation into cities, and it will be helpful to divorce social welfare and public services from local household registration identification in order to eliminate rural-urban differences and ensure social inclusion for all.

Meanwhile, rural migrant workers' land transfer issues need to be addressed. Recently, the government has begun to gradually implement rural land transfer policies, which promote "legal, voluntary, and compensated" land transfers to protect rural residents' interests. The government needs to formulate special acts for land transferal as well as improve existing rules and regulations, establish a healthy land transfer market, create a mechanism for calculating land transfer prices, and actively monitor and manage land transfer practices.

4.4. Encouraging new government policies concerning migrant workers

The *Twelfth Five-Year Plan [for the] National Essential Public Services System* released by the State of Council in 2012 proposes the development target of "establishing a complete essential public services system and promoting the equality in essential public services". The *National New-Mode Urbanization Plan (2014–2020)* further emphasizes the need to "follow the principle of people-oriented urbanization, reasonably guide migration, promote the citizenization of migrated rural population in an orderly manner, and steadily enforce the full coverage of essential public services for permanent residents". Therefore, the essence of rural migrant workers' citizenization and assimilation lies in the equality of essential public services, and the realization of full provision of essential public services for permanent residents to allow rural migrant workers to enjoy the fruits of the reform and opening-up policy (Ma et al., 2015).

The State Council released *Opinions about Further Promoting Household Registration System Reform* in 2014 to annul existing differences between agricultural and non-agricultural populations, and establish a uniform urban and rural household registration system. It indicated the termination of the agricultural and non-agricultural household registration management mode, which had been in place in China for over half a century. It also suggested that the residence permit be taken as a base to establish an essential public services supply system that is tied to length of residence, and that the range of the public services provided for the residence permit holder be continuously widened. According to the implementation practice in different provinces and cities, people can apply for a residence permit after living in a place for more than six months, and the residence permit holder gains equal rights to employment, basic public education, basic healthcare service, basic pension service, housing security, public culture services, license processing services, etc.

The *Thirteenth Five-Year Plan* passed in late October 2015 further emphasized "promoting the people-oriented new-mode urbanization, deepening the household registration system reform, and encouraging capable rural populations to work and live in cities with their family members and strive for equal rights and obligations as urban residents; implementing the residence permit system, and trying to realize the full coverage of the permanent population in terms of essential public services".

In his 2017 government work report, Premier Li Keqiang mentioned the issue of migrant workers three times. First, he called for accelerating the citizenization of rural migrants, deepening the reform of the household registration system and relaxing the conditions for rural migrants to be settled in urban areas. He said: "We must act swiftly to ensure that long-term urban residents without urban residency are issued residence cards, thus enabling them to enjoy, as provided for by law, the right to access compulsory education, employment, medical care, and other basic public services".

Second, he called for the development of small and medium-sized cities and small towns in the central and western regions to accommodate more migrant workers for employment and entrepreneurship. Specifically, he said, "we will promote the development of small towns and small and medium-sized cities in the central and western regions to help more rural migrant workers find employment or start businesses in urban areas closer to home so that they do not have to choose between earning money and taking care of the families they leave behind".

Thirdly, in regard to education of rural migrants, Li said that "over 21 million training opportunities should be provided for migrant workers to improve their skills.... We will continue to help see the increased enrollment of students from poor rural areas into key colleges, and improve and implement policies enabling children who live with their migrant worker parents to go to secondary school or take college entrance exams in their city of residence".

These general policies are meant to ensure migrant workers and their families' wellbeing. The hope is that the detailed policies and their implementation will meet these citizens' needs, and that public services in China may be accessible to all without Hukou requirements by 2020.

5. CONCLUSION

Rural-urban migrant workers (or new urban citizens) are important participants in China's social development. They are at the core of China's urbanization process and overall economic growth. After the transformation of the Chinese economy, the Hukou system, which was once effective and necessary, became a barrier: it blocked rural migrant workers from gaining access to welfare and social services in the cities in which they reside. For instance, rural migrant workers cannot enjoy the same employment, education, public health, medical care, pension, and housing security services as their native urban counterparts. Evidently, the traditional urban-rural dual household registration systems need to be reformed to allow the assimilation of all rural migrants into the cities they are part of. China's social reality also calls for a universal essential social benefits and public services system for all.

The Chinese government is actively promoting the new phase of urbanization, which is human-centered and includes the integration of industrialization, environment, resources and the development of cities of different sizes. Meeting the needs of new urban residents will be one of the major tasks. Breaking down institutional and sectorial barriers and eliminating policy obstacles will speed up citizenization of rural migrant workers and their families. Once this population can truly settle down in the cities, their productivity and consumption power will be the new engine of China's further growth.

ACKNOWLEDGMENT

The study is sponsored by the Fundamental Research Funds for the Central Universities (RW150112).

REFERENCES

Chen, Zhenggao (2016, March 15). Press Conference Concerning Issues on Housing Provident Fund for Rural Migrant Workers. http://zhishi.fang.com/xf/qg_138951.html.

China Daily (2015). Jīfēn luòhù: Points system for household registration. http://www.chinadaily.com.cn/opinion/2015-12/14/content_22705970.htm.

Dong, Weizhen (2015). Chinese Migrant Workers' Healthcare Challenges And Innovative Strategies. *American Review of China Studies* 16(2).

Dong, Weizhen (2016, July 13). Social Determinants of Health in Rural China. Talk at session *Social Determinants of Health and Policy Implications in Transitional Societies*, International Sociological Association conference. University of Vienna.

Francis, Fukuyama and Cao, Yi (2003). Social Capital, Civil Society and Development. *Marxism & Reality* 64(2): 36–45.

Ge, Shoukun (2013, September). Understand the scientific contents of the new urbanization thoroughly. *Qunzhong*. http://www.chinacity.org.cn/csfz/fzzl/114482.html.

Huang, Wei (2016). Is migrant workers' points accumulation into urban household registration a beautiful fairy tale? *Statistics and Management* 7: 33–34. http://www.cqvip.com/qk/82802a/201607/669443169.html.

Huang, Ziyi (2017, January 20). 2016 China's urbanization rate is 57.35%, increase of rural migrants slowed down. *Financial News*. http://china.caixin.com/2017-01-20/101047161.html.

Jin, Chongfang (2011). An Empirical Analysis of Human Capital of Peasant Workers and Their Urban Assimilation: A Case Study of Peasant Workers In Shaanxi Province. *Resources Science* 33(11): 2131–2137.

Lei, Hui and Lei, Yu (2012, January 4). Guangdong will stop using the label "farmer workers". *Nanfang Daily*.

Li, Fengtao (2014, March 11). The Process of Citizenization of Migrant Workers Was Halted, the Completion of Urbanization Must Be in 2050. *China Economic Weekly*. http://finance.sina.com.cn/china/2014/03/11/001818464788.shtml.

Li, Hui (2014, April 10). How Long Will Be Part from Migrant Workers' Identity. *Guangming Daily*.

Li, Peilin (2003). *Migrant Workers: Socio-economic Analysis of the Migrant Workers in China*. Social Science Literature Press.

Li, Rongbin, et al. (2013).Analysis on the Current Situation and Influencing Factors of the New Generation of Migrant Workers' Citizenship. *Youth Studies* 1: 1–11.

Liao, Xiaodong and Wei Xin (2003). *Xiaokang Zhongguo Tong* (*Comfortable Living: Pain of China*). Chinese Social Sciences Press, p. 449.

Lin, Huochan (2016, April 26). How to Develop New Mode Of Urbanization through the Old One. *Economic Daily*: 5.

Ling, Lan (2000). Investigation on Occupational Hazard Awareness Level among Migrant Workers. *Zhejiang Journal of Preventive Medicine* 12(1): 36–37.

Liu, Chuanjiang, et al. (2009). *Study on the Second Generation Migrant Workers in China*. Shandong People's Publishing House.

Lu, Huan and Wei, Shen (2009). What's the Result of "Opening Chest Examining Lung". *Xinhua News*. http://news.xinhuanet.com/video/2009-08/13/content_11875975.htm.

Lu, Xueyi (2007, April 30). Analyzing the label of migrant workers. *People's Daily*.

Ma, Yonghao and Pang, Cuiyu (2015). Citizenization of Migrant Workers and Complete Coverage of Basic Public Service for Permanent Population under the View of New Urbanization. *Agricultural Economy* 35(2): 83–85.

Ministry of Education (2012). Migrants' children must meet 3 conditions in order to take college entrance exam not in their Hukou location. 2012-11-28, Xinhua.

Mursal, Adam and Dong, Weizhen (2018). Education as a key determinant of health: A case study from rural Anhui, China. *Journal of Health and Social Sciences* 3 (1): 59–74.

National Bureau of Statistics of China (2015). The Monitoring Survey Report on Migrant Workers in 2014. http://www.stats.gov.cn/tjsj/zxfb/201504/t20150429_797821.html.

National Bureau of Statistics of China (2016). The Monitoring Survey Report on Migrant Workers in 2015. http://wenku.baidu.com/view/ca74b4a8ddccda38366baf25.html.

National Bureau of Statistics of China (2017, January 21). National Economy Fulfilled a Good Start with "Thirteenth Five".

National Women's Federation Research Group (2013). A Report on the Situation of Rural Left-behind Children and Floating between Rural and Urban Children in China. People.com.cn, 2013-05-10. http://acwf.people.com.cn/n/2013/0510/c99013-21437965.html.

Pan, Qi (2013, February 6). It's Hard to Safeguard the Legal Rights of Over 6 Million China's Migrant Workers with Pneumoconiosis Because They Had No Labor Contract. *Legal Weekly*. http://finance.sina.com.cn/china/20130206/074114516659.shtml.

Peng, Xizhe, et al. (2014). Points Right-Benefit System: the universal beneficial choice that considering household registration reform's multi-objectives. *Population and Economics*, no.1.

Qian, Zhengwu (2012). Social Exclusion: The Major Reason for the Slow Progress of the Migrant Workers' Citizenization. *The World of Survey and Research*, no. 2: 41–45.

Ren, Juanjuan (2012). Research on New Generation Rural Migrant Workers' Citizenization and Factors Exerting Influence on the Issue: A Case Research of Xi'an. *Lanzhou Academic Journal*, no. 3: 118–125.

Research Group of the State Council (2006). *The Survey Report of Chinese Migrant Workers*. Chinese Yanshi Press.

State Council Research Institute (2006). *Report on Chinese Migrant Workers' Studies*. China Yanshi Press.

Sun, Dechao and Mao, Sujie (2012). The Status and Improvement Ways of the Basic Public Service for the Migrant Workers. *Jilin University Journal Social Sciences Edition* 52 (3): 153–158.

State Council (2014, July 24). Opinions on Further Promote the Reform of Household Registration System.

Tan, Yong (2015, December 8). Farmers in Puyang City Receive Various Levels of Subsidies when Purchasing Homes. *Henan Daily*. http://www.henan.gov.cn/zwgk/system/2015/12/08/010605518.shtml.

Tian, Feng (2010). A Study of the Income Gap between Urban Workers and Migrant Workers. *Sociological Studies*, no. 2: 87–105.

Wang, Zhulin (2010). The Capital Dilemma and Way Out for Migrant Workers' Citizenization. *Issues in Agricultural Economy*, no. 2: 28–32.

Wang, Yijie (2012). Points system can hardly help the rural migrants to fulfill their "urban dream". *Countryside, Agriculture, Farmers*, no. 3B: 35–37.

Wu, Yemiao (2009). The Equivalent Construction of Public Services and Peasant Workers: Core System and Promotion Path. *Urban Problems*, no.11: 64–69.

Wu, Yilin and Gu, Bin (2013). Research on the Statistical Monitoring of the Equalization of Essential Public Services in China. *Modernization of Management*, no. 3: 1–3.

Xiong, Fengshui (2015). Migrant Workers' Demands, Government Preferences and Equalization of Essential Public Services. *Journal of Qinghai Nationalities University*, no.1: 65–70.

Xu, Jianling (2008). Measurement of the Process of Migrant Workers' Citizenization: Theoretical and Empirical Analysis. *Issues in Agricultural Economy*, no. 9: 65–70.

Yan, Deru and Yue, Qiang (2014). On the Realization of the Equalization of Essential Public Services in Urban and Rural Areas. *Study & Exploration*, no. 2: 43–47.

Yang, Tao and Zhang, Aiping (2014). Study on the Migrant Workers' Citizenship in the Perspective of the Equalization of Essential Public Services. *Youth & Juvenile Research*, no. 4: 6–12.

Yang, Weimin (2015, November 9). Urban Residents' Housing Needs Are Met, 34m^2 Per Person. http://politics.people.com.cn/n/2015/1109/c1001-27794777.html.

Yu, Jianrong (2008). Equalization of Essential Public Services and the Problem of Migrant Workers. *China Rural Survey*, no. 2: 69–74.

Zhang, Bei (2014, January 23). The Monthly Income of Migrant Workers Who Master Technique Has Exceeded 10 Thousands, 6 Thousands Farmers Will Stay in Qingdao City during the Chinese New Year. *Qingdao Evening News*. http://news.qingdaonews.com/qingdao/2014/01/23/content_10244896.htm.

Zhang, Fei (2011). The Status and Influencing Factors of Citizenization of New Generation Rural Migrant Workers. *Population Research* 35(6): 100–109.

Zhao, Changxing and Yu, Bo (2014). Study on Social Exclusion and the Construction of Social Support System for Migrant Workers. *Journal of Xidian University (Social Science Edition)* 24(5): 39–43.

Zheng, Bingwen (2008, October 27). Thinking from the Phenomenon of Latin America to Surrender Flows of Migrant Workers. *Xinhua News*. http://news.xinhuanet.com/comments/2008/10/27/content_10257943.htm.

Zhong, Bing (2015). Analysis on the Equalization of Essential Public Services of Migrant Workers. *Macroeconomic Management*, no. 8: 71–74.

Chapter 4
Migrant Workers' Healthcare Access and Policy Implications

Weizhen Dong[1]

ABSTRACT
Migrant workers are arguably the most vulnerable people in today's urban China. Their vulnerability is most evident in the matters such as living situation, income level, working conditions, and access to social security and healthcare. Migrant workers' health status is crucial to their very livelihoods in the cities in which they reside while encountering various health challenges. However, the reality is unfortunate. There are a number of healthcare access barriers that migrant workers experience. Although informal healthcare providers are offering much-needed affordable basic care services to their fellow migrants, it is far from sufficient. Ensuring migrant workers' access to healthcare requires innovative strategies. Given the fact that the strongest social tie for this group is the one with their workplaces, a workplace intervention will be the most economical and practical solution.

1. INTRODUCTION
Healthcare access is key to any population's wellbeing. In China, healthcare access for 274 million migrant workers is problematic due to its linkage to the nation's residential registration system. China's economic reform resulted in the loosening of residential restrictions, but not the residential registration system (*hukou*) itself, which is tied directly to various social welfare programs.

China has been reforming its healthcare system since the 1990s, but the trajectory of the reform has evidently overlooked some vulnerable populations' healthcare access needs. This chapter discusses the challenges faced by one of such populations—migrant workers and their families—and explores ways in which an improvement of their lives would be possible without waiting for governmental policy change.

2. MIGRANT WORKERS AND THE DUAL SYSTEM IN CHINA
2.1. Hukou
Hukou is a residential registration system established shortly after the founding of the People's Republic of China. The government implemented different welfare policies for urban and rural residents. For example, a land-based system was designed for the rural residents, whereas the system for urban residents was based on employment. When the country had very limited resources and a massive population, the *hukou* system helped to ration food and other neces-

---
1. An earlier version of this chapter appeared in *The American Review of China Studies*, Fall 2015.

sities, thus effectively preventing unnecessary suffering and death. The country's distribution of resources was based on one's residential registration, and one could only access such resources as education, healthcare and employment from where his or her *hukou* was located (Dong, 2008).

Once the *hukou* system was in place, Chinese citizens were no longer free to move from one place to another, not even between cities. Children of residents, no matter where they were born, simply followed their parents' *hukou* registration locations.

The economic reform started in 1978 saw rural land redistribution and the implementation of the "Responsibility System", resulting in many rural surplus labourers wanting to go to cities where they could find jobs with better incomes. According to Chinese official censuses, the migrant population in China increased from 6.57 million in 1982 to 48.41 million in 1995 and 144.39 million in 2000 (Shen, 2003; Liang, 2004). In 2005, a sample survey showed the migrant population had reached 147.35 million (National Bureau of Statistics of China, 2005). In 2010, the number had reached 211 million, with an average age of 27.3 years (*People's Daily*, June 29, 2010). In 2011, it increased to 253 million; by 2012, the number was 261 million. The number of migrants is expected to continue to rise, with some analysts saying that it will have reached 300 million by the year 2015 (Editorial, *China Daily*, 2011). The main economic sectors open for migrants are manufacturing, construction, transportation, agriculture, services, and domestic service (e.g., working as maids).

The household residential registration (*hukou*) system ensures each person has a permanent place of resident registration. Since *hukou* is, in fact, a social benefit eligibility system, most rural migrants face constraints at work and in day-to-day life (Dong, 2003, 2008). Without *hukou*, they cannot access public education, public housing, healthcare, and social security in the city in which they live, and they do not enjoy the same rights and opportunities as city natives (Chan, 2012). The traditional rural-urban divide in China, therefore, is perpetuated and reinforced by the household registration system.

2.2. Rural-urban migrant workers

According to a survey by the National Bureau of Statistics of China, migrant workers in China account for 47 percent of the total urban labour force (2014). This group has been and still is playing a very important role in China's economic development, and they form the salient backbone of the nation's impressive economic development (Editorial, *China Daily*, 2011).

Migrant workers tend to hold low-income precarious jobs. Their working and living environments tend to be unstable and/or unhealthy, and they tend to have received fewer years of formal education and health education than their urban counterparts (Zhang et al., 2005). Migrant workers earn lower wages than native city residents, and a large percent of them have to financially support their families in rural areas. All of these challenges make them vulnerable to physical and mental health issues. Many suffer from mental illness including long-term depression (Dong, 2003; Murphy, 2006; Park and Wang, 2010; Tian, 2010; Mai and Peng, 2011).

Table 1. Proportion of Migrant Workers with Social Insurance (%)

Type of Insurance	2008	2009	2010	2011	2012	2013	2014
Pension Plan	9.8	7.6	9.5	13.9	14.3	15.7	16.7
Injury Insurance	24.1	21.8	24.1	23.6	24.0	28.5	26.2
Health Insurance	13.1	12.2	14.3	16.7	16.9	17.6	17.6
Unemployment Insurance	3.7	3.9	4.9	8.0	8.4	9.1	10.5
Maternity Insurance	2.0	2.4	2.9	5.6	6.1	6.6	7.8

Source: National Bureau of Statistics of China, 2015. Note: There is no data on social security programs in the statistical report concerning migrant workers after 2015.

Table 1 shows that only a minority of the population had some social benefits by the end of 2013, which included unemployment insurance (9.1 percent), pension plan (15.7 percent), and health insurance (17.6 percent). Only 6.6 percent of women had maternity insurance (National Bureau of Statistics of China, 2014).

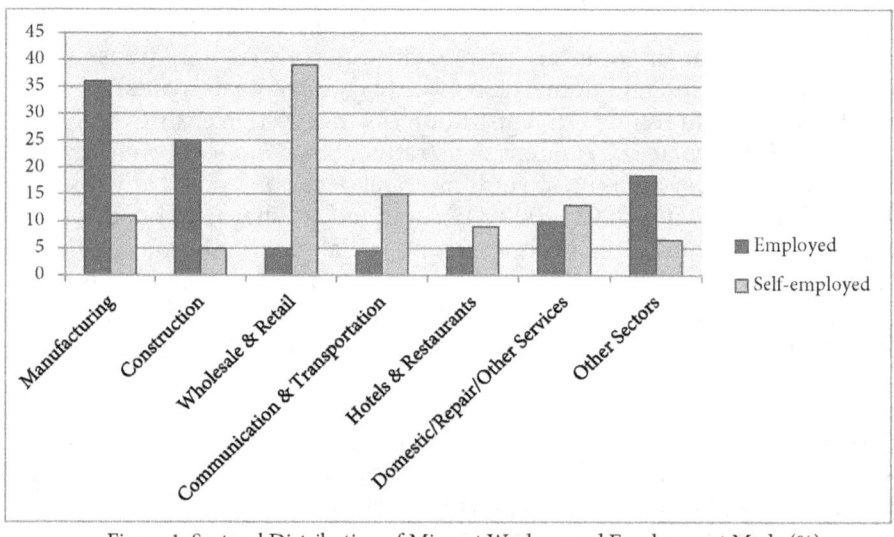

Figure 1. Sectoral Distribution of Migrant Workers and Employment Mode (%)
Manufacturing 31.4%; Construction 22.2%; Wholesale and Retail 11.3%; Communication and Transportation, Warehousing and Postal Service 6.3%; Hotels and Restaurants 5.9%; Domestic Services, Repair and Other Services 10.6%; Other Sectors 12.3%. Source: National Bureau of Statistics of China, 2014. After 2014, no new statistics of the same type are available but there is data on overall distribution of employment of migrant workers.

Economic reform relaxed restrictions on residential movement but did not alter the existing social welfare system, which is still linked to one's *hukou* location. Thus, migrant workers do not have the same rights to social benefits through their residence or employment as do their urban counterparts. For example, they are not likely to be entitled to any pension or medical benefits, and most of their children cannot enroll at public schools in the cities where they live.

Table 2. Migrant Workers' Living Arrangements, 2013 (%)

Index	Workplace Accommodation	Group Rent	Rent	City Home	Village Home	Other
Total	46.3	18.5	18.2	0.9	13.0	3.1
Municipalities and Provincial Capitals	51.2	21.6	20.4	0.7	3.2	3.0
Prefecture-level Cities	49.7	20.5	19.9	0.9	6.4	2.7
Small Towns	39.0	13.9	14.9	1.2	27.3	3.8

Source: National Bureau of Statistics of China, 2014

Most rural-urban migrants tend to live on the outer edges of cities. Almost half live in company dormitories or on construction sites—construction workers typically live in tents at the site where they work, while some build their own simple shelters (see Table 2). The nature of their accommodations is precarious and in most cases unhealthy. Their living places are usually crowded, dark, damp, and lacking in fresh air (Shen, 2003; Yamaguchi & Shinya, 2006; Dong, 2008).

Table 3. Migrant Workers' Living Arrangements 2015–2016 (%)

Living Arrangements	Rent	Home Owner	Workplace Accommodation	Other
2015	64.8	17.3	14.1	3.8
2016	62.4	17.8	13.4	6.4

Source: National Bureau of Statistics of China, 2016, 2017

In 2013, quite a high percentage of migrant workers were provided with workplace accommodation (Table 2); however, by the year 2015, the proportion of workplace accommodation was sharply reduced, from 46.3 percent to 14.1 percent, and it was further reduced to 13.4 percent in the year 2016 (Table 3). This means most migrant workers have to pay for their housing. Meanwhile, they still earn a limited income (see Figure 2, next page).

In short, the main challenges facing this population group are (1) low wages compared with other (native) urban dwellers (see Figures 2 and 3, next page); (2) few social benefits compared with other groups in urban China, and (3) a high level of uncertainty because of their lack of urban *hukou* status, which is the basis for entitlement to urban social security programs' various benefits.

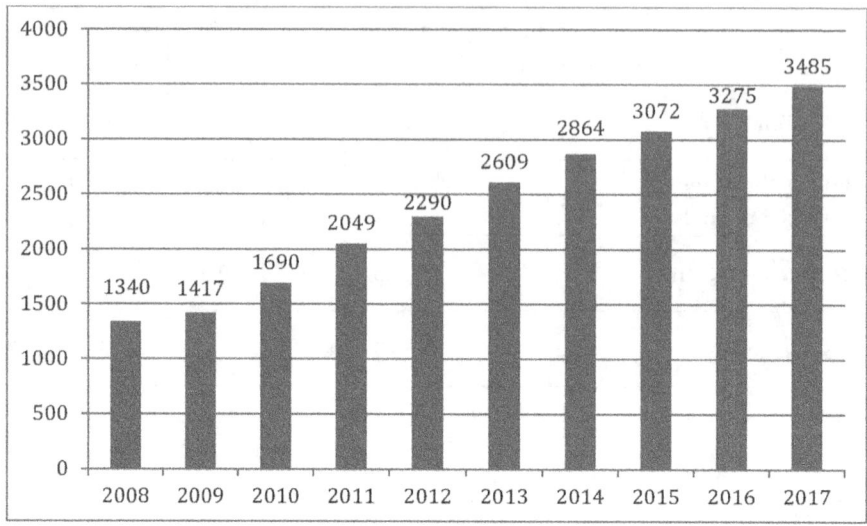

Figure 2. Migrant Workers' Per Capita Monthly Income (2008–2017)
Source: National Bureau of Statistics of China, 2017. Unit: Yuan ¥

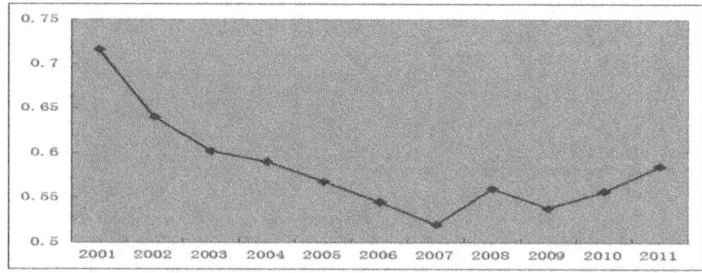

Figure 3. Relative Wages of Rural Migrants and Urban Formal Employees (2001–2011)
Source: National Bureau of Statistics of China. Formal real wages are average urban wages reported in China Statistical Yearbook (2012), rural migrant wages are from NBS rural household surveys and rural migration monitoring surveys.

2.3. Migrant Workers' Health and Healthcare Challenges

A study reveals that 84 percent of migrant workers have only achieved secondary school or a lower level of education (Bai et al., 2008). Lack of sufficient essential education affects their health knowledge base and their ability to acquire relevant information when necessary. Meanwhile, they face other difficulties in life. A study shows that 57 percent of rural-urban migrants reported unknown causes of pain, 26.2 percent experienced psychological problems, and 24.5 percent had sleeping issues (Tang et al., 2006). Despite poor health knowledge, most migrants also receive limited to none health education while working in factories or service sectors.

A study on rural migrants' reproductive health revealed that 58.2 percent of migrants lacked adequate knowledge of sexually transmitted diseases (STDs). Moreover, while 43.1 percent of the female migrants in a study believed they had contracted a STD, only half of them had visited doctors (Zhang et al., 2005). A study in Guangzhou City found a high prevalence of self-reported reproductive tract infection symptoms and also found that unmarried migrant workers were more vulnerable to sexual and reproductive health risks (Lu et al., 2011). A study also showed that female migrants are more likely to contract STDs (81.9 percent) than their male counterparts (18.1 percent) (Wang et al., 2011).

Childbirth-related mortality rates among migrant workers are very high as well, since most migrant women would find healthcare too costly to use relevant services. The high cost of healthcare services and the lack of healthcare insurance have resulted in under-utilization of healthcare services by rural-urban migrants. This has led to a series of ineffective health-seeking behaviors such as unsupervised self-treatment, going to unregulated underground clinics, or failing to seek medical care altogether (Hong et al., 2006; Li and Zhang, 2012).

Table 4. Migrant Workers' Working Hours

Index	2012	2013	2014	2015	2016
Working months in the year	9.9	9.9	10.0	10.1	10.0
Average working days in a month	25.3	25.2	25.3	25.2	25.2
Working hours in a day	8.7	8.8	8.8	8.7	8.7
Daily working hours over 8 Hours (%)	39.6	41.0	40.8	39.1	37.3
Weekly working hours over 44 hours (%)	84.4	84.7	85.4	85.0	84.4

Source: National Bureau of Statistics of China, 2017.

Rural-urban migrant workers are at high risk for infectious diseases and injuries, since more than half of them are working in the manufacturing and construction sectors (see Figure 1). Additionally, their long working hours and heavy workload prevent them from finding any time for leisure and relaxation, or for hospital visits when necessary. Table 4 shows their highly demanding working hours in the past several years, and the hours in each category saw nearly no change at all. This makes this group a high-risk population today and in the foreseeable future. It also shows the difficulty migrant workers are facing when accessing healthcare services.

Until the 1980s, basic healthcare services were provided at minimal or no cost in urban China, where all residents were almost completely covered by the two major insurance systems, the government insurance scheme (GIS) and the labour insurance scheme (LIS). Since the beginning of the economic reforms, coverage by the two systems has fallen significantly while the requirement for co-payments emerged. As a result, Chinese healthcare system reform over the recent decades has had a profoundly negative impact on service utilization, particularly by the poor and vulnerable. Migrants are largely excluded from the plan that replaced the LIS, the urban employees' basic healthcare insurance scheme (Dong, 2003, 2008).

Healthcare costs have vital implications for individuals who are at risk. A significant number of migrant women who have forgone prenatal care have then given birth with the assistance of untrained midwives and have also forgone antenatal care (Zhan et al., 2002; Jiang, 2007) because healthcare is costly. Only 6.2 percent of migrants have some kind of healthcare insurance (Bai et al., 2008) and lack health- and healthcare-related knowledge. In 2010, only 26.8 percent of migrants had limited medical care subsidies (People's Daily, June 29, 2010).

When workers with urban *hukou* become ill or suffer from injury, they can enjoy healthcare at least partly paid for through healthcare insurance; yet when migrant workers experience similar setbacks, they do not have such benefits. In fact, Chinese healthcare system reform in the recent decades has had a profoundly negative impact on service utilization, particularly by the poor (Dong, 2006). Migrants are largely excluded from the urban employees' basic healthcare insurance schemes (Dong, 2003). These costs have important implications for individuals who are at risk.

China has clarified its residence policies to facilitate domestic migrants' settling in small and medium-size cities as permanent residents, which was a move intended to further promote urbanization (Xinhua News, 2012). Census data shows that the population of Beijing, the capital of China, exceeded 19 million in 2010. Of Beijing's 19 million people, migrants from elsewhere accounted for about seven million (*Xinhua News*, 2012).

3. MIGRANT WORKERS' HEALTHCARE ACCESS IN SHANGHAI

A study of Shanghai migrant workers found that this group faced severe barriers in accessing medical care (*Laodongbao*, April 17, 2012).

These migrants work in restaurants, manufacturing (producing electronics, clothes and shoes, etc.) and the construction sector. Most received middle school education (71 percent), while 20 percent received only primary school or lower levels of education; 78 percent of migrant workers had lived in Shanghai for more than 2 years, and the monthly income of nearly half of them (46 percent) ranged from ¥2000 to ¥3000.

3.1. Burden of illness

Among these workers, 85 percent had encountered illness, yet 15 percent of them chose to forgo care. Nearly half (48 percent) preferred to seek care at underground clinics, where the healthcare providers did not receive proper professional training and had no license to practice medicine. Although most migrant workers are in their prime working years, they have a deep fear of being ill. Some of them expressed their fear by calculating how much it would cost them if they were to get sick. One worker in the study said that a hospital visit would cost him two to three days' income. While treatment for a common cold can cost up to ¥200, unpaid time off from work and the transportation cost of visiting a hospital would together cost much more.

While illness costs workers money, it may also cost them their jobs, which are lifelines for their entire families. For example, a worker's income may support his parents and parents-in-law (four elderly people), his two children and his wife. If he is too ill to work, it will change his family members' lives forever. Rather than take time off work and risk losing his job, the worker will buy antibiotics if he has a high fever and painkillers if he suffers from conditions such as a stomach ache, and then go to work as usual (Li and Zhang, 2012).

Table 5. Dispensable Income Difference between Urban and Rural Residents (2013–2017)

Dispensable Income/Person	2013	2014	2015	2016	2017
Urban Residents (Yuan/Year)	26467.00	28843.85	31194.83	33616.25	36396.19
Rural Residents (Yuan/Year)	9429.59	10488.88	11421.71	12363.41	13432.43

Source: *China Statistical Yearbooks,* 2014–2018

Table 5 shows that there is a visible dispensable income gap between urban and rural residents in China. Migrant workers are working and living in the cities but they have to support their family who are living in their home village. When lacking healthcare coverage, finding affordable alternative became a natural choice for them.

3.2. User-friendly Underground Clinics

A study found that 47 percent of migrant workers sought care at underground clinics, which are defined as clinics without licenses issued by the appropriate professional authorities. Migrant workers prefer not to go to regular hospitals because of high costs. They would forgo care if the problems are minor and do not affect their ability to work. If the illness cannot be ignored, they would go to an underground clinic run by their fellow villagers.

According to migrant workers, these clinics are run by former "barefoot doctors" from their home villages. Serving their fellow villagers and their new migrant friends and family in the city has become their new career. These clinics do not have any signs on their doors, but they are literally "open" 24/7—migrant workers can knock on their door at any time asking for help. They provide very economical treatment with low-cost drugs or traditional Chinese medicines. Moreover, these "doctors" do not face language barriers with the migrant workers they treat, since they themselves are from the same village or a nearby region. Having said that, these "doctors" are careful not to treat anyone not referred by people they already know. Migrant workers and their "doctors" have a trusting relationship and they understand each other well.

However, when an illness is very serious that it requires special medical attention, migrant workers often choose to go back to their home village (Zhang et al., 2015; *Laodongbao* Editorial, 2012), since medical care in rural areas is less costly and their family and relatives in the village can take care of them.

3.3. Information Access as an Issue

The Shanghai government initiated programs to enhance healthcare access for this population group such as the "¥20 medical care plan"; however, implementation and information dissemination were not as effective as hoped. During the study, migrant worker participants were asked about the local government's healthcare programs, but none of them had heard anything. This means migrant workers experience an information access barrier as well.

4. DISCUSSION AND A PROPOSAL

China's dual system has created two classes of citizens. Although many migrant workers have never worked in the rural fields, they retain their "peasant" identities because of their parents' rural residential status. Their contribution to the Chinese economy is no less important than their urban native counterparts, but their pay is usually much less. As Figure 3 shows, their incomes are less than 60 percent of those of their city counterparts. Their migrant status has restricted them to certain jobs and not others, and their educational background has disadvantaged them in securing skilled positions.

To date, many studies have been conducted on the vulnerability of migrant workers. However, not much action has been taken to actually improve their situation, and most people, affected or otherwise, are still waiting for government policies to address these issues. Thus, this population's unfortunate status has persisted for decades.

As we have noted, migrant workers' long work hours and their accommodation arrangements with their employers (Table 2 and Table 3) mean that their only strong social ties are with their workplaces, no matter how precarious their jobs and living situations happen to be. Thus, it is only logical to use the workplace to aid them, for example by making the workplace the workers' household for the purposes of residential registration, which will also serve to establish their eligibility for social benefits. This method could be the swiftest, most economical way of meeting migrant workers' basic needs before the government finds other ways to address the issue.

With appropriate intervention strategies, the workplace of migrant workers can serve as a starting point for migrant workers to receive education in health promotion, preventive care and basic healthcare. Migrant workers' healthcare access can also be improved through a collaborative network including company/factory administrations, workplace clinics, and neighbourhood community healthcare providers.

Migrant workers do care about their health, but they currently face serious barriers in healthcare access, including cost, time constraints, lack of knowledge, in some cases a language barrier, and the fact that official healthcare institutions may not be as accessible or friendly to migrant workers as less formal settings. Therefore, I propose a *workplace intervention strategy* for the wellbeing of Chinese migrant workers. Healthcare professionals should be invited to carry out health promotion activities at the workplace, in the form of lectures, seminars and posters. As well, workplace medical clinics should be set up that meet the basic medical care needs of migrant workers and other members within the community, and underground clinic healthcare providers should be retrained and assigned to appropriate posts where their knowledge and experience could be best utilized to serve migrant workers.

Providing migrant workers with healthcare knowledge at their workplaces will empower them, and workplace-based clinics will ensure their basic access to timely healthcare. Annual checkups and other preventive care services at workplace can also reduce healthcare costs and prevent unnecessary suffering. No doubt employers would be interested in making this happen, since healthier workers are happier workers, and happier workers are more productive and more efficient. Meanwhile, re-trained underground clinic doctors could serve as bridges for the migrant workers to access local healthcare facilities when necessary.

5. CONCLUSION

China has entered an intensified urbanization process. However, rural migrants are not well assimilated into urban society due mostly to the country's traditional residential administration system, which tends to be a barrier for the new urban dwellers trying to access social security programs and other social resources and services in the city they live. Migrant workers often do the jobs that urban natives do not care to do, and are vulnerable in many ways. Improving living conditions and healthcare access is particularly crucial to migrant workers' wellbeing, and requires action even before the government enacts reforms of the household registration system reform and institutes the relevant policy changes. Knowing this population group's strong employment ties, a workplace intervention strategy can effectively support the group in accessing healthcare and housing as well as urban residential status. A workplace healthcare station can provide a cost-effective health safety net to migrant workers. Other workers and personnel can also benefit from such convenient preventive medical care services. It will be a much needed health protection measure that eventually reduces unnecessary time loss due to illness and injury, reducing healthcare expenditures.

Moreover, such an approach will eventually help rural migrants fully assimilate to urban society.

REFERENCES

Bai, W.P., Zhang, W.Z., Bai, M. (2008). *Peasant Workers' Living Conditions Survey, China National Conditions and Strength*, Vol. 1.

China Radio International (CRI) (January 25, 2008). Migrants in Guangzhou. http://english.cri.cn/4026/2008/01/25/44@317459.htm.

Dong, Weizhen (2003). Healthcare financing reforms in transitional society: A Shanghai experience. *Journal of Health, Population and Nutrition*: 223–234.

Dong, Weizhen (2006). Can healthcare financing policy be emulated? The Singaporean medical savings accounts model and its Shanghai replica. *Journal of Public Health*: 209–214.

Dong, Weizhen (2008). Cost containment and access to care: The Shanghai health care financing model. *The Singapore Economic Review*, 53 (1): 27–41.

Du, Huimin and Siming, Li (2010). Migrants, urban villages, and community sentiments: A case of Guangzhou, China. *Asian Geographer* 27 (1–2).

Editorial, *China Daily* (2011, December 1). Rights of migrant workers. http://www.chinadaily.com.cn/opinion/2011-01/12/content_11831899.htm.

Gao, J., et al. (2002). Health equity in transition from planned to market economy in China. *Health Policy and Planning* 17: 20–29.

He, Na, et al. (2006). Sexual behavior among employed male rural migrants in Shanghai, China. *AIDS Education and Prevention*, 18(2): 176–186.

Hong, Yan, et al. (2006). Too costly to be ill: Health care access and health seeking behaviors among rural-to-urban migrants in China. *World Health Popul.* 8(2): 22–34.

Huang, Yun-Qing (2003). A probe into the floating population's fertility problems in Guangdong. *South China Population* 2(18): 45–51.

Jiang, Yuxia (2007, December 17). Pregnant migrant woman's death in Beijing sparks call for government aid to poor. *Window of China*. http://news.xinhuanet.com/english/2007-12/10/content_7226612.htm.

Li, Pei and Xinci Zhang (2012, April 17). Survey on rural migrant workers' health care channels. *Laodongbao*.

Liang, Zai, and Zhongdong Ma (2004). China's floating population: New evidence from the 2000 census. *Population and Development Review* 30(3): 467–488.

Liu, H., et al. (2005). Risk factors for sexually transmitted disease among rural-to-urban migrants in China: Implications for HIV/sexually transmitted disease prevention. *AIDS Patient Care STDs* 19(1): 49–57.

Liu, Yuanli (2004). China's public health-care system: facing the challenges. *Bulletin of the World Health Organization* 82(7): 532–538.

Lu, Ciyong, et al. (2011). Sexual and reproductive health status and related knowledge among female migrant workers in Guangzhou, China: A cross-sectional survey. *Eur J Obstet Gynecol Reprod Biol* (2011), PMID 22071111.

National Bureau of Statistics of China (2005). *Bulletin of Main Data about 1% National Population Sample Survey*. http://www.stats.gov.cn/tjgb/rkpcgb/qgrkpcgb/t20060316_402310923.htm.

National Bureau of Statistics of China (2013). National Monitoring and Survey Report on Rural Migrant Workers in 2012. http://www.stats.gov.cn/tjsj/zxfb/201305/t20130527_12978.html.

National Bureau of Statistics of China (2014). National Monitoring and Survey Report on Migrant Workers in 2013. http://www.stats.gov.cn/tjsj/zxfb/201405/t20140512_551585.html.

National Bureau of Statistics of China (2015). National Monitoring and Survey Report on Rural Migrant Workers in China in 2014. http://www.stats.gov.cn/tjsj/zxfb/201504/t20150429_797821.html.

National Bureau of Statistics of China (2016). Monitoring and Survey Report on Rural Migrant Workers in 2015. http://www.stats.gov.cn/tjsj/zxfb/201704/t20170428_1489334.html.

National Bureau of Statistics of China (2017). Monitoring and Survey Report on Migrant Workers in 2016. http://www.stats.gov.cn/tjsj/zxfb/201704/t20170428_1489334.html.

National Bureau of Statistics of China (2018). Monitoring and Survey Report on Migrant Workers in 2017. http://www.stats.gov.cn/tjsj/zxfb/201804/t20180427_1596389.html.

Rozelle, S., Taylor, J. E., and DeBrauw, A. (1999). Migration, remittances, and agricultural productivity in China. *American Economic Review* 89: 287–291.

Shen, Jianfa and Yefang Huang (2003, April). The working and living spaces of the "floating population" in China. *Asia Pacific Viewpoint* 44(1): 51–62.

Tang J. et al. (2008). Study of employment insurance system innovation for peasant-workers to work in a city. *Western Forum*, Vol. 1.

Wang, Pan, Wu Tao and Cheng Yunjie (2012, January 30). Rural-urban shifts put China on development alert. *Xinhua News*. http://news.xinhuanet.com/english/indepth/2012-01/30/c_131383031.htm.

Wang, Yaolin (2002). Small city, big solution? China's *hukou* system reform and its potential impacts. *DISP* 151: 23–29.

Xinhua News (Feb. 24, 2012). China clarifies residence rules to smooth urbanization. http://news.xinhuanet.com/english/china/2012-02/24/c_131429783.htm.

Yamaguchi, Y. Shinya, M. (2006). Affordable housing for rural migrant workers in urban China. *East Asia Social Policy.* http://www.welfareasia.org/4thconference/papers/Yamaguchi_Affordable%20housing%20for%20rural%20migrant%20workers%20in%20urban%20China.pdf.

Xu, Qian, et al. (2007). Promoting contraceptive use among unmarried female migrants in one factory in Shanghai: A pilot workplace intervention. *BMC Health Services Research* 7: 77–85.

Zhao, DX, et al. (2002). Status and needs of sexual health among women migrant workers in Taiyuan. In *Status, perspective and strategy of reproductive health among adolescents and unmarried youth*, pp. 231-243, Gao, ES, et al. (eds.). Shanghai: The Second Military Medical University Press.

Zhan, Shaokang, Sun Zhenwei, and Erik Blas (2002). Economic transition and maternal healthcare for internal migrants in Shanghai, China. *Health Policy and Planning* 17: 47–55.

Zhang, CX, et al. (2006). Investigation on smoking behaviors and smoking-related knowledge and attitude among secondary school teachers. *Zhonghua Liu Xing Bing Xue Za Zhi* 27(3): 234–7.

Zhang, Luwen, et al. (2015). Internal migration and the health of the returned population: a nationally representative study of China. *BMC Public Health* 15: 719.

Chapter 5
Aging-Related Welfare Policies in China
From Income Security to Elder Care Services

Baozhen Luo, Heying Zhan

ABSTRACT
This chapter provides a description of the historical development of aging-related welfare programs in China since 1949. More attention will be paid to developments since 2000. First, we provide a brief overview of the general direction of welfare policies in three distinct periods—the planned economy period between 1949 and the beginning of economic reform in 1979, the period of economization, and the period of welfare expansion. Then, we focus on two major areas of social policies that are specifically targeted toward the aging population: income support (social insurance and public assistance/aid in rural and urban areas respectively) and elder care services (family care, institutional care, and community-based care). Lastly, we evaluate the strengths and weaknesses of each area and make suggestions for policy makers to address the weaknesses.

1. INTRODUCTION

Since the establishment of the People's Republic of China in 1949, the Chinese government has undergone several shifts of focus. Before the economic reforms of 1979, the Chinese government, led by the Chinese Communist Party (CCP), defined the nation-state of the mainland as a so-called planned economy based on the public ownership of industrial enterprises and agricultural production. After 1979, the Chinese government shifted its focus to economic development of the whole nation, a process known as "economization of the nation" or "depoliticization of the economy" (Chen 2012: 3). The CCP's effort has yielded unprecedented economic growth in China since then. However, little attention was paid to the establishment of a welfare state until recently, when widespread social problems (e.g., unprecedented social inequality on all levels) started to emerge in all corners of Chinese society. It was then that the CCP realized the urgent need to extend social welfare provisions and create policies to address issues such as social injustice, social insurance, and public aid. Meanwhile, the considerable revenue growth due to rapid economic development allows the government the financial ability to enact various welfare programs.

One of the most urgent issues faced by China today is its rapid process of population aging, especially with the Chinese baby boomers entering old age. In 2014, China's 60-plus age group accounted for 15.5 percent of its total population, about 212 million (the 65-plus population is roughly 138 million) (National Bureau of Statistics of China, 2014; Xinhua News Agency, 2015). The elderly dependency ratio (the number of elders 60+ to every 100 15–64-year-old workers) in 2005 was 10.67; this number increased to 13.7 in

2014 (National Bureau of Statistics of China, 2014). It was projected by the United Nations that people over age 65 will account for 18 percent of China's population, reaching 350 million, by 2050, at which time China is expected to have nearly 500 million people aged 60 and above, exceeding the entire population of the United States (Xinhua New Agency, 2015).

Additionally, Chinese elders are living longer than ever. The average life expectancy was 67.8 in 1981 and 71.4 in 2000. This number increased to 76.34 in 2015 (National Bureau of Statistics of China, 2016). Unlike developed countries, China is not generally considered financially prepared for the aging of society, even though the country has become wealthier in general. Meanwhile, family structure is going through a verticalization process, with a lower fertility rate largely due to the one-child policy and increasing numbers of generations due to elongated life expectancy. Family members are increasingly unavailable to take on or overburdened by elder-care responsibilities (Luo, 2012; Zhang, 2007). How to take care of such a large aging population financially and physically is probably one of the most pressing issues on the agenda of Chinese policymakers. Observing these needs, over the past two decades the Chinese government has been taking cautious steps to gradually reform and expand its public pensions and elder-care service programs in an attempt to cover citizens in both rural and urban areas.

2. INCOME SUPPORT

Income support as a welfare program can be divided into two types: public assistance/aid and public pension (social insurance) programs. The public assistance programs in China, as in the West, are means-tested, and provide basic benefits for the most disadvantaged. The social insurance programs provide income security for people who have earned entitlement through employment prior to retirement (Quadagno, 2011). Since 1949, the CCP has been continuously practicing and introducing different schemes of income support for the aging population in urban and rural areas. Below, we will illustrate the pension systems and the public assistance programs in urban and rural areas respectively.

2.1. The multilayered public pension system in urban China

The current old-age public pension system in urban China consists of three separate schemes based upon one's employment and residence—those working for government and public institutions, for enterprises, and for urban residents outside of the workplace. The first two schemes were established in 1951, as one nationwide pension system. However, since the early 1990s, these two systems have been separated and operated differently. The scheme for government and public institutions is a noncontributory benefit system (roughly similar to a traditional defined benefit system in the U.S.) financed through central revenues—employees are not required to make individual contributions. Today, this system covers roughly 40 million participants, with a pension benefit replacement rate of 90 percent after retirement (Chen, 2015; Zhen, 2012). This has made public servant jobs particularly desirable among youth and has overburdened the public pension system.

On the other hand, the scheme for enterprises was financed through individual enterprises. Since the 1980s, the number of retirees has increased disproportionately compared to the number of employees. Compounded by changes during the era of restructuring of the state-owned enterprises (SOE) in the 1990s, the enterprises were facing a major "pension crisis". In order to address this pension crisis, a nationwide reform of the enterprise pension system—changing from a noncontributory system to a contributory system—took place between the early 1990s and the mid-2000s (Zhen, 2012). Today, the system which now covers all urban non-public-servant employees (in state-owned and non-state-owned enterprises) is operated as a defined-contribution (DC) system funded by a 20 percent employer contribution and 8 percent employee contribution—a total of 28 percent of a worker's salary. By the end of 2015, the pay-as-you-go system had roughly 320 million participants, with 80 million retiree beneficiaries and 240 million contributors (Chen, 2015).

This division between the schemes for the public servants and the enterprise workers, coined a "Two-Orbit System", has called into question the fiscal burden on general revenue caused by the noncontributory nature of the public-servant system. This is due to changing demographics, which has led to increasing dissatisfaction over inequity among urban non-public-sector workers. Not only do enterprise workers have to make individual contributions to their retirement plan, their average monthly pension is also significantly lower than those working in the public sectors. For instance, in 2013, the average yearly pension received by an enterprise worker was 20,400 RMB whereas the same number was 28,392 RMB for a public servant (Ministry of Human Resources and Social Security of PRC, 2013). To address such inequality and tension, in December 2014, the Chinese central government passed new public-pension legislation, which will gradually merge the two orbits by transforming the public servant scheme into a contributory system, essentially making the system for the public servants the same as the one for enterprise workers (Hu, 2015).

It was not until 2009 that the CCP started working on establishing a pension system for the informal sector to include the large number of urban residents who do not work for the government, public institutions, or enterprises. This new scheme, enacted in 2011 by the State Council through the *Guidelines for Establishing Pensions for Urban Residents*, covers all urban residents with a two-tiered benefit program—a basic pension and an individual account pension. The basic pension, which does not require individual contributions, is funded through central government and local governments. Participation in the individual account is voluntary. After age 60, a participant can get a monthly minimum of 55 RMB from the basic pension plus a monthly sum equal to 1/139 of the total funds accumulated in the individual account after making 15 years of contributions (Xu & Zhang, 2013).

2.2. URBAN: PUBLIC ASSISTANCE PROGRAM
Until 2000, no public assistance program in China targeted the poor—young or old. Welfare was provided by the family. Government assistance was only available for the older people of the "Three Nos"—those with no children, no work ability, and no source of income. Most people in urban areas belonged to

a work unit. Because of the active role of work units in provision of care, only a small portion of older people were in need of public assistance.

In the early 1990s, with the nationwide transition to a market economy, the work-unit-based social relief system became unsustainable due to increasing financial constraints. The consequence was the rapid emergence of a large number of "new urban poor". Some of these new urban poor were workers laid off during the restructuring of SOEs. Due to their poor economic performance in the market economy, many SOEs collapsed, and were thus unable to afford pensions or any type of financial assistance for their former employees. Gradually, the increasing rate of poverty and ever-growing income gap among urban residents started drawing attention from the central government as social unrest among the poor grew quickly (Xu & Zhang, 2013).

In 1999, the State Council enacted a national public assistance program called the Minimum Living Standard Guarantee System for Urban Residents (Dibao, Minimum Guarantee). The urban Minimum Guarantee program is a means-tested program operated at the local government level. It expanded its criteria from the "Three Nos" to all individuals whose average household income fell below the lowest local living standard. The amount varied greatly across cities and counties according to varied local living standards. Initially, all funds were expected to be drawn from local government revenues. Realizing the local governments' difficulties and/or some level of unwillingness to cover the needs of the increasing number of urban poor, the central government substantially increased its funding for the Minimum Guarantee program to almost 60 percent of the total expenditures in 2008 (Ministry of Civil Affairs, 2010). In June 2010, around 23 million urban residents were Minimum Guarantee recipients, among whom 3.4 million, about 14 percent, were people 60 and above (Ministry of Civil Affairs, 2010; Xu & Zhang, 2013).

2.3 Rural residents' public pensions: From non-existence to national coverage

The need for a pension system for the rural population was largely ignored until the early 1980s. In a few wealthier regions where village and township enterprises flourished, various community-funded and administered pension systems were experimented with (Xu & Zhang, 2013). In 1992, the Ministry of Civil Affairs issued the Basic Plan of Rural County-Based Pensions. It stated that the funding responsibilities should be shared by three parties—the individuals, collectives (such as village and township enterprises and collective farms), and the government. However, the government's financial contribution was largely in the form of a tax deduction for the collectives, which was rather small. Peasants between 20 and 59 years old were eligible to participate on a voluntary basis (Ministry of Labor and Social Security, 2006). By 1997, a county-level pension system was implemented nationwide covering over 90 percent of counties, in both economically developed and less-developed regions. However, starting in 1998, the number of participants declined dramatically by over 30 percent and some programs in less-developed regions had to be discontinued due to financial restraints at the community level (Chow & Xu, 2002).

While the central government was working on reforming the urban pension system, great effort was also made to reform the failing rural pension system. In 2009, the New Rural Pension System (NRPS), which is similar to the pension scheme established for urban residents in informal sectors, was launched to provide some level of pension support for the rural elderly population with significantly more financial contribution from the central government (Ministry of Human Resources and Social Security, 2009). The central government fully or partially funds the basic pension for all 60+ elders as a universal benefit/entitlement. Although the amount is small (a minimum of ¥55 per month, roughly $9 dollars in 2009), it signifies the Chinese government's commitment to a more extensive public pension scheme. Within one year of implementation, in 10 percent of rural counties in China the number of beneficiaries increased from 15.56 million to 28.63 million, and the number of participants increased from 87 million to 102.77 million. The government has made plans to increase the benefit level incrementally and intends to extend NRPS to all rural elders by 2020 (Xu & Zhang, 2013). By the end of 2013, the NRPS covered more than 500 million people with the contribution flows outpacing the retiree payments (Chen, 2015; Zhen, 2012).

In 2014, China's State Council made an executive decision to merge the rural and urban systems and established one unified national resident public pension system. This move was taken based on two rationales: (1) to increase administrative efficiency, since the two systems are operated quite similarly; and (2) to address increasing rural-urban division/inequality, though its effect in this regard is much more arguable (Hu, 2015).

As one of the most important yet discriminated-against workforces, rural-urban migrant workers are in a unique situation when it comes to the pension system. They are legally categorized as rural residents based upon the household registration (*hukou*) system. Because of their lack of urban hukou, they are treated as a "floating population", although they work in urban enterprises (not state-owned). They do not fit in the complicated and multilayered employee and resident system. In 2009, a specific policy was enacted by the Ministry of Human Resources and Social Security to include rural migrant workers in some type of pension system (Zhen, 2012). This system functions in conjunction with the system for enterprises and the NRPS (later the rural/urban residents unified national system). Funding is shared by individual participants (4 to 8 percent of wages) and enterprises (12 percent of wages); then, upon returning to their rural hometowns, the participants also have the choice of transferring the fund to the resident system (Findlaw.cn, 2015).

2.4. RURAL PUBLIC ASSISTANCE PROGRAM

The rural public assistance program for the needy went through similar changes to the urban public assistance program. Before the economic reform, most rural elders were cared for by their families in commune-based welfare systems. Only a very small number of elders, mainly the "Three Nos", received aid from the government. For those with no family caregivers or any source of income, a special community-based social relief program called "Five Guarantees Household" (*Wubaohu*) was established in early 1950s. The Five Guarantees included food, clothing, housing, medical care, and a proper burial.

The decollectivization of rural economy inevitably led to the collapse of the commune-based welfare system. In 2006, the "Five Guarantees" program was finally turned into a state-run program with funding from both the central and local governments. "Five Guarantees" elders were cared for individually in villages or collectively in "Elder Care Homes" (*Yanglao Yuan*) administered by county governments (Feng, 2012).

With strong financial support from the central government, the means-tested "Minimum Guarantee" (*Dibao*) program was extended to most rural areas in 2007. The elderly population accounted for more than 30 percent of total recipients. In 2009, the average Minimum Guarantee allowance was about ¥64 per month (Ministry of Civil Affairs, 2010). Xu and Zhang (2012) estimated that about 12 percent of the rural elderly population received public assistance from the government in 2010, which included "Five Guarantees" elderly recipients and those on the Minimum Guarantee program.

It is important to note that government public assistance programs were only provided when family resources were completely absent or exhausted. The Minimum Guarantee program, using families as receiving units, includes all adult children's income as household income to measure a senior's eligibility. The result is the disqualification of many poor elders who may not receive any or sufficient financial support from their adult children.

3. ELDER CARE SERVICES

Providing adequate elder care services is another major challenge for the Chinese government brought about by population aging. The social policies related to elder care services for the aged can be categorized into three areas: family care, institutional care, and community care. According to the 2013 *State Council's Opinions on Speeding Up the Development of Elder Care Services*, and based on previous trial policies, the government set the strategic goal of "establishing a comprehensive and moderately-scaled elder care services system which covers both rural and urban areas by 2020, following a model of family care as the foundation, community care as the relying platform, and institutional care as a support". The implementation of this policy is largely left to local governments, which seem to have largely interpreted it in a quantitative manner with percentage divisions among the different actors. For instance, this model is operationally implemented as "90–6–4" in Beijing, i.e., 90 percent of elders age in place (at home), 6 percent are to be cared for in/by the community, and 4 percent in an institution. In Shanghai, the ratio is "90–7–3" (Yang, 2014; Polivka & Luo, 2013). This simplistic approach is quite problematic. The authors will provide further analysis and critique in the discussion section. Other cities may vary in the percentage share of community and institutional care, but primary care is understood to be provided in and by the family across the board.

3.1. FAMILY CARE

Traditionally, elder care has been provided by adult children at home under the norm of filial piety (*xiao*), which states that children are obligated to obey and respect their elderly parents and provide them with physical, financial, and emotional care. As Levin (2008) insightfully summed up, "For thousands of years, filial piety was China's Medicare, Social Security, and long-term care, all woven into one single-family value."

Since the early 1950s, the CCP has institutionalized filial piety by writing it into laws intended to enforce family elder care. It was stated in the 1954 Constitution that "parents have the duty to rear and educate their minor children, and the adult children have the duty to support and assist their parents". In 1996, the Law Protecting the Rights of the Elderly of the People's Republic of China formally laid out adult children's obligations toward their elderly parents in providing housing, medical care, property protection, and other care (China Law Education Website, 2011). This law was revised in 2013 and further reinforced the family's centrality in provision of elder care (Luo, 2015). These important steps of enforcing filial piety and family care correspond to the lack of a comprehensive government welfare system to provide elder care.

The implementation of another important family policy, the 1979 one-child policy, has placed tremendous pressure on adult children to fulfill their moral and legal obligation of familial elder care. The one-child policy quickly and successfully reduced the country's high birth rate; however, it has created the unintended consequence of inadequate family care for the rapidly aging population—care of Chinese baby boomers by the one-child generation children. In urban areas, the family has gradually evolved into an inverted pyramid with four grandparents, two children, and one grandchild (Zhan, 2002). In rural areas, where a comprehensive pension and health care system is still largely underdeveloped and the poverty rate is still high, families are facing a much bigger challenge, even though implementation of the one-child policy in rural areas was more relaxed (if the first child was a girl, a rural couple was allowed to have a second child). With rapid economic growth, adult children of the one-child-policy cohort, in both rural and urban areas, are increasingly unavailable to fulfill their duties of elder care provision, even though they may continue to feel morally obligated for these filial responsibilities (Luo & Zhan, 2012). People in urban areas are facing growing demands on their time from work and child care, whereas rural families are facing the enormous challenges brought about by the migration of adult children from rural to urban areas (Zhang, 2007). In many cases, although elderly parents may be able to receive more financial support, physical care, especially for the frail, is severely lacking (Zhan 2002; Luo & Zhan, 2012).

As discussed in the previous sections, the central government has taken actions to extend public pension and public assistance benefits to cover all elders in both urban and rural areas, and in formal and informal sectors. However, the benefits provided by some of the programs are simply not sufficient, especially the new pension schemes for rural and urban residents and those in the informal sectors. Indeed, familial care is and will continue to be the main source of support for most of elders in China.

To address these challenges, Chinese governments have made major moves to relax the one-child policy in hopes of a higher fertility rate and a lower dependency ratio in the future. The relaxing of the one-child policy with the aim of facilitating family care started at the local level and gradually moved to the national level. For instance, in 2003, the municipal government of Beijing first implemented a policy which stated that if both husband and wife are only children, they are allowed to have two children. In 2013, the central government took a big stride forward in relaxing the policy nationwide, allowing couples to have two children if at least one was an only child. However, its impact was very limited as only a small fraction of qualified couples applied for permission to have a second child (271,600 out of 11 million) (Luo, 2015).

In 2015, the Chinese government officially abandoned the one-child policy when revising the Population and Family Planning Law, which allowed all couples to have a second child starting in 2016 (Li, 2015). However, again, the effectiveness of this new population policy is under question as today's couples are simply overwhelmed by three layers of responsibilities—work, child care, as well as elder care—in an increasingly competitive society and thus are reluctant to have a second child (Li, 2015).

3.2. INSTITUTIONAL CARE

Between the 1950s and the 1980s, institutional care facilities, largely in urban areas, were used as social relief institutions for very needy elders—those with no children, no income, and no relatives (the Three No's) (Chen, 1996; Feng, et al., 2012). They were usually government-owned, funded, and operated. The number of such facilities remained minimal. It was estimated that there were only about 870 institutions throughout the nation in 1988 (Chen, 1996).

Changes in financial support from the government (central and local) to welfare institutions played an important role in shaping the growth of institutional care facilities in China. In the 1990s, the push for decentralization and privatization dramatically reduced governmental financial support for welfare institutions. In the meantime, new social policies encouraged the growth of non-profit elder care institutions. As a result, former government-owned institutions had to seek funding from other sources besides government (Shang, 2001), while the number of private elder care homes mushroomed because of favorable tax policies and government subsidies at both local and central levels (Zhan, 2012).

In the 2000s, as local government experienced great growth in revenues, some municipal and provincial governments offered subsidies for nonprofit and nongovernment elder care institutions. For instance, in the city of Nanjing, each occupied bed could receive a subsidy in the amount of ¥200–¥400 per month (Feng et al., 2011; Zhan et al., 2012). Newly constructed and remodeled care homes may also qualify for lump-sum reimbursement. Consequently, some major cities experienced a boom in the elder care sector in the 2000s (Feng et al., 2011).

Since 2009, after the National Development and Reform Commission clarified the government's initiative to heavily invest in institutional care, many major and medium-sized cities started rapid development of large-scale elder care facilities, taking advantage of favorable policies from the local government such as tax exemptions, subsidies for new and existing beds, land allotment or leasing for new construction, and reduced utility rates (Feng et al.,

2012; Yang 2014). However, such development often occurred in a hasty manner without thoughtful design and planning; especially lacking was a careful needs assessment of elders' functional needs and the need for different levels of medical care. Many facilities, some of which are very large scale with 1,000 to 2,000 beds, are not equipped to provide high levels of professional care for those in need of it, and as a result have very high vacancy rates (40 to 50 percent). Yang (2014) described this phenomenon as a "Great Leap Forward" of institutional facility development.

At the same time, these lucrative policies have also attracted attention from real estate developers, venture capitalists, and other large domestic and foreign corporations, which intend to develop high-end facilities for those elders who can afford high-cost care. Consequently, the government's preferential policies and public funding often end up helping the most privileged and most healthy elders, rather than those who are in most need of long-term care and public financial support. Such a mismatch in resource investment and population needs has caused massive waste in public resources.

3.3. COMMUNITY CARE

Community played an important role in providing care for the elders, particularly for disadvantaged elders before the economic reforms. People belonged to collectives, work units in urban areas, and communes or farm communities in rural areas. Family, especially adult children, took the greatest share of responsibility for elder care. However, when a family caregiver was not present, the community stepped in and took care of the disadvantaged elders through the "Five Guarantees" program.

The economic reform's restructuring of state-owned enterprises in urban areas and decollectivization in rural areas have resulted in the collapse of the community care system in China. During this process, many workers were laid off or became self-employed. For rural elders, at the beginning of the decollectivization process the government continued to push for village and town enterprises to take on the responsibility of community care for the "Five Guarantees" elders. However, for the large part, Mao-era community care was gone soon after economic reform swept through the entire nation.

The void left by the end of community elder care was quickly occupied during the first decade of the 21st century by the nationwide development of a pension system, public assistance program, and health care reform to address increasing social inequality. Predicting that care for the rapidly growing elderly population could be extremely costly, the central government is searching for innovative ways to provide such care through cost-effective models (Feng et al., 2012; Luo, 2015). The initiation of community-based elder care services was based upon the government's understanding of three realities: first, adult children are increasingly unavailable to provide physical care for aging parents; second, elder care institutions are still largely underdeveloped, quality of care is in need of improvement, and most families could not afford institutional care; third, most elders desire to age at home for personal and cultural reasons (filial piety). In urban and rural areas, different community-based care models, aiming to supplement family care with some paid formal services, were tested.

In urban areas, a nationwide movement to promote community-based care has taken place since 2001 under the slogan of "establishing a harmonious society". To address these challenges, starting in 2001, China's Ministry of Civil Affairs began a national "Starlight Plan" (Xinguang Plan) dedicated to building community-based long-term care services through local administrative units. The local governments have established community service coordination centers which contract with qualified local service agencies (nonprofit and for-profit) to provide various services for local residents. Whenever a senior needs help, he/she can call the community coordination center. The coordination center will then contact a local service agency and ask them to send staff to provide the needed service. Beneficiaries pay according to their income level, although all the programs are heavily subsidized by the local government (Ministry of Civil Affairs, 2012). Since the Starlight Plan programs were initiated in 2001, 9873 Senior Centers and over 300,000 Starlight Elder-Homes have been established across the nation (Wu & Du, 2012).

Most of these experiments in home and community-based services only occurred in a few cities. In 2006, the government established five principles as an important component of the 11th Five Year Plan to ensure the wellbeing of elders—"older people should be supported, have medical care, be contributory to the society, be engaged in lifelong learning and live a happy life". Since then, these initiatives have resulted in rapid growth of home and community-based services in large and small cities nationwide. In 2010 in Shanghai, for instance, about 210,000 elders received community-based care services (Wu & Du 2012: 426). In some developed areas, such as Ningbo in Zhejiang province, these community services have been gradually expanded to rural areas (Yu et. al, 2012).

Compared to their urban counterparts, rural communities have fewer resources and fewer options and thus more challenges. The migration of adult children to the cities left elders to care for themselves and often take care of their grandchildren in addition. A "mutual assist elder care" model, which is characterized by younger seniors taking care of older seniors, has gained popularity among rural communities and local and central governments. This model was first invented in Feixiang county, Hebei province in 2008, where a village old-age home was established to house those in critical need of care, with the caregivers being younger, more able-bodied elders. The government subsidized some of the cost for each elderly resident (Chinanews, 2011). This mutual assistance elder care model was promoted nationally as an exemplary rural elder care model. The central government set aside ¥3 billion ($490 million) to push forward this model in the next three years (Chinanews, 2013).

4. DISCUSSION

The shift of CCP's policy focus from economic development to social welfare programs has yielded great improvements in the provision of financial, medical, and physical care for most, if not all, Chinese elders. With the goal of creating a harmonious society in mind, the CCP implemented many new welfare schemes, reformed the old systems, and greatly increased fiscal support for local governments and communities. These changes were demonstrated through improvements in pension programs and long-term care support. However, the nation is still facing great challenges brought about by systematic problems such as unequal distribution of resources, discriminative infrastructure, and lack of thoughtful design of and proper regulations for elder care services. Many more policies need to be put in place to fundamentally improve the well-being of the majority of elders in China.

4.1. MULTI-DIMENSIONAL INEQUALITY: ALLEVIATION AND PERPETUATION OF SOCIAL STRATIFICATION IN CHINA'S OLD AGE SECURITY SYSTEM

The social security systems in many developed countries can be described as a double-edged sword, since they tend to decrease inequality on the one hand, but perpetuate it on the other. For instance, an elderly person's Social Security benefit in the U.S. is based upon a person's consistent contributions to the system for at least 10 years. It tends to reward those working full time and in professional occupations and punishes those working in part-time jobs who have an interrupted work history (most likely women). However, in large part the Social Security system is designed to alleviate social inequality. Higher earners receive a lower income replacement rate (28 percent) whereas low earners receive a much higher replacement rate (78 percent). Spousal benefits, survivor benefits, and dual entitlements are also put in place to support elderly women in their later years (Quadagno, 2011).

China's old age security system also appears double-edged. On the one hand, during the past decade or so, the Chinese government has made great strides in providing some income support for all citizens, including the most disadvantaged (e.g., rural residents, new urban poor, etc.). The current system, with its multilayered schemes, does provide a cushion for all. On the other hand, the comfort level and the size of "cushion" varies greatly among different populations. The current system perpetuates existing social inequality across sectors and rural/urban areas.

It is not difficult to picture a pyramid representing the multilayered pension system in China (see Figure 1), a structure which is largely based upon employer types and household registration (rural or urban) and reflects ever-growing inequality. Those at the very bottom are rural elders, making up almost 66 percent of the 60+ population in China. They used to have no pension coverage at all and now receive minimum coverage under the current reforms, something which is a great improvement but still insufficient for a financially comfortable old age. They will have to continue to rely on their families for financial support. In urban areas, those who do not have formal employment experience, about 7.3 percent of the 60+ population, face a similar situation as the elderly in rural areas. They also receive minimum coverage and need to rely on family in later life.

Then, there is the two-orbit pension system, which created a large income gap among urban retirees depending on employer type. Those who worked at enterprises (20.2 percent of the 60+ population) receive modest public pensions, which on average are significantly lower (almost three times less) than those who worked in government and public institutions, and find themselves on the entry level of the pyramid (6.5 percent of the 60+ population) (Pei &

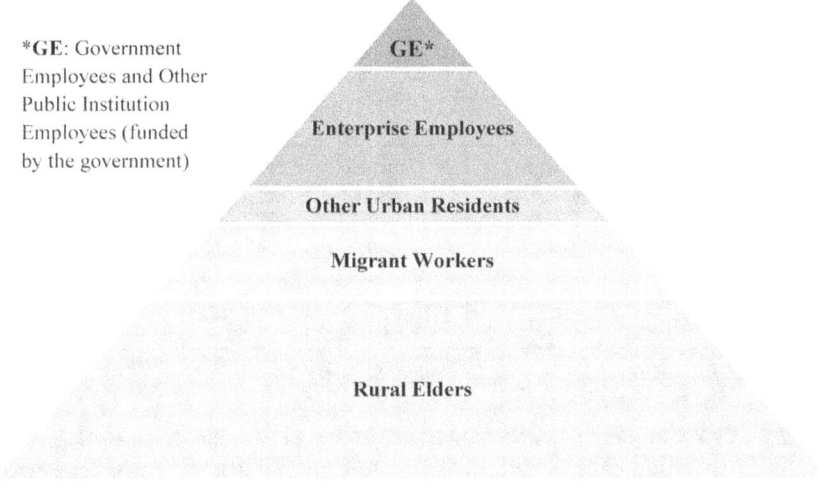

Figure 1. Pyramid of China's Social Security System

Xu, 2011). Zheng's (2015) study estimates that the current pension benefit replacement rate for public service employees is over 90 percent whereas it is below 50 percent for other urban employees. Table 1 shows the large gap in income and pensions across different populations in China.

As shown above, China's pension system is in a way institutionalized to perpetuate inequalities through employment type and the urban/rural divide. Two major efforts have been made to reduce social inequality and address social tension. The first, which we believe to be the most effective effort, lies in the public aid program (Minimum Guarantee Program) targeted at those below the poverty line in both urban and rural areas. This program, however, does not challenge the fundamental and systematic hierarchal structure of welfare distribution due to the nature of its targeted population. The second major effort is the 2015 legislation aiming to eliminate the two-orbit retirement system in urban China by transforming the pension system for public services workers (approximately 40 million participants) into a contributory system similar to the one for other urban employees (approximately 320 million participants). This legislation also goes hand in hand with an incremental increase in basic retirement benefits for urban employees. Because the gap in benefit replacement rate is so large and potential local resistance may be provoked by the reduction of benefits for the more privileged retirees, the author argues that the effectiveness of this legislation in changing the current benefit hierarchy may only be achieved through gradual and persistent administrative enforcement.

All in all, within a short period of time, the Chinese government has made significant improvements in providing later-life income support for its citizens. There is no doubt that today's and tomorrow's Chinese elderly population has greatly benefited from the redistribution of the wealth created by 30 years of rapid economic growth. However, the deeply entrenched hierarchy within the current income support systems and the ongoing pension reforms will continue to test Chinese citizens' tolerance for social inequality and the Chinese

Communist Party's willingness to address social inequality to strengthen its legitimacy.

Table 1. Income and Pension Benefits across Different Employment-Based Populations

	Rural / Urban Residents	Migrant Workers	Enterprise Employees	Government Employees
Average Income (RMB¥/Year)	15,792	27,480	47,284	48,451
Average Pension (RMB¥/Year)	859	N/A	20,400	28,391

Source: *2013 China Human Resources and Social Security Annals.*

4.2. Elder Care Services: Inequality, Effectiveness, and Regulation

In the area of elder care services, it is evident that the Chinese government continues to expect family and adult children to be the main providers of elder care, specifically through the further institutionalization of filial piety and the abandoning of the one-child policy. However, it is important to recognize that the level of effort invested by the government to expand institution-based and community-based services in the past few decades is impressive. These efforts include several new or revised government legislative policies and incentives to encourage the involvement of nongovernment actors, including the private sector as well as civil society. Chinese governments and policymakers are definitely responding to the ever-increasing demands for elder care services including the long-term care needs of families.

However, as with the public pension system, uneven distribution of public resources in formal care services is a major problem, especially in regard to differences across regions and between rural and urban areas. Similar to other public programs, budgetary and operational matters involving elder care services are largely left to local governments. While this mechanism has propelled a proliferation of experimentation, innovation, and horizontal policy learning at local levels, it also widened the already existing gap across localities. The level of service development is closely tied to the local government's revenue, with the more developed eastern provinces significantly surpassing the central and western regions. For instance, in the city of Shanghai and the provinces of Zhejiang and Jiangsu, community-based services have become widespread whereas in provinces such as Gansu and Jiangxi, such programs are still quite rare.

Furthermore, most of the high-quality institutional care facilities and community-based services are located in urban China and often tied to the location of individuals' household registration (*hukou*), especially among those facilities owned and heavily subsidized by the government. Also, institutional care is usually unaffordable for rural elders, even with a modest government subsidy. Community-based services have also been largely limited to urban areas with very low levels of development in rural areas. The lack of basic health care and other infrastructure in rural China poses serious practical limitations to the development of elder services. Without reforming the household registration system and increasing infrastructure investment in rural China, the gap between rural and urban elders will continue to grow.

Besides uneven distribution of resources, the effectiveness of the existing institutional care services and community-based programs (e.g., the Starlight program) in meeting the demands for elder care is also questionable. There is a serious mismatch between resources and demand in both areas. For instance, the government's preferential policy and funding for institutional facility development seem to favor those who are already the most privileged and most healthy elders rather than those who are in most need of long-term care and public support.

The fact that current policies and resource allocation tilt toward institutional care also goes against most Chinese elders' preference for aging in their own homes and communities.

Further, most of the community-based services are targeted toward elders who only need occasional support in instrumental activities of daily living (IADL). It does not address the needs of those who are less mobile and in need of regular (up to 24/7) intensive care for their activities of daily living (ADL). Also, the quality of care provided by contracted agencies is still low as no systematic regulations have been established for proper training of caregiving staff and standardizing the services based upon needs. Although the elder caregivers may be able to provide basic care, the needs for more skilled caregivers are simply not met. Other professional care such as rehabilitation, mental support, spiritual support, palliative care, and hospice care are still quite rare in institutional care facilities and almost non-existent in community programs.

On the other hand, some scholars and policymakers who are working on creating financial systems to support long-term care (e.g., a long-term-care insurance system in Qingdao) seem to narrowly understand long-term care as purely medical in nature and ignore two other important aspects—personal care and social care, which could effectively reduce the cost of medical care if financed and delivered properly. It becomes increasingly clear that policymakers are treating eldercare services in a compartmentalized manner, both conceptually and in practice. For instance, different ministries are in charge of the financing and delivery of the three different aspects of care, and are in fact often working at odds with each other. There is an urgent need to develop a more comprehensive conceptualization of long-term-care support and services by integrating medical, personal, and social care, and perhaps even establishing one single administrative unit to oversee all of the elder care services.

Lack of a professionalized elder care workforce presents another pressing challenge. Most of the formal caregivers in China today receive almost no professional training and are especially unequipped to provide skilled long-term care. In the search for cost-effective ways of providing formal elder care services, the government may need to not only continue supplying financial and material support, but also find innovative and thoughtful ways to provide more and better professional care services in the community.

5. CONCLUSION AND POLICY RECOMMENDATIONS

To address China's aging-related issues from a policy level is particularly challenging for many reasons. The problem largely lies in the reality that economic growth has not been distributed evenly. While urban areas and the eastern regions savored the fruits of economic reform, a large portion of the population in rural areas and the western regions of the country is still struggling with poverty. The ever-increasing rural-urban divide, uneven regional development, and multilayered social security system, compounded by massive social and familial transformations, have left China's most disadvantaged elders to survive on their own. It is perhaps not an exaggeration to describe such an uneven distribution of income security and elder care services as a sharp division between the haves and the have-nots.

While recognizing the great efforts made by the state to improve the coverage of social insurance and public aid, we argue that the current multidimensional system continues to perpetuate inequality and divide the nation. The recent waves of welfare reforms indicate that the main concern of the state is ensuring social stability to maintain the political regime, rather than the wellbeing of its citizens. As a result, the reforms have been mostly carried out within the pre-existing discriminative structure, which continues to divide people by rural/urban registration and employment type. We believe that a fundamental shift is necessary to move the government's ideological focus away from a preoccupation with political stability to a greater concern for citizens' wellbeing and sustainable economic and social development over the long run. The Chinese government's new governing theory—"the New Normal," which aims to restructure the economy and further develop care-focused service sectors—seems to be steering in the right direction.

While greatly expanding the level of financial and service investment, China's policymakers are also searching for ways to utilize limited resources wisely and innovatively to efficiently take care of a large aging population and reach out to elders at different social levels. Being innovative, however, requires thoughtfulness in policy design and should not sacrifice quality. This is an area that zealous local policymakers, who can be described as entrepreneurial, often ignore. For instance, the simplistic approach of a quantitative division for elder care service planning (the 90–7–3 or 90–6–4 models) is quite problematic as it does not take into consideration elders' variations in levels of functional abilities, financial wellbeing, and health status, and devalues the important process of needs assessment in policy planning for elder services. The nationwide promotion of the Starlight Plan and Mutual Assistance Model, while much less costly compared to institutional care, may not be cost-effective, due to the lack of professionalization of service providers and government regulations on quality control. Future policies need to pay more attention to the provision of quality care through public investment in the building of social infrastructure related to caregiving jobs, such as a comprehensive system of university and vocational training for various administrative and direct-caregiver positions in the elder care sector.

Last but not least, to fully cope with the challenge of population aging and improve the livelihoods of all people, the making of policies and investment of financial resources are necessary but may not be sufficient. They need to go hand-in-hand with a reinterpretation of the relationship between the state and the citizens and a more cautious approach in integrating the market into the provision of social services (e.g., learning from the Great-Leap-Forward development of elder care institutions). Traditionally, the Chinese people are used to the idea that emperors or governments always impose taxes; welfare or benefits are favors or "grace" that emperors or governments bestow on the people.

With the rapid growth of the Chinese middle class and the increase in citizens' educational levels, Chinese people's desire to participate in public decision-making and their social consciousness of citizenship rights are likely to be raised. Until then, perpetuation of social stratification based on place of residence and type of employment will likely continue to be part of China's social reality. Aging well is likely to be an inspirational goal for intellectuals but only wishful thinking for the majority of rural elders for years to come.

REFERENCES

Chen, P. (2015, Winter). China's retirement system: What does the future hold? (Interview with Zheng, Bingwen) Available online at https://us.dimensional.com/media/323321/Chinas-Retirement-System-What-Does-the-Future-Hold.pdf.

Chen, S. Y. (1996). *Social Policy of the Economic State and Community Care in Chinese Culture: Aging, Family, Urban Change, and the Socialist Welfare Pluralism*. Avebury: Brookfield.

Chen, S., & Powell, J. L. (Eds.). (2013) *Aging in China: Implications to Social Policy of a Changing Economic State*. New York: Springer.

China Law Education (2011). http://www.chinalawedu.com/falvfagui/fg21752/29797.shtml.

Chinanews (2011, February 16). A visit to Qiantuan village: A new mutual assistance elder care model. http://www.chinanews.com/gn/2011/02-16/2847648.shtml.

Chinanews. (2013). An investment of 3 billion yuan to establish mutual assistance elder care model across the nation. http://www.chinanews.com/gn/2013/02-21/4581992.shtml.

Chow, N., & Xu, Y. (2002). Pension reforms in China. In C. J. Finer (Ed.), *Social Policy Reforms in China: Views from Home and Abroad*. Aldershot: Ashgate.

Feng, Z.L., et. al. (2011). An industry in the making: The emergence of institutional elder care in urban China. *Journal of America Geriatric Society* 59: 733–744.

Feng, Z. L, et al. (2015). China's rapidly aging population creates policy challenges in shaping a viable long-term care system. *Health Affairs* 31(12): 2764–2773.

Findlaw Website. (2015). Policies on social insurance policies for migrant workers. Available online at http://china.findlaw.cn/laodongfa/laodongbaoxian/yanglaobaoxian/yanglaobaoxiangainia/1189858.html.

Hu, N. J. (2015). Public pension system unified: Replacing general revenue expenditure with social insurance. *Chinese Economy Report* 2: 50–52.

Levin D. (2008, July). Aging in China: A tradition under stress: Who will care for the nation's elders? *AARP Bulletin*. Available from: http:// www.aarp.org/politics-society/ around-the-globe/info-07-2008/ aging_in_china_a_tradition_ under_stress.html.

Li, W.A (2015). China's "Second-Child for All" policy. *Southern Weekly*. Available online at http://www.infzm.com/content/112655.

Luo, B. (2015). China will get rich before it grows old: Beijing's demographic problems are overrated. *Foreign Affairs* 94(3): 19–24.

Luo, B. & Zhan, H.J. (2012). Filial piety and functional support: Understanding intergenerational solidarity among families with migrated children in rural China. *Ageing International* 37(1): 69–92.

Ministry of Civil Affairs. (2010). *China civil affairs statistical yearbook—2010*. Beijing: China Statistics Press.

Ministry of Human Resources and Social Security. (2009). *Guidelines for experiment of the New Rural Pension System*. http://www.mohrss.gov.cn/ncshbxs/NCSHBXSzhengcewenjian/200909/t20090901_83916.htm.

Ministry of Human Resources and Social Security. (2013). Annual report on human resource and Social Security development. Available online at: http://www.mohrss.gov.cn/SYrlzyhshbzb/zwgk/szrs/tjgb/201405/t20140529_131147.html.

Ministry of Labor and Social Security (2006). *Basic Policy*. http://www.molss.gov.cn/gb/ywzn/2006-02/15/content_106550.htm.

National Bureau of Statistics of China. (2016) Report on National Economy and Social Development for the Year of 2015. http://www.stats.gov.cn/tjsj/zxfb/201602/t20160229_1323991.html.

National Bureau of Statistics of China (2014). *Annual Data on Population*. Available online at http://data.stats.gov.cn/easyquery.htm?cn=C01&zb=A0301&sj=2014.

Pei, X. and Xu, Q. (2011). Old age security, inequality, and poverty. In Chen, S. and Powell, J. (Eds)., *Aging in Perspective and the Case of China* (pp. 133–149). Nova Science Publishers.

Polivka, L. and Luo, B. (2013). The future of retirement security across the globe. *Generations: Journal of the American Society on Aging* 37(1): 39–45.

Quadagno, J. (2011). *Aging and the Life Course*. 5th edition. Boston: McGraw-Hill.

Shang, X. (2001). Moving toward a multi-level and multi-pillar system: Changes in institutional care in two Chinese cities. *Journal of Social Policy* 30 (2): 259–281.

The Central People's Government of the People's Republic of China (2011). Guidelines for establishing pensions for urban residents. http://www.gov.cn/zwgk/2011-06/13/content_1882801.htm.

Wu, C.P & Du, P. (2012). *Aging Society and Harmonious Society*. China Population Publishing House.

Xinhua News Agency (2015). Aging population, changing attitudes drive China's senior care boom. Available online at http://news.xinhuanet.com/english/2015-12/20/c_134935216.htm.

Xu, Y., & Zhang, X. (2013) Pensions and social assistance: The development of income security policies for old people in China. In Chen, S., & Powell, J. L. (Eds.), *Aging in China: Implications to Social Policy of a Changing Economic State* (pp. 43–59). New York: Springer.

Yang, T. (2014). Exploring home and community-based long-term care social policies. *Learning and Practice* 6: 82–91 (in Chinese).

Yu, J., Chen, Y., Peng, Z., & Tong, Z. (2012). *Allow the Society to Operate Smoothly: A Study of Social Development in Haishu District, Ningbo City*. Beijing: Renming University Press.

Zhan, H. J. (2002). Caregiving burden and the future burden of elder care in China: A lifecourse perspective. *International Journal of Aging and Human Development* 54: 267–291.

Zhan, H.J., Luo, B, & Chen, Z.Y. (2012). Institutional elder care in China. In Chen, Sheying and Powell, Jason (Eds.), *Aging in China: Implications to Social Policy of a Changing Economic State—International Perspectives on Aging* (pp. 221–235). Springer.

Zhang, H. (2007). Who will care for our parents? Changing boundaries of family and public roles in providing care for the aged in urban China. *Care Management Journal* 8(1): 39–46.

Zhen, L. (2012). The basic old-age insurance of China: Challenges and countermeasures. Available online at http://www.worldpensionsummit.com/Portals/6/Zhen%20Li_Basic%20old%20age%20insurance%20in%20China.pdf.

Chapter 6
Aging and Elder Care in Shanghai

Xin Yang, Weizhen Dong

ABSTRACT

Shanghai has become an aging society: 4.84 million of its residents are 60 years and older. While its residents' longevity deserves much celebration, the rapid aging trend and the burden of elder care are beyond imagination. What is at stake are not only the wellbeing of elders and their caregivers, but also the stability and sustainable development of the entire region. Projecting the aging trend may enhance public preparedness, and examining potential supply and demand gaps may help improve intervention and access improvement. The current trajectory of elder care facility development requires modification in order to meet the needs of seniors in Shanghai: namely, to provide more affordable and easy access to community-based elder care centers instead of high-end luxurious and/or suburban ones.

Collaborations among communities and relevant stakeholders such as government, family, and nonprofit organizations could result in innovative ways of meeting the elder care challenge. As the first city in China to tackle the aging issue, Shanghai's lessons and experiences will be valuable for the rest of the nation.

1. INTRODUCTION

The aging of society is a global phenomenon and China is no exception, particularly in its major urban centers. The elderly population in China aged 65 and over grew from 63 million to 144 million between 1990 and 2015. Its proportion to the entire population increased from 5.57 percent to10.47 percent. Over the same period, the average family size decreased from 3.96 persons to 3.10 persons (National Bureau of Statistics of China, 2016). Among the different regions of China, the aging trend in Shanghai has been particularly rapid. By the end of 2015, 30.2 percent or 4.36 million of Shanghai registered residents were 60 years of age (the official retirement age for men and professional women) or older. Presently, Shanghai's average life expectancy at birth is 83.37 years (men 80.98, women 85.85). It is the highest in China, partly due to its dynamic economy and prolific resources (Dong et al., 2017; Shanghai Municipal Commission of Health and Family Planning, 2017; Shanghai Municipal Government, 2018).

This trend in Shanghai will not slow down any time soon. By the year 2030, 7.9 million of the city's residents will be 60 years of age and older. The city's current supply of elder care services does not meet its residents' needs. The main challenge lies in accessibility and affordability, as well as quality of care—namely, imbalance in location (downtown vs. suburban), cost (luxury vs. basic elder care), and scale. The development of community elder care centers will have a positive impact on the state of Shanghai's elder care and its senior residents' lives.

This chapter aims to project Shanghai's aging trend, to examine and analyze the elder care supply and demand reality in Shanghai, and to explore ways in which the megacity could potentially tackle the relevant issues successfully.

2. METHODS

This study's data include China's national census and other relevant censuses. The cohort-component method is employed for the projections of population trends in Shanghai. We predicted the future population size and age structure through age-shift calculations based on the set of fertility, mortality and population sex ratio data and other parameters, specifically (1) population by age and sex from the sixth population census of China in 2010; (2) mortality by age and sex from the Shanghai Municipal Center for Disease Control and Prevention in 2009; (3) total fertility rate based on the China national population census in 2010 (TFR = 0.72); and (4) sex ratio at birth based on the sixth census data in 2010 (the most recent available).

The procedure for making cohort-component population projections was developed by Whelpton in the 1930s. It can be thought of as an elaboration of the ideas encapsulated in the demographic balancing equation

$$P(t+n) = P(t) + B(t) - D(t) + I(t) - E(t)$$

where $P(t)$ is the population at time t, $B(t)$ and $D(t)$ are number of births and deaths occurring between t and $t+n$, and $I(t)$ and $E(t)$ are the number of migrants and of emigrants from the city during the period t to $t+n$.

Sources used for the analysis are publicly accessible, in the form of journal articles, national statistics reports and government websites. The keywords used for searching the materials include *census, statistics on population structure, aging studies, aging in Shanghai, elder care institutions, elders' welfare institution*, and *homecare*. We also included data from the *Shanghai Longitudinal Survey on Elderly Residents' Living Status and Their Desires* since 1998.

3. AGING IN SHANGHAI

Shanghai is China's major industrial and financial center. Due to its dynamic economic development, its openness and its cultural diversity, the city's population growth has been particularly rapid in recent decades. It has doubled in size since the 1990s. By 2015, the proportion of the elderly aged 60 and above was 30.2 percent, a total of 4.36 million people (see Figure 1 and Table 1 on the next page).

Figure 1 and Table 1 show us that the proportion of registered elder residents in Shanghai has been constantly increasing, and their share of the whole population is also increasing.

The elder population itself is also aging, with the proportion of that population aged 80 years and above increasing. Between 1953 and 2015, the percentage of the population aged 80 years and above rose from 3.1 percent to 17.9 percent of all elderly residents (i.e., those 60+ years in age). Growth in the last 15 years is almost as great as during the 40 years prior to the year 2000. According to census data, the percentage of registered elderly aged 60 years and above in Shanghai was 14.2 percent in 1990; those aged 80 years and above made up 9.1 percent of that population. By the end of 2015, 5.4 percent of Shanghai residents were 80 years or older; and they made up 18 percent of the total elderly population, double the 1990 figure (Shanghai Municipal Bureau of Statistics, 2016).

Table 1. Aging Trends among Shanghai Registered Residents (1953-2015)

Year	60+/total population (%)	65+/total population (%)	80+/60+ (%)	80+/65+ (%)
1953	3.7	2.0	3.1	5.7
1964	6.1	3.6	4.4	7.5
1982	11.5	7.4	7.9	12.3
1990	14.2	9.4	9.1	13.7
2000	18.2	14.1	12.4	16.0
2010	23.4	16.0	18.1	26.4
2015	30.2	19.6	17.9	27.5

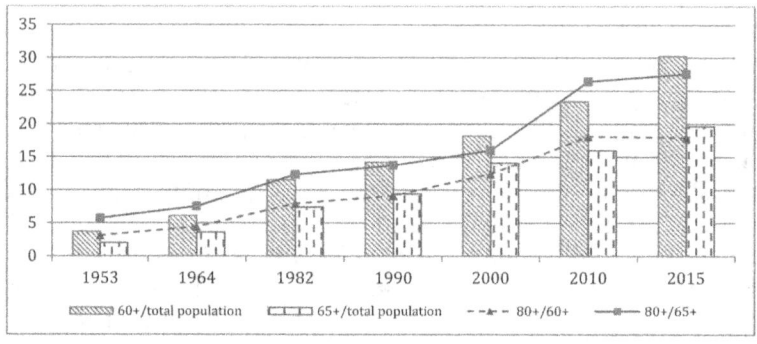

Figure 1. Aging Trend among Registered Residents in Shanghai (1953-2010)

Data resource: 1. *The Historical Statistical Data of Economy and Social Development of Shanghai* (1949-2000), Shanghai Municipal Bureau of Statistics, China Statistics Press: 2001. 2. Shanghai government website: http://www.shanghai.gov.cn/shanghai/node2314/node2319/node12344/u26ai25463.html 3. *Shanghai Statistical Yearbook*, 2001-2016; 4. Census data; and 5. Monitoring statistical information of elderly population in Shanghai, Shanghai Research Center on Aging, http://www.shrca.org.cn/5764.html.

In terms of overall projections, we assume that, first, total fertility rate and mortality by age and sex are likely to remain at the current level for the next 15 years; second, the annual net increase of residents will likely be 400,000 until 2020, and then 350,000 from 2021 to 2030; and third, the age structure of incoming migrants will remain the same as before. Total fertility rate (TFR) in different projections (1) increases from 0.72 to 0.9 between 2010 and 2030; (2) increases gradually from 0.72 to 1.2 between 2010 and 2030; and (3) increases rapidly from 0.72 to 1.4 between 2010 and 2030 (see Figure 2).

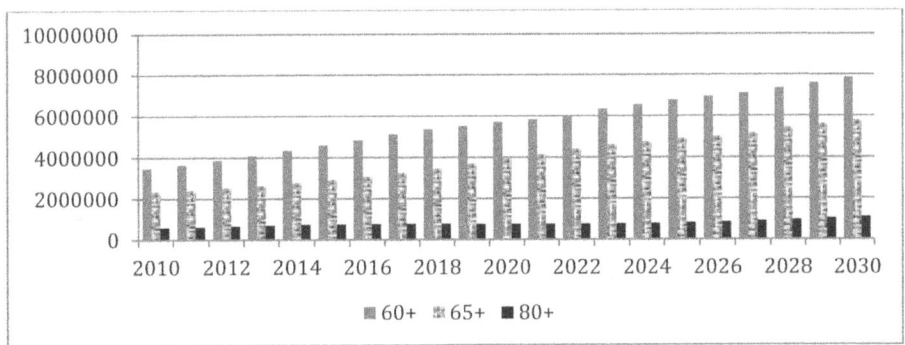

Figure 2. Projection of Aging Trends in Shanghai (2010–2030)

Based on recent trends, we predict that the population of Shanghai will rise gradually to 30 million by year 2030. The number of registered elderly residents aged 60 years and above will grow linearly and the speed of aging will accelerate. With a medium-speed projection, the size of this population group will reach 7.9 million by 2030. The proportion of elderly residents will reach 26 percent of the total population, which includes both the registered population and migrants. This figure is lower than the proportion in the registered population alone, which will be over 40 percent (see Figure 2). This is because the inflow of young migrants will help reduce Shanghai seniors' share of the total population. During the period 2010–2025, the number of elderly 80 years and above will continue to rise at the same rate, and will be well over 800,000 by the year 2026.

4. HEALTH STATUS OF THE ELDERLY AND ELDER CARE DEMAND IN SHANGHAI

The demand for elder care service depends on self-care ability and health status. Table 2 presents the ADL status of senior groups of different ages in 2013, based on data collected through the *Shanghai Longitudinal Survey on Elderly Residents' Living Status and Their Desires since 1998*.

Self-care ability is classified into three categories, based on an assessment of daily living activities of respondents. An elderly person who is able to care for himself or herself is given the self-care status. An elderly person who requires minimal assistance with daily life is assigned a partially disabled status. An elder who requires assistance all year round with all tasks is given the completely disabled status. The survey data shows that 87.62 percent of the elderly aged 60 years and above can live independently. Of those aged 60 to 64 years, more than 96 percent are able to live independently, but less than 30 percent can live without help when they are over 90; self-care ability diminishes with age. Only 3.82 percent of those aged 60 to 64 need assistance, but that proportion rises to over 70 percent for those 90 and older (see Table 2).

Table 2. The ADL* Status of Shanghai Elders in 2013

Age group	Self-care %	Partially Disabled %	Completely Disabled %
60-64	96.19	3.22	0.60
65-69	93.32	6.51	0.17
70-74	90.55	7.96	1.49
75-79	82.74	14.21	3.05
80-84	67.24	24.57	8.19
85-89	49.43	40.34	10.23
90+	27.27	49.35	23.38
Total	87.62	9.89	2.49

*ADL (activity of daily living) is a set of measurements used to evaluate elders' self-care ability.
Data resource: Shanghai Research Center of Aging, Shanghai Academy of Social Science, Shanghai University and the National University of Singapore (2013): *Shanghai Longitudinal Survey on Elderly Residents' Living Status and Their Desires*.

4.1. SOCIAL TRANSITION, DEMOGRAPHIC CHANGE AND ELDER CARE DEMAND TRAJECTORY

Traditionally, caring for elders was a family matter, with the responsibility shared among the elders' children. During the nearly four decades' implementation of the one-child policy, the traditional mode of elder care became problematic. Elder care has become a growing burden to society, and the social norms on elder care are being challenged as well.

As Figure 3 shows, Shanghai's average household size has declined from 3.09 persons in 1990 to 2.69 persons in 2015. At the same time, the proportion of families with at least one person aged 60 years and above is rising (Shanghai Municipal Bureau of Statistics, 2016). During this period, the proportion of elderly persons living alone increased as well. By the end of 2015, there were 987,000 seniors living alone, and 281,000 of them were 80 years of age or older (Shanghai Research Center on Aging, 2015).

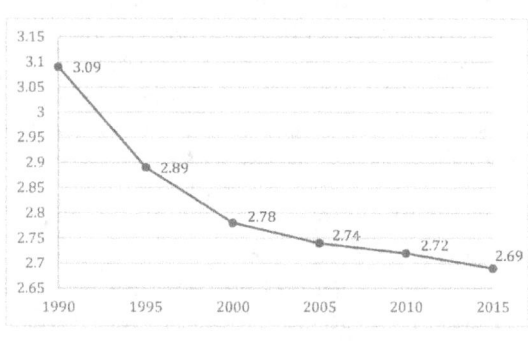

Figure 3. Average Household Size in Shanghai (1990–2015)

Source: Shanghai Municipal Bureau of Statistics website, http://www.stats-sh.gov.cn/tjnj/nj16.htm?d1=2016tjnj/C0201.htm.

According to the theory of expansion morbidity (Gruenberg, 1977; Kramer, 1980), the longevity of patients and disabled people will be extended because of the improvement of health promotion measures and medical care. As a result, the proportion of people living with functional defects will rise in tandem with the increase in average life expectancy. This theory has been verified by a study in China (Du and Li, 2006). Therefore, the average survival period for the disabled elderly is likely to be extended along with the increase in average life expectancy generally. These elders will require assistance in their daily lives. The demand for institutional care can be estimated based on the proportion of elders who are completely disabled, and the demand for family and community care estimated based on the proportion of elders with partial disability. Given that age is a key factor in one's health status, we can use the rate of disability by age.

In 2012, the number of seniors who needed institutional care was around 96,000; in other words, the total demand for institutional elder care beds was 96,000 in 2012. Meanwhile, about 381,900 elderly persons required family and community care. Assuming the disability rate by age of resident remains the same, the demand for institutional, family and community elder care will rise among those 80 years of age and older, and this population's size will grow rapidly in the next 15 years. The number of Shanghai residents 80 and older—the oldest of the old—will reach 195,590 by 2030.

4.2. SUPPLY OF ELDER CARE IN SHANGHAI

There are different types of elder care in Shanghai, including institutional elder care (welfare institutions and elder care wards in hospitals), community elder care, and home care. Currently, 139 of the 660 elders' welfare institutions in Shanghai have medical care resources, and 353 of them have contracts with community healthcare centers for in-house healthcare delivery services privileges (Wu, 2015).

Until the 1990s, institutional elder care service was only provided to seniors who had no income, no working capacity and no family support. With the aging of the population and the changing family structure, more elderly residents are willing to live in a welfare institution, and Shanghai's elderly welfare institutions were opened to all the elderly in the city. In order to increase the supply of institutional services, the government strengthened fiscal support and promoted investment in elderly welfare institutions by offering incentives such as tax relief, priority status in land-use permission, and financial assistance.

4.2.1. Institutional elder care

There are four types of elderly welfare institution in Shanghai: (1) Those established by the municipal government or district governments, with large-scale, extensive facilities, high-quality services, and lower costs; (2) those sponsored by large-scale state-owned enterprises or public service units (in the past, these institutions were only accessible to their employees as part of the welfare system, but with the collapse of the planned economy system, some of these institutions were closed and the rest were opened to the local community); (3)

quasi-public institutions set up by neighborhood committees and villagers' committees, which usually follow a small-scale, flexible operation mode and provide inconsistent service quality; and (4) private institutions invested in by non-state-owned enterprises or individuals.

Due to government policy guidance, the number of beds in elder care institutions started to increase from 1997 onward, and especially after 2005. The number of beds was 16,532 in 1997, and rose by about 4,000 per year over the next seven years. From 2005 on, its annual growth exceeded 10,000 beds. The total number of beds reached 114,907 in 2014, and 126,000 by the end of 2015 (Shanghai Municipal Bureau of Statistics, 2016).

4.2.2. Community care

Community care in Shanghai is a form of social support for senior residents. It relies on families, community networks, and professional teams. The services provided include house cleaning, cooking, personal hygiene and basic healthcare. The mode of service includes individual homecare as well as group care in daycare centers. The growth of community daycare centers for the elderly over the past ten years was rapid. In 2005, there were only 83 such centers; by 2015, the number had increased by 5.3 times to 442, as Table 3 shows.

Table 3. Elders in Community Daycare Centers (Shanghai, 2005–2016)

Data Year	Number of day care centers	Elders in day care centers	Elders in community day care centers	Elders receiving government subsidies
2005	83	2,100	54,800	39,400
2006	108	3,500	105,000	59,600
2007	128	4,800	135,000	68,400
2008	229	6,400	177,000	103,000
2009	283	8,000	219,000	129,000
2010	303	9,000	252,000	130,000
2011	326	9,000	262,000	133,000
2012	313	11,000	272,000	126,000
2013	340	12,000	282,000	130,000
2014	381	14,000	295,400	130,000
2015	442	15,000	305,500	131,800
2016	488	20,000	--	126,600

Data resource: 1. Shanghai Municipal Bureau of Statistics website, http://www.stats-sh.gov.cn/tjnj/nj16.htm?d1=2016tjnj/C2118.htm, http://www.stats-sh.gov.cn/tjnj/nj13.htm?d1=2013tjnj/C2118.htm, http://www.stats-sh.gov.cn/tjnj/nj10.htm?d1=2010tjnj/C2018.htm, http://www.stats-sh.gov.cn/tjnj/nj08.htm?d1=2008tjnj/C2121.htm; 2. Shanghai Statistical Yearbook 2017.

Some communities have set up seniors' self-help groups as an innovative form of elder care. Members of such groups receive free care services by taking care of other members of the group. Service hours are recorded as the basis for care providers to receive the free care services they require. The members can also pay ¥365 a year as a mutual care fee, something which also saves them money. After paying for 15 years, the member will be eligible for four hours a day of free services when they require them (Zhang, 2006).

4.2.3. Family care
Spouses and children are still the most important caregivers for the elderly in Shanghai. The longitudinal survey on living arrangements of the elderly shows that more than 85 percent of the population was cared for by their families in 2013. The percentage of family members who are caregivers in the under-80 group rose compared to 1998, while the percentage of caregivers in the 80+ group decreased substantially from 86.0 percent to 79.5 percent. In the latter group, the proportion who received services from domestic helpers and professional caregivers had risen significantly.

Most of those aged 60 to 79 years can still live independently. However, those who are 80 years and older tend to be less healthy, and the proportion of disability or partial disability in this group tends to be much greater, creating a heavy elder care burden for their families. Thus, some families would consider institutional care as their preferred, if not only, option.

5. DISCUSSION

Elderly care in an aging society is a challenging issue for both the government and the general public. In Shanghai, there are several government bodies closely involved in elder care affairs. The Civil Affairs Bureau of Shanghai is responsible for the construction of the elderly welfare institutions and service supply. The Shanghai Municipal Commission of Health and Family Planning is responsible for the construction of elderly welfare institutions and medical care services. The Social Security Bureau of Shanghai is responsible for fundraising and payments. Policy coordination amongst these departments is very important. However, since each agency has its own priority and mission, finding common interests and achieving common good require the central government's policy guidance.

5.1. Effective Supply and Utilization of Elder Care
5.1.1. Utilization: Hospital vs. non-hospital care
As in many other countries and regions, healthcare insurance in China covers hospital costs but not those for long-term care, a fact which encourages the elderly to choose hospital care over other options. Welfare institutions for the elderly, such as retirement homes, are rather costly, but if an individual stays in a hospital, health insurance would cover a high proportion of the expenses. This practice is wasteful of medical care resources, since most elderly persons do not require hospital care at all.

The rate of elder care bed utilization dropped from 83.4 percent in 1997 to 77.9 percent in 2000, and further to about 65 percent in 2012. Two factors explain the drop: first, there are more elder care facilities and beds in suburban Shanghai but more elders living in downtown Shanghai; and second, some newly operating facilities are too pricy for ordinary elders (Wu et al., 2015; Dong et al., 2017).

5.1.2. Accessibility: Downtown vs. suburb

About half of Shanghai seniors live in the downtown area, but only a third of the city's elderly welfare institutions are located in downtown Shanghai, while 47 percent of institutional elder care beds are in suburban Shanghai but only one-third of the elder population is located there (see Table 4). The mismatch in demand and supply caused the rate of bed utilization to fall between 2004 and 2012 (see Figure 4).

Table 4. The Distribution of Institutional Beds and Elders in Shanghai (2015)

Region	Number of Beds	% of Total	Number of Elders	% of Total
Pudong Area	25010	19.74	823,100	18.88
Downtown	42500	33.54	1,961,900	45.00
Suburban	59211	46.72	1,574,500	36.12
Total	126721	100.00	4,359,500	100.00

Data resource: Statistical Information of Elderly Population Monitoring in Shanghai in 2016.

Currently, 33.2 percent of Shanghai's registered population, or 4.84 million, is 60 years and older. Shanghai has 703 nursing homes with 140,400 beds in total (Xinhua, 2018). There is no more recent data on bed utilization rates; Figure 4 shows the rates from 2014 to 2012. It seems these elder care facilities are facing challenges in selling their services.

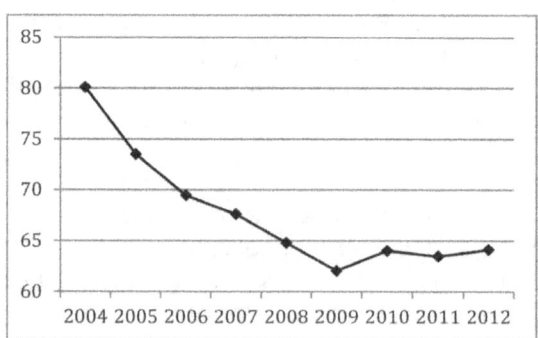

Figure 4. Elder Care Bed Utilization Rate in Shanghai (2004–2012)

Data source: Shanghai Aging Committee (2013), Monitoring Statistic Information of Elderly Population in Shanghai in 2012.

5.1.3. Service supply: Undefined mode of care vs. need-based care
Many homes for the elderly and elder care facilities located in Shanghai lack well-defined parameters of services. For example, since these institutions prefer to accept healthy elders, they leave those truly in need of care—with disabilities or chronic illnesses—excluded from the city's elder care system. This fact serves as a reminder that a variety of elder care institutions are needed to provide different modes of services, such as independent living homes, assisted living apartments, nursing homes, and palliative care centers.

5.1.4. Quality of care: Professionalization vs. lack of training for caregivers
There is a serious shortfall in human resources devoted to elder care in Shanghai. Currently, most caregivers for the elderly are middle-aged female rural-to-urban migrants. They tend to have junior high school education or less and have had little training for elder care. Since caregiving jobs carry great responsibility but with low pay and low occupational status, very few native local residents are interested in this profession, especially those with high levels of education. There is an urgent need for the training and professionalization of caregivers, whether they work in homecare, community care, or institutional care.

Institutional care is a necessary alternative for seniors who are disabled or chronically ill. The government should also find measures to ease the burden on family caregivers. Supporting informal family caregivers can effectively ease the burden placed on community care and institutional care services.

6. CONCLUSION
Shanghai is aging rapidly. Its senior population comprises a great proportion of the city's residents. Projected future growth of the city's elderly population is alarming. There will be serious challenges associated with the demographic shift.

Some government measures have been developed to assist family caregivers, such as respite care supplied by day care centers for the elderly. Different stakeholders can also support informal caregivers both directly and indirectly, including improving community-based services and encouraging relevant non-governmental organizations to devote resources to elder care.

Clearly defining the roles of existing elder care welfare institutions can help both caregivers and the elders who require services. Division of care will help elders in need to receive services they deem necessary and appropriate, and avoid an institutional bias towards admitting only healthier individuals. Developing elder care facilities where elders currently reside is very important. It can meet the needs of the elders and their families, and address the issue of utilization rates.

Finding intelligent and caring ways of tackling the elder care reality promises to enhance every citizen's quality of life. Ensuring the wellbeing of society's senior members is an integral part of building a healthy population, and each one of us is responsible for that mission.

REFERENCES

Dong, W., et al. (2017). Determinants of self-rated health among Shanghai elders: A cross-sectional study. *BMC Public Health* 17: 807.

Du, P., and Li, Q. (2006). Disability-free life expectancy of Chinese elderly and its change between 1994 and 2004. *Population Research* 30 (5): 9–16.

Gruenberg, E.M. 1977. The failure of success. *Milbank Q* 55 (1): 3–24.

Institute of Urban and Population Development Study, Shanghai Academy of Social Science (2012). The study of admittance standard of elderly welfare institution directed by Shanghai municipal government[R]. Sponsored by Shanghai Municipal Civil Affairs Bureau.

Kramer, M. 1980. The rising pandemic of mental disorders and associated chronic diseases and disabilities. *Acta Psychiatrica Scandinavica* 62 (285): 382–97.

Ministry of Civil Affairs of China (2001, February). *Standards of Social Welfare Institution for Elderly (MZ-008 2001)*.

Shanghai Municipal Bureau of Quality and Technical Supervision (2013). *Assessment for Elderly Care (DB31/T684-2013)*.

Shanghai Municipal Commission of Health and Family Planning (2015). *Shanghai Residents' Life Expectancy over 83 Years for the First Time*. WenHui News website. http://wenhui.news365.com.cn/html/2017-01/26/content_521464.html.

Shanghai Municipal Government (2018). The average life expectancy of Shanghai residents has risen to 83.37 years. http://www.shanghai.gov.cn/nw2/nw2314/nw2315/nw17239/nw22560/u21aw1284581.html.

Shanghai Municipal Government (2010). *Shanghai Municipal Government's Advices on Eldercare Institutions' Development during the "12th Five-Year Period" in the City*. Shanghai Municipal Government, China. Available online at http://www.shanghai.gov.cn.

Shanghai Municipal Statistics Bureau (2001). *The Historical Statistical Data of Economy and Social Development of Shanghai (1949–2000)*. China Statistics Press, China.

Shanghai Municipal Statistics Bureau & Survey Office of the National Bureau of Statistics in Shanghai (2001–2011, 2013). *Shanghai Statistical Yearbook*. China Statistics Press, China.

Shanghai Municipal Statistics Bureau & Survey Office of the National Bureau of Statistics in Shanghai (1999–2002). *Shanghai Statistical Yearbook*. China Statistics Press, China.

Shanghai Research Center on Aging, Shanghai Academy of Social Sciences, Shanghai University & the National University of Singapore (2013). *Shanghai Longitudinal Survey on Elderly Residents' Living Status and Desires*.

Wu, R. (2015, June 29). One "60+" elderly person among every three Shanghai residents. *Xinmin Evening News*.

Wu, Y., et al. (2015). Study on eldercare institutions in China. *Scientific Research on Aging* 3: 8.

Xinhua News (2018, March 29). One-third in Shanghai residents aged 60 or over. http://www.xinhuanet.com/english/2018-03/29/c_137074836.htm.

Zhang, X. 2006. *The Pattern Choosing of Shanghai Elderly Long-Term Care on the Background of Aging Population* (Master's thesis). Shanghai Jiao Tong University.

Chapter 7
Housing Policy
A Comparative Study of Shanghai and St. Petersburg

Xiaowen Lu

ABSTRACT
Under the planned economic system, China and the former Soviet Union both adopted universal welfare housing policies, and regarded housing as public property. Housing marketization began in China in the 1990s, and progress was rapid. For the most part, urban Chinese families sought to improve their housing situation by participating in the open real estate market; however, drawbacks such as quickly rising house prices and excessive marketization began to appear. As a result, both the Chinese central and Shanghai local governments formulated new social policies to better address the needs of low-income families.

Meanwhile, under the enormous economic reforms in Russia, all public housing was transferred to families, but some social security functions of housing were maintained and consolidated. A pattern in which social welfare and open market housing existed side by side was adopted. Under the influence of different economic development situations and different social policies, the housing situations in major cities in China and Russia began to demonstrate their distinctive features. Keeping the proper balance between the open market and welfare needs is a common problem in improving housing conditions in both nations.

1. THE EVOLUTION OF THE HOUSING SYSTEM AND POLICIES IN CHINA AND RUSSIA

1.1. THE CHANGE IN SOCIAL SECURITY HOUSING POLICIES IN CHINA AND SHANGHAI

Since the new China was founded in 1949, efforts to ensure housing security in China and Shanghai can be divided into four periods:

1.1.1. 1953–1979: Government-oriented welfare housing distribution
In the 1950s, the government took charge of the housing supply for urban residents, and China established a national housing supply system. At the same time, housing construction was included in the national capital construction plan. Local governments and work-units obtained funds from the national budget to build public houses assigned to workers. The housing system emphasized social welfare, so adequate housing was regarded as a right. Housing distribution was based first on occupational rank and then on the number of family members. Residents paid only a nominal rent. In Shanghai, the government used direct housing distribution to help families with housing difficulties first, addressing the housing problems of 454,500 families (Shanghai Local Chronicles Office, 2008).

The work-unit and government housing policy benefited families by providing housing through the welfare system. Nevertheless, the inefficiently planned economy led to a shortage of material resources. With the rapid increase of the urban population and the obvious lack of new housing construction and supply, many problems accumulated, including an overall shortage of houses, cramped living spaces, old and low-quality houses, and lack of housing maintenance. Most families in Shanghai faced housing difficulties and the imbalance between supply and demand became more acute. By the late 1970s, Shanghai faced a serious housing crisis because the government could not provide enough houses for its citizens.

1.1.2. 1980–1986: Workplace-oriented housing: Self-built and self-distributed
National, local, enterprise and public institutions invested in and distributed housing to the population using the "self-built and self-distributed (by the workplace)" principle. Following government housing policy, enterprise and public institutions began investing in housing by considering the degree of housing difficulty as the main factor. In Shanghai, the housing problems of 236,200 families were addressed during this period (Shanghai Local Chronicles Office, 2008).

1.1.3. 1987–1999: Emphasis on solving the housing problem
Shanghai entered this period of large-scale housing solutions by consolidating administrative resources. Between 1987 and 1988, the housing difficulties of households with less than 2.0 square meters per capita were addressed, and in 1991, the housing difficulties of households with less than 2.5 square meters per capita were resolved. At that time, a total of 47,000 households benefited from these two programs. In 1995, the problems of 13,000 households with less than 4.0 square meters per capita were settled. By 1999, Shanghai had addressed the housing difficulties of an additional 120,000 households with less than 4.0 square meters per capita, benefiting nearly 500,000 residents (Shanghai Local Chronicles Office, 2008).

In July 1998, the State Council issued the "Circular of the State Council on Further Deepening the Reform of the Urban Housing System and Speeding Up Housing Construction," which proposed a multi-level urban housing supply system with a focus on establishing and improving the common-property security housing system (i.e., economically affordable housing). It also implemented different housing supply policies for households with different incomes. The government or work-units provided minimum-income households with low-rent housing, and allowed low-and-middle-income households to purchase economically affordable housing (China Statistics, 2012; Shanghai Real Estate Yearbook Editorial Office, 2012).

1.1.4. 2000–present: "Four in One" affordable housing with emphasis on low-rent housing
The solutions implemented between 1987 and 1999 brought about significant social and economic benefits, but the government's approach still did not meet requirements for the development of a modern society and the improvement

of urban residents' living quality. Therefore, Shanghai required new housing policies to address the difficulties faced by the lowest-income households. In addition, housing problems not addressed by the open market needed to be resolved. In 2000, Shanghai took the lead in China in establishing a low-rent housing system (Shanghai Real Estate Year Book Editorial Department, 2001). In 2002, Shanghai started the construction of resettlement housing and renovation of old areas and old housing, and implemented a subsidy policy for mortgages for low-income households (Shanghai Real Estate Year Book Editorial Department, 2003). In August 2007, the State Council issued *Opinions on Solving Housing Difficulties of Urban Low-Income Families*, which specifically listed low-rent housing as a focus for the first time, and established that at least 10 percent of land transfer net income should be utilized as a low-rent housing guarantee fund. In 2008, Shanghai began to implement a new renovation policy (Shanghai Real Estate Year Book Editorial Department, 2009).

In 2009, Shanghai explored the feasibility of implementing a public rental housing policy (Shanghai Real Estate Year Book Editorial Department, 2010). In June 2010, the Ministry of Housing together with six other departments issued "Guidance on Accelerating the Development of Public Rental Housing," thus launching a public rental housing construction program nationwide (Shanghai Real Estate Year Book Editorial Department, 2011).

In recent years, Shanghai has been constantly improving the basic housing security system and its supporting policies, building a multi-level, multi-channel "Four in One" housing security system to meet the city's needs (Han, 2012). The "Four in One" housing security system refers to a hierarchical housing security system based on various types of housing-needy households in the city, including low-rent housing, economically affordable housing, public rental housing, and resettlement housing, which is the result of reallocation due to city projects. According to this system, low-rent housing mainly targets urban, low-income, housing-needy families; economically affordable housing is mainly for urban middle-income housing-needy families; and public rental housing is for young workers, introduced talents, migrant workers and other resident population. Meanwhile, with the renovations of old areas, Shanghai has been allocating resettlement housing to improve the living conditions of low-income, housing-needy households in the old towns. The "Four in One" housing security system offers solutions to all kinds of households in need of government housing security through different channels and means, effectively settling many housing problems (Han, 2012).

1.2. Historical review of housing situations in Shanghai and St. Petersburg

1.2.1. Historical review of the housing situation in Shanghai

Since the 1950s, China has gradually built up its national housing supply system, in which the government fully assumed the responsibility of providing housing for urban residents, and housing construction was included in the national infrastructure plan. Local governments and work-units obtained housing investment from the national budget, and then built public housing and allocated it to workers as one of their rights and entitlements under the social welfare system. Urban residents acquired housing from the state or work-unit and only paid a nominal rent. This public housing system, in which the state supplied housing, had led to many problems including a lack of housing, limited living space, low quality of housing, and insufficient housing maintenance. The main reasons for these housing problems were rapid population growth, insufficient housing investment and supply, as well as lack of order in land use planning. By the late 1970s, the government was unable to provide adequate housing for urban residents, so society suffered from a severe housing crisis. Under such circumstances, the government began to carry out housing system reform. The main strategies covered commercialization of housing, privatization of public housing, and the development of an open housing market. In the past 20 years, housing reform has been characterized by slow progress and frequent policy changes.

After 1949, Shanghai became the first city to build a Workers' Village, and the "new-type workers' housing" (*Xin Gong Fang*) or "public housing" (*Gong Fang*) became the general name for workers' apartments constructed after the 1950s. (The housing was constructed based on the model established by the Russian Khrushchev administration.) Public apartment buildings built before the 1970s offered no independent kitchen or sanitary facilities in each unit, while almost all of the buildings constructed after the 1980s incorporated both independent kitchen and sanitary facilities within each apartment unit. Public housing was the major type of housing built in Shanghai in this period.

Shanghai began to construct public housing in 1950, with a total area of 13,000 square meters. By 1986, the total area of public housing reached 32.62 million square meters, accounting for 44 percent of the city's housing stock. By 2006, this proportion reached 89 percent. In the late 20th and early 21st century, the proportion of the total area of almost all other types of housing except for public housing declined in Shanghai, especially in the mid-1990s. In other words, through reform, public housing has become the most important type of housing for residents living in Shanghai. This translated into a fundamental improvement in the living conditions of Shanghai residents. By 2009, for urban residents, floor space was 34 square meters per capita, living space was 17.2 square meters per capita, and the residential housing set rate reached 95.6 percent (see Table 1).

The Institute of Sociology of the Shanghai Academy of Social Sciences surveyed a total of 1200 households in 1987. According to the findings at that time, the average housing area of each household was 24.78 square meters, with the largest being 100 square meters and smallest only 4 square meters. The survey showed that the average size of each household was 4.39 members, so the average housing area for Shanghai residents at that time was only 5.76 square meters per capita.[1] Housing without independent kitchens or washrooms was still the norm; about half of Shanghai households had no private kitchen, 25.1 percent of households had kitchens in the hallway or on the stairs, and 34.4

---

1. According to data in the *Shanghai Statistics Yearbook*, the average size per household was 3.55 persons, even though the average living space back then was only around 7 square meters.

Table 1. Residential Investment and Completed Construction Area in Shanghai (1978 to 2010)

Year	Residential investment (100 million Yuan)	Proportion of investment in total social fixed investment (%)	Completed residential floor space (10,000 square meters)	Per capita urban living space (square meters)
1981	10.02	18.4	1 380.70	4.5
1982	11.03	15.5	1 363.63	4.7
1983	11.18	14.7	1 347.79	4.9
1984	15.88	17.2	1 788.44	5.0
1985	25.47	21.5	2 112.04	5.4
1986	28.24	19.2	1 790.01	6.0
1987	36.28	19.5	1 874.90	6.2
1988	44.84	18.3	1 758.29	6.3
1989	35.82	16.7	1 246.58	6.4
1990	42.94	18.9	1 339.02	6.6
1991	48.92	18.9	1 160.61	6.7
1992	61.23	17.1	1 379.18	6.9
1993	77.14	11.8	1 017.54	7.3
1994	300.65	26.8	1 349.24	7.5
1995	433.76	27.1	1 746.82	8.0
1996	466.99	23.9	1 872.65	8.7
1997	458.22	23.2	2 179.68	9.3
1998	404.96	20.6	1 963.51	9.7
1999	378.82	20.4	1 731.55	10.9
2000	443.90	23.7	1 724.02	11.8
2001	466.71	23.4	1 743.90	12.5
2002	584.51	26.7	1 880.50	13.1
2003	694.30	28.3	2 280.79	13.8
2004	922.61	29.9	3 270.43	14.8
2005	936.36	26.4	2 819.35	15.5
2006	854.15	21.8	2 746.80	16.0
2007	853.13	19.1	2 843.62	16.5
2008	871.52	18.0	1 899.40	16.9
2009	922.81	17.5	1 522.07	17.2
2010	1 232.96	23.2	1 415.44	17.5

Data source: *Shanghai Statistics Yearbook*, China Statistics Press, 2011.

percent of the households shared kitchens with others.

In addition, 52.08 percent of households used commodes, and only 21.92 percent of the households in Shanghai had both public flush toilets and bathtubs. Especially in the older areas of Shanghai, many houses had no sanitary facilities. Therefore, during winter, only 16.5 percent of residents took a shower on a daily basis, 27.1 percent once or twice a week, 44.4 percent once a week, 10.5 percent once or twice a month, and about 1.5 percent never took a shower in the winter. In summer, it was common for children or young men in some alleys to take a shower directly under a tap. For cooking or heating, 51.5 percent of the households used pipeline gas, 8.8 percent used liquefied gas, and the other 39.7 percent used coal stoves.

Annual residential data shows that before 1990, living expenses were only a small part—less than 5 percent—of total household expenditure. However, since 1990, people's living expenses have gradually increased, rising to around 10 percent by 2005. From this change, we can conclude that it was during this time that Shanghai residents strove to improve their living conditions and buy property for housing. In fact, we can see different stages and forms of improved housing conditions from the changes in the data. If in the 21st century Shanghai citizens seek to improve their living conditions through the open housing market, then in the 1990s they sought to do so through the housing welfare policy. From 1990 to 1995, expenditures on household equipment and services grew particularly quickly, far exceeding housing expenses, which suggests that at this stage people purchased more home appliances. This was a big step toward the improvement of quality of life. Since the late 1990s, living expenditures have been higher than expenditures for household appliances and services, and the gap is increasing. This trend has continued through the first decade of 21st century, indicating that Shanghai residents have entered an era of improving living conditions by purchasing housing on the real estate market (see Figure 1).

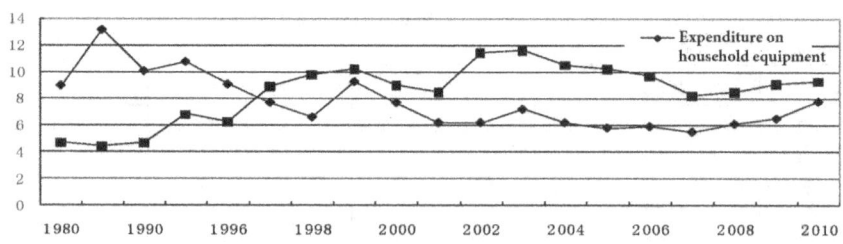

Figure 1. Shanghai Households' Expenditure on Appliances and Services

Source: Shanghai Statistical Yearbook, 1980–2011.

Consistent with the above change, housing has become an important asset for Shanghai families. Between 1991 and 1994, the Shanghai Municipal Government developed plans for selling houses to residents, commencing sales in 1994. In March 1991, the Shanghai Municipal People's Government formulated

"Reform Plans on the Shanghai Housing System," and established the principle of "Realize housing commercialization, and change the rule of low rent and free housing distribution". In April, the Shanghai Municipal People's Government issued 14 rules for the implementation of the reform plan, which was implemented step by step from May 1. In May 1994, the Shanghai Municipal Government endorsed "Interim Procedures on the Sale of Public-owned Housing" (Shanghai Real Estate Year Book Editorial Department, 1995). On June 15, the Shanghai Housing System Reform Office and the Shanghai Real Estate Administration printed and distributed *Rules for the Implementation on the Sale of Public-Owned Housing* (Shanghai Real Estate Year Book Editorial Department, 1995). It also issued a series of policies, known as the "94 Plan", for the privatization of public-owned housing, marking the beginning of the Shanghai housing system commercialization reform (Shanghai Real Estate Year Book Editorial Department, 1995).

The "94 Plan" confirmed the principle of "Purchase houses voluntarily, with the property owned and maintained by the owners". The "94 Plan" also specified the range of public-owned housing that could be sold, that is, sets of public-owned housing alone, which were limited to standard sets of multilayer and high-level worker housing used for living alone. In addition, the "94 Plan" specified conditions for housing purchasers, who had to be tenants of public-owned housing with permanent residence in the city or residents not younger than 18 years old, and workers who were entitled to public housing. Each household could have only one chance to purchase public-owned housing at its cost price (State Council, 1994).

The "94 Plan" gave the purchaser some favorable terms. According to the rules, the purchaser could enjoy a seniority privilege and housing allowance, free housing property tax, deed tax and deferral of rent, and free fixed asset investment regulation tax for newly built public-owned housing. The "94 Plan" included discounts of 1.2 percent for each year of work and a one-time 5 percent discount, while purchasers still received the original housing allowance. In addition, people who could pay the entire purchase price in cash at the time of the sale would get a 20 percent discount. Under the "94 Plan", when teachers in primary and secondary schools, retirees included, purchased public-owned housing at its cost price, the area could be increased 8 square meters according to the control standard. The "94 Plan" also confirmed that purchasers enjoyed sole ownership of the house, and it could be traded after five years (State Council, 1994).

After the 1990s, the real estate market emerged in Shanghai, and houses could be purchased on the open market. Through either public housing purchase or open-market purchase, about 80 percent of residents of Shanghai now are homeowners. The number of residents purchasing through the real estate market is rising especially quickly, to more than 50 percent (*Shanghai Statistical Yearbook,* 1990–2010).

In recent years, housing prices have risen rapidly in Shanghai and other major urban centers. As a result, China has implemented strict measures to help control prices. Meanwhile, China specified that the local governments must build affordable housing and public rental housing. In the future, improvement in economic and social policies will decide the evolution of living conditions in Shanghai. It is impossible to solve the housing problem through the open market and social welfare policy alone.

Table 2. Shanghai Property Ownership by Type of Housing (%)

Type	2008	2009	2010
Public rental housing	17.4	16.3	16.4
Private rental housing	4.2	3.7	3.5
Original private housing	0.7	0.7	0.7
Reformed private housing	37.8	37.2	37.4
Commercial housing	39.1	41.3	41.1
Others	0.8	0.8	0.9

Source: *Shanghai Real Estate Yearbook*, 2009–2011.

1.2.2. Historical review of the housing situation and policy changes in St. Petersburg

During the Soviet era, housing was allocated to residents by the state for free. During World War II, almost all the houses located in the European part of the Soviet Union were destroyed, leaving many people homeless. The housing area for residents of the former Soviet Union was 6.0 square meters per capita in 1946. By 1950 the figure had fallen to less than 5.0 square meters per capita. After World War II, the Soviet government gave great priority to housing construction. Beginning in 1957, Khrushchev's administration developed a clear objective of providing each household with an independent living space with a standard of 9.0 square meters per capita. The basic principle of housing in this period was "simplicity and economy"; external appearance and internal decoration were not taken into account. Each household's living space was small but separate, thus ending the embarrassing situation of several households sharing the same apartment (Epihina, 2012). From then on, the Soviet Union began to build up to 2 million square meters of new living space each year (Epihina, 2012). Since all the housing was based on essentially the same plans, it all appeared similar. Most apartment blocs were box-like five- or six-story buildings, with no reliefs or decorations. The construction materials were mainly blue or red bricks. Westerners dubbed such houses "Khrushchev tube-shaped apartments" (Epihina, 2012). Though "Khrushchev tube-shaped apartments" lacked decoration and were below Western standards for area and quality, they could be considered reasonably designed and fully furnished. These apartments basically solved the national housing shortage caused by the war, and significantly improved the housing conditions in the former Soviet Union (Epihina, 2012). With the administration of Leonid Brezhnev, a cooperative housing mechanism co-funded by the state and individuals was introduced. Namely, tenants provided part of the money to make up for insufficient national housing funds, and housing maintenance costs were shouldered by the state. In the 1980s, living space increased to 12 square meters per capita, but the housing supply in Moscow, Leningrad and other cities was still quite limited (Epihina, 2012).

During Gorbachev's reforms, the "All-Union Outstanding Builders" contest planned to solve housing problems faster by increasing the number of stories in new apartment blocs. However, the result was not ideal, leading to an extended construction period and higher construction costs (Epihina, 2012).

After the collapse of the Soviet Union, Russia launched a large-scale reform of the housing system, with the goal being a transition to a market-oriented system. The new system included systems of property rights, changes in the distribution of the housing supply, as well as welfare policies relating to housing.

In 1985, 77.2 percent of housing in urban areas was owned by the government, of which 50 percent belonged to the state and 50 percent belonged to cities, government departments and agencies. Cooperatives accounted for about 7 percent of housing, while the remaining 22.8 percent was privately owned. However, regulations of that period stated that the building of private houses was not allowed in cities with populations over 100,000. By 1985 there should have been no private housing in big cities. Consequently, there were no private housing property rights in St. Petersburg in 1985 (Epihina, 2012).

To improve the housing situation and boost housing construction during Gorbachev's administration, the government reformed housing policy mainly through legal changes, and allowed the state to lend money to individuals to promote private ownership of housing. Russia began to prepare legislation and policies to allocate housing through the open market with the financial and fiscal burden of housing construction transferred from the central government to municipalities and individuals. In 1988, the selling of national apartments to individuals was legalized. This privatization process was very slow in the beginning, and did not accelerate until 1992. On the other hand, the law encouraged housing construction by cooperatives and individuals. With the collapse of the Soviet Union, privatization campaigns were prevalent throughout the economy, but the housing sector still experienced the slowest changes.

Market-oriented construction accelerated noticeably after changes in Russian federal housing law at the end of 1992. The total housing floor area grew to 36.3 million square meters by 2003, almost 1.7 times that of 1990. From the beginning of 2001, the housing construction growth rate remained at more than 6 percent. The growth rate between 2001 and 2002 was 6.6 percent, and between 2002 and 2003 7.4 percent. However, the growth rate for private housing construction was more impressive. From 1990 to 2003, the amount of private housing increased by 2.5 times, and private housing retention rate reached 41.8 percent (Epihina, 2012)..

On April 25, 2005, when Russian President Vladimir Putin delivered the State of the Union message to the Parliament, he stated that Russia had almost realized the complete privatization of public housing. Putin claimed: "If we add the housing increase from 1997 to 2003, we have a total of 227.6 million square meters, of which private housing accounted for 142.9 million square meters, or 62.79 percent. The Russian housing privatization level is now close to that of the western developed countries" (Epihina, 2012). This meant Russia had basically completed the task of housing privatization.

At the same time, utility costs were adjusted. In the past, residential utility bills were subsidized by local government, so the burden on local finances was heavy. Many local governments defaulted on huge debts to heat, electricity, natural gas and other utility enterprises. In addition, due to a lack of funds, housing and utility pipelines were not maintained. Public facilities aged seriously, causing frequent accidents and endangering residents' safety. In order to bridge the huge gap between rent and actual housing costs in the welfare housing system, Putin decided to reform housing utilities and planned to gradually increase the proportion of utility charges paid by residents. Over a five-year period, starting in 1994, residents would gradually assume responsibility for full rent and public service charges for public housing. For 1994 and 1995, public service charges would not exceed 10 percent of household income; for 1996 and 1997, not more than 15 percent; and for 1998, not more than 20 percent. By 2005, residents would shoulder 100 percent of the cost of utility bills. But at the same time, it was stipulated that if public service fees accounted for more than 22 percent of total household income, the government would provide appropriate subsidies. Russia is now addressing the inadequate development of public utilities by establishing owners' committees, introducing competition and applying energy-saving technologies (Epihina, 2012).

By 2004, Russia's living space increased to 19.7 square meters per capita, but the housing problem for low-income residents was not completely resolved. The Russian housing market faced many problems: most people needed improved housing, but could not afford it; the existing housing did not meet the needs of residents; the state lacked an effective long-term housing credit system as well as effective policies for allocation and transfer of residential land; municipal departments lacked residential land and urban construction planning; public housing utilities had deteriorated seriously because of age; the construction process for social security housing was slow; approval procedures for construction documents were complex; fraud in the housing trade caused ineffective protection of shareholders' interests; housing prices rose continually; and so forth. With the deepening of housing reform, housing allocation and consumption began to shift to market allocation and price-based market consumption (Epihina, 2012).

In line with the "Outline for Solving Russian Federal Housing Problems from 2002 to 2010", the state carried out an in-depth reform, including cancelling sector monopolies, introducing competitive mechanisms, setting up mechanisms to attract domestic and foreign funds, conserving resources, encouraging investment in fields of centralized resources and improving contractual relations between housing public service departments and consumers (Epihina, 2012).

The Russian government also established targeted welfare policies for some special social groups. The National Priority Project for Affordable Housing provides budget support for young families in need of housing or improved living conditions. The state can contribute part of the money for the purchase or construction of a house, or provide a down payment for the mortgage. Those eligible for support are married couples, both spouses under 30 years old, or single-parent households with the parent under 30. The federal project also guarantees that veterans and the disabled can have ready-made houses as set forth in the Russian federal laws "On Veterans" and "On Social Services for Disabled Citizens." From 2006 to 2007, the state invested 8.4 billion rubles to improve the living conditions of 30,100 people (Danilova et al., 2012).

In addition, the state distributed subsidies as housing coupons to demobilized soldiers and residents transferred from Baikonur, the Arctic, nuclear radiation accident zones, and other forced immigration areas. The value of housing coupons they received was based on the market price of the housing they planned to buy. In 2010, the government provided 13.3 billion rubles for these people, addressing the housing problems of 132,000 households. The subsidy standards for this group include 33 square meters for single-person households, 42 square meters for two-person households and 18 square meters per capita for three or more-person households (Danilova et al., 2012).

1.3. Summary

By comparing changes in housing policy and provision in these two countries and cities, we can draw some preliminary conclusions. After the introduction of market-oriented housing policies, disadvantages in addressing housing problems through the open market alone were exposed; different systems for social welfare housing were necessary to satisfy public needs. Although Russia enjoyed a faster marketization than did China, it took a very cautious approach in the supply of housing and covering the costs of public utilities, and has gradually transferred to market-oriented housing while retaining some social welfare features.

2. COMPARATIVE ANALYSIS

As we have seen, St. Petersburg shares many similarities with Shanghai in its housing situation. In both cities the housing stock mainly consists of two- and three-bedroom apartments, a legacy of the former national urban housing welfare systems in the two countries. There is a higher proportion of three-bedroom apartments in Shanghai. More than 40 percent of Shanghai households live in a three-plus-bedroom apartment, while in St. Petersburg, the proportion is less than 30 percent. For two-bedroom or smaller apartments, Shanghai's proportion is about 35 percent, while St. Petersburg's is more than 50 percent. Almost the same proportion of households in both cities live in public housing with shared sanitary and kitchen facilities. We can conclude that Shanghai residents enjoy more living space than those in St. Petersburg, and the overall housing structure in Shanghai is also sounder.

Data for St. Petersburg did not include living space, which could be obtained only for Shanghai, where the area of a house is usually measured in two ways. One is by *floor space*, including bathrooms, kitchens, public areas, and the other is *living space*, including bedrooms and family rooms. The Shanghai survey shows that the average floor space for Shanghai households is 65.23 square meters, and the average living space is 35.32 square meters. According to the *Statistical Report on National Economic and Social Development of Shanghai* issued by the Shanghai Municipal Statistics Bureau in 2009, the average floor space for urban residents was 34 square meters and the average living space was 17.2 square meters with a housing set rate—the proportion of hous-

Table 3. Distribution of housing types

	St. Petersburg			Shanghai		
	Frequency	Percentage	Cumulative percent	Frequency	Percentage	Cumulative percent
Detached house	6	0.5	0.5	0	0	0
1 room apartment	154	11.8	12.3	186	11.6	11.6
2 rooms apartment	495	38.1	50.4	376	23.5	35.1
3 rooms apartment	348	26.8	77.2	489	30.5	65.6
4 rooms apartment	35	2.7	79.8	162	10.1	75.7
Public housing with shared bathroom and kitchen	198	15.2	95.1	234	14.6	90.3
Hotel renting	14	1.1	96.2	0	0	90.3
Rented housing	45	3.5	99.6	118	7.3	97.7
Others	5	.4	100.0	37	2.3	100.0
Total	1300	100.0		1604	100.0	

Table 4. Ownership of housing property

	St. Petersburg			Shanghai		
	Frequency	Percentage	Cumulative percent	Frequency	Percentage	Cumulative percent
Private housing	1013	78.0	78.0	993	61.9	61.9
Public housing	220	16.9	95.0	456	28.4	90.3
Rented housing	54	4.2	99.2	118	7.3	97.6
Others	11	0.8	100.0	38	2.4	100.0
Total	1298	100.0		1604	100.0	

ing that includes facilities like independent washrooms and kitchens which are used solely by the occupying family—reaching 95.6 percent by the end of 2009 (Shanghai Real Estate Yearbook, 2010). Because living spaces in rural areas are generally better than in the urban center, the result of this Shanghai survey is close to the Municipal Statistics Bureau's figures: more than 80 percent of housing units include their own bathroom and kitchen, with the living space exceeding 10 square meters per capita (Shanghai Real Estate Yearbook, 2010).

According to the Shanghai survey, single room apartments have an average living space of 21.9 square meters with an average floor space of 38 square meters; two-room apartments have 36.16 square meters and 65 square meters respectively; and three-room apartments have 85.55 square meters and 105 square meters respectively. More than 40 percent of the Shanghai respondents enjoy a floor space of over 100 square meters.

The surveys also show that St. Petersburg has a higher percentage of private housing ownership than Shanghai. (According to data published by Shanghai Municipal Statistics Bureau in 2010, the proportion of families who own housing property in Shanghai is 79.2 percent.) Table 3 shows a relatively high ratio of private home ownership in both Shanghai and St. Petersburg after the large-scale housing privatization and family ownership process. From this it can be inferred that both countries exploited housing privatization and commercialization to alter the original overall social welfare model for housing during subsequent economic reforms.

According to the Shanghai survey, among families who own their homes, 33 percent purchased the work-unit house or public house where they had been living, 31.2 percent accepted a new apartment to replace homes razed for urban reconstruction, and another 33 percent bought new homes through the housing market. Thus, one-third of the families who have full home-ownership in Shanghai improved their living conditions entirely through the market access, about one-third got their home through relocation, and the rest obtained the housing property at a very favorable price.

The price for public housing sales is very low. According to the Shanghai survey data, the average purchase price is about 30,000 yuan, and the average floor space for such homes is 56.15 square meters, with an average living space of 42.33 square meters. However, the average market price for a home is 432,800 yuan with an average living space of 60.24 square meters. This comparison shows that those who have bought houses in the market are enjoying better living conditions at the moment.

The Shanghai survey also presents very interesting chronological information regarding housing acquisition. The housing relocations occurred around 1997, the public housing purchases were concentrated around 1998, and the commercial housing market began around 2002. The conclusion can be drawn that the development of Shanghai's real estate market followed a planned path. The first step in developing the Shanghai real estate market was to build low-cost homes to relocate some families while razing their original homes to provide initial space for urban redevelopment. The second step was to sell public housing, which provided many families with the basic economic means to improve their housing condition; however, in Shanghai there is a public housing purchase regulation stating that five years after the purchase, the house can be sold in full ownership exempt from any transaction tax. Finally, the third step was the rapid development of the real estate market since 2002. Obviously, the prosperity and rapid development of the Shanghai real estate market since 2002 is closely related to the public housing resale and tax provision.

The Shanghai survey illustrates the steep rise in housing prices due to the rapid development of the real estate market. Public homes originally purchased for 30,000 yuan sold for an average market price of 637,600 yuan in 2009; the average price of homes obtained on the open market for about 400,000 yuan rose to 945,800 yuan; and the price for homes acquired through demolition and relocation reached an average of 658,200 yuan. By 2009, the average private property value had reached 758,600 yuan in Shanghai.

3. CONCLUSIONS

Due to differences in the questions asked in the surveys, a direct comparison cannot be made between Shanghai and St. Petersburg in some aspects. In particular, a comparison of the housing situation for different social classes could not be made. Nevertheless, some conclusions can still be drawn:

1. Most social groups have acquired varying levels of economic interest through the reform of the housing system. The surveys found that nearly 80 percent of families own homes with private property rights in the two cities and these homes constitute a significant proportion of family or personal wealth, often even the greater part of the family wealth. This is a significant sign of economic and social change in the two countries and cities discussed. The transformation from housing as a social welfare provision to home ownership as a significant source of wealth is a substantial symbol of the economic, social and political transition of both China and Russia from the former planned economy system.

2. Universal property ownership has an economic and social role that should not be underestimated. Because of differences in the surveys that were carried out, a clear contrast could not be drawn between the data collected in Shanghai and St. Petersburg. However, according to the data obtained in Shanghai, the existing housing ownership system is of vital importance for the stable life and economic development of Shanghai citizens, especially for the development of the real estate economy. First, the majority of citizens, Shanghai permanent residents in particular, own their own homes. This means that they have a minimum living guarantee and a fixed asset. In recent years, the number of housing heritage disputes among Shanghai permanent residents has increased, which indicates that housing has become the most important symbol of family fortune. Second, large-scale housing privatization and marketization has had an enormous impact on the economy, especially the real estate economy. The Shanghai data shows that the start of the Shanghai real estate market boom exactly conforms to the listing date of the sale of public houses in Shanghai. This suggests that many Shanghai citizens sold or rented their homes after they obtained them through low prices around 2002, subsequently purchasing a new home to improve their lives. This promoted the development of the real estate market, and many residents enhanced their own wealth as they improved their housing conditions. Third, with more than 80 percent of Shanghai permanent residents owning real estate, Shanghai has one of the highest home ownership rates. With a huge migrant population in China, rental housing has become an important way to obtain residence in China's major cities. A complete or relatively complete residential leasing market is realized due to advances in the privatization of housing ownership. The large and quickly developing leasing market seems to have sprung up overnight. This has helped to avoid the emergence of slums caused by the influx of large number of migrants, especially poor rural migrants. Although Shanghai now has a migrant population of about 10 million, the slums that often appear during the process of large-scale urbanization in many cities did not occur in Shanghai.

3. As a result of differences in economic development, the effects of housing privatization in China and Russia differ materially. The housing privatization

process in Shanghai occurred in tandem with China's economic development, while St. Petersburg encountered a period of economic stagnation after housing privatization, which consequently had a smaller impact on the economic development. For this study, I made many trips to Moscow and St. Petersburg to study issues related to housing and found the housing problem is still a core issue in improving quality of life in Russia, especially in its major cities. Due to rising prices of newly constructed homes, the wealth transferred to families or individuals has been devalued in the privatization process. Although many people have their own homes, the value of the existing home is far below the purchase price of a new home. In Shanghai, a real estate development bubble has already emerged, and non-residential speculative commercial purchases of property have raised housing prices, so families are now unable to buy homes due to limited economic means. Therefore, a significant part of the government's social policy has become the provision of indemnificatory housing.

4. Following the large-scale housing privatization process, the two countries and the two cities still face a problem that seems much like that at the beginning of the process, but which is fundamentally different in nature. That is, the government still holds responsibility for the living arrangements of its citizens. The government should not leave the issue to the market, which we know cannot solve the problem.

REFERENCES

Danilova, E.N., V.A. Yadova, P. Davjej (Eds.) (2012). *Epoch of Change: Comparative Study of St. Petersburg and Shanghai at the Beginning of the 21st century*. Logos: Moscow. [In Russian and Chinese.]

Epihina, Yulia (2012). Chapter 4: Comparison of everyday life. In *Epoch of Change*, ed. Danilova. [In Russian and Chinese.]

Han, Zheng (2012, 21 January). Speech on developing a "Four in One" housing security system. http://www.shanghai.gov.cn/shanghai/node2314/szzcnew/node9816/u21ai476652.html.

Lu, Xiaowen (2012). Chapter 9: Comparison of housing. In *Epoch of Change*, ed. Danilova. [In Russian and Chinese.]

Shanghai Local Chronicles Office (2008). *Shanghai Local Chronicles, Vol. 27: Housing and Real Estate*. http://www.shtong.gov.cn/node2/node2247/node4586/index.html.

Shanghai Statistics Bureau (2011). *Statistics Yearbook of Shanghai 1980–2011*. China Statistics Press: Shanghai.

Shanghai Local Chronicles Editorial Office (1995–2016). *Shanghai Local History*. http://www.shanghai.gov.cn.

Shanghai Real Estate Year Book Editorial Department (1995–2016). *Shanghai Real Estate Year Book*. http://www.zgtjnj.com.

State Council (1994). The State Council's decision on deepening the reform of urban housing system.

Chapter 8
Employment and Income Policy

Weizhen Dong, Xin Le

ABSTRACT
Employment and income policies are critically important to peoples' wellbeing. China's employment and income distribution policies have shifted dramatically: from full employment and lifetime employment with low levels of income and high levels of welfare coverage to massive layoffs and large income gaps. The transition through economic reform changed the employment and income distribution landscape. China gained its wealth from economic reforms, but not all citizens benefited from the country's rapid economic growth. The current income distribution system needs rebalancing, and vulnerable groups' interests need to be better considered in policymaking. Informal employment arrangements are on the rise, especially among rural-urban migrants. Training and retraining are reliable mechanisms for providing more employment opportunities and higher incomes. Developing new policies under which different social groups' interests are reflected and protected and which combine growth with justice will be essential for China's future development.

1. INTRODUCTION

China has experienced a fundamental social and economic change since it became a socialist country in 1949. Shortly after the establishment of the socialist system, Mao's government introduced Soviet Union-style full employment and lifetime employment policies as well as an egalitarian income distribution policy. In the post-Mao era (since 1978), major economic reform policies shifted the nation from a planned economic system to a "socialist market" one. In 1984, the "equal income distribution" principle was replaced by a policy grounded in the principle that "efficiency comes first with consideration of fairness". By 1992, a socialist market economic system had emerged. In 1997, the decentralization trend continued, and the government allowed the market to play a role in income distribution, which led to the widening of income gaps—between sectors, between regions, and between urban and rural areas. In fact, the Gini coefficient for family income in China has stood above 0.5 since 2005, largely due to regional and urban-rural income disparities (Xie and Zhou, 2014).

With regard to rural poverty, the State Council has reaffirmed the importance of poverty reduction with a particular emphasis on improving the income level of rural residents, stating that "the urban-rural gap and the difference in citizens' income is relatively large, income is irregularly distributed, there are obvious problems of grey income and illegal income; and some people are living in difficult conditions" (State Council, 2013).

This chapter discusses China's transition from an egalitarian system in the early decades of the People's Republic to a very unequal system in the post-Mao era. It discusses government policy changes in regard to employment and income distribution at different stages of China's development, as the country was on its way to becoming the world's second-largest economy.

2. FULL EMPLOYMENT, LIFETIME EMPLOYMENT AND EQUAL BUT LOW INCOMES (1949-1977)

Chairman Mao Zedong's government created an egalitarian society through its social policies, although the Chinese inherited a country that suffered from decades of war, foreign invasion, oppression, and widespread poverty. China's planned socialist economy promoted public ownership of the means of production and services. The scale and quantity of production were planned and controlled by the central government, which also regulated revenues and the distribution of goods, etc. The Chinese government faced unprecedented economic and societal challenges, particularly because of a severe lack of resources; but China's planned economic system was regarded as positive and successful in creating favorable conditions for the country's economic recovery. As Piazza (2014) states, from the 1950s to the 1970s, China had reduced poverty and improved the living conditions of the Chinese people through its egalitarian policy, increased production of food, and improved access to basic education and public health.

2.1. Full time employment and lifetime employment

China implemented a full-time and lifetime employment system at the beginning of the socialist regime. State-owned and collectively owned sectors were encouraged to recruit as many people as they could, and the hiring was done through the government's labour departments, which assigned jobs to new graduates from various educational institutions. Once the enterprises and institutions reviewed their respective new employees' files, they had the autonomy to assign them to different posts. It was very common to find these employees working in the same workplace until retirement (Mann, 1986; Dong, 1996).

This practice ensured that every working-age adult had a job. Even those with disabilities were assigned to appropriate positions, and were paid the same as their able-bodied counterparts. People took job opportunities for granted, since there was no competition involved. Promotion, however, was based on job performance.

2.2. Equal pay and low incomes with high benefits

An equal income distribution policy was set up within the planned economic system. During the period, enterprises and institutions were almost all state- or collectively owned, with production and revenues distributed equally. Salary increases were only linked to one's job tenure (i.e., years of employment). For example, the head of an institution and a staff member at that institution had no pay difference other than that due to job tenure (Dong, 1996).

During this period, each work unit constituted a small society, which took care of its members' pay, social benefits (i.e., housing, healthcare for the employee and their family, training, theatre and game tickets, and funerals). And the trade unions took care of their members' financial wellbeing by providing a safety net, which meant supporting their eligible members with regular or one-time subsidies and loans. Most of the workplaces had free childcare and healthcare facilities. Therefore, although the income level was low, employees were provided with many benefits, including housing, childcare, and healthcare (Dong, 1996).

3. THE TRANSFORMATION OF EMPLOYMENT AND INCOME DISTRIBUTION POLICIES

The economic reforms initiated in 1978 transformed China dramatically. Along with the privatization and marketization, China's economic system gradually changed from a planned system to a market one, which was termed a *socialist market economic system*. The new economic system differed fundamentally from the former one. It endowed individuals and enterprises with the right to make independent economic decisions and assume related liabilities. The market played a central role in the distribution of resources, with the government controlling the economy indirectly at the macro level.

China's income distribution policy experienced three main reforms from 1978 to 2012. Fundamental changes in income distribution policy took place during these economic reforms.

3.1. 1978–1983

In 1978, the need for "economic development" was set as the primary policy by the government. It identified the basic governing plan of the Chinese Communist Party (CCP). To implement the central policy, the income distribution principle was changed from "equal distribution" to "efficiency comes first with consideration of fairness". Guided by this central policy and distribution principle, the government leader then encouraged "letting some people get rich first", which was an obviously new direction for the socialist country.

Rural China was the main battlefield during this period of reform. During the early 1980s, the rural agricultural household production responsibility system was implemented in most rural areas. The responsibility system clarified rights along with responsibilities and interests for both the collective and individual citizens. For instance, a farmer's income was now directly tied to productivity for the first time. This responsibility system stimulated productivity. It provided more opportunity for farmers to improve their incomes. All of these changes contributed to improvement in income levels and the reduction of the income gap between rural and urban residents.

In short, the agricultural household production responsibility system changed the income distribution policy in rural areas. It had a very strong impact on later reforms in China and on income disparity.

3.2. 1984–1991

After the Third Plenary Session of the 12th Congress of the CCP in 1984, the economic reforms' focus was shifted from rural areas to urban areas. In 1987, an agreement on establishing a "planned commodity economy" system was reached at the 13th Congress of the CCP. It was a big step in the development of China's economic system. The planned commodity economy was the intermediate step between the planned economic system and the market economic system.

3.2.1. Introduction of labour contract system and unemployment insurance
Minister of Labour and Personnel Zhao Dongwan introduced the new employment policy in his report to the Standing Committee of the National People's Congress: abolishing permanent employment was intended to give both enterprises and workers the right to make their own choices (Mann, 1986). State-owned enterprises would be given the autonomy to dismiss workers who repeatedly violated work rules. In order to provide a safety net to those who were laid off due to enterprises' bankruptcy or were fired, as well as provide benefits to contract workers, China would introduce an unemployment insurance system (Mann, 1986).

It was the first time that any worker had to face the possibility of being fired from their job. The unemployment insurance system would help to ease the shock and insecurity.

Table 1. Personnel in a Chinese Factory

Category	Total (Persons)	% of Total
Front-Line Production	780	45.88
Ancillary Staff (cleaning, checking)	520	30.58
Supervisory Staff	150	8.82
Engineers and Technicians	50	2.94
Administrative & Cadres	200	11.76
Total	1,700	100

Source: Feuchtwang et al. (1988), *Transforming China's Economy in the Eighties*, p. 112.

As Table 1 shows, a large proportion of the people working in an average factory in China worked in non-production-related posts. Once market regulations were applied and market competition brought pressure on labour costs, almost all of the enterprises had to reduce their burdens. Moreover, many in administrative positions did not have the proper educational background and relevant skills. In fact, at the time there were more than 20 million superfluous workers in state-owned enterprises alone. Reducing the number of staff members in administrative posts also reduced the underemployment rate in the enterprises (Dong, 1996).

Another challenging issue facing the state-owned and collective enterprises was the welfare system. These enterprises were responsible for their employees' and their respective families' healthcare, housing, various paid leaves and subsidies, leisure activities, as well as retirees' healthcare, etc. These costs became a heavy burden once these enterprises started to compete with newly established firms and enterprises. Thus, laying off non-essential personnel became a logical course of action. The labour contract system provided policy grounds for the massive nationwide lay-offs.

During the process, women workers were more vulnerable than their male counterparts. A higher percentage of women was laid off during the period. Some enterprises urged women employees to take early retirement at 45 or even 40 years of age. This was partly because of gender bias, since women were perceived as less productive and took more time off for family matters, especially during their childbearing years. They might also be perceived as entitled to more work-related benefits and more paid leaves because of their reproductive role (Dong, 1996). The shape of women's participation in the labour force has been different ever since, although the government noted developments and issued the Law on the Protection of Rights and Interests of Women in 1992 (NPC, 1992).

In 1986, open unemployment emerged for the first time in China's modern history with the introduction of the labour contract system. By 1990, 59 percent of the labour force was either unemployed or underemployed (Majid, 2015). The government anticipated the vast wave of unemployment in urban China, and issued the interim provisions of its unemployment insurance policy (1986). Although the main elements of the unemployment insurance system, such as the scope, object, source of funds, payment standards, and management institutions were described, it assumed the core structures of the planned economy would be retained, something which was reflected in its funding sources and scale of coverage, limitation of guarantees, and the fact its operation was more akin to unemployment relief.

3.2.2. New income distribution

The income distribution policy resulted in corresponding changes under the "planned commodity economy system", with one's income determined by the quantity and quality of work. One could also receive income based on one's contribution of production factors, which included capital, technology, management, and information.

Under this income distribution policy, salaries of workers were linked with the productivity and profits of their employers for the first time. The "planned commodity economy" allowed state-owned enterprises to manage themselves to some extent. The reforming framework stimulated the emergence and the development of new kinds of enterprises, such as township enterprises, individual and privately owned enterprises, and the "three-capital" enterprises, i.e., Sino-foreign joint ventures, Sino-foreign cooperative enterprises, and foreign investment enterprises in China. Compared to the former egalitarian distribution policy, the new policy was far more complex, with different kinds of distribution mechanisms co-existing at the same time.

The emergence of the new income distribution policy was the outcome of various social and economic changes. The transition to the new policy was rapid. Such deep reforms rearranged the social and economic order, which led to two key outcomes.

First, the transition resulted in the rapid growth of income gaps among different enterprises, different sectors, and among workers from the same enterprise. In the mid-1980s, a number of high-income households appeared. They were known as the "¥10,000 households". Prior to this, there were hardly any households with savings reaching ¥10,000. Meanwhile, the income gap between rural and urban residents rose again due to the much more rapid income increase in the cities.

Second, after the introduction of the market to the nation's economic system, demands to reform state-owned enterprises grew inevitably. The mindset of the old ownership and management style of state-owned enterprises did not match the realities of the new market economic system. In order for such enterprises to survive amid fierce market competition, large numbers of surplus workers were laid off. During the planned economy period, however, the state-owned enterprises had employed as many workers as they could. Data from the National Bureau of Statistics of China (NBS) shows that the total number of urban employees in 1978 was 95.1 million, of whom 74.5 million worked for state-owned enterprises, making up 78.3 percent of all urban workers. The percentage of employees who work in urban state-owned enterprises has dropped dramatically during the last three decades; of 359.1 million urban employees, only 67 million of them worked for state-owned enterprises in 2011, 18.7 percent of the total (NBS, 2012).

3.3. 1992–2006

The socialist market economic system was established in 1992 during the 14th Congress of the CCP. China had just begun a decades-long rapid economic growth period.

The essence of socialism is the liberation and development of productive forces, the elimination of exploitation and polarization, and the ultimate achievement of common prosperity. The socialist content of the concept "socialist market economy" included public ownership of land and the major means of production, the egalitarian distribution of income, and the leadership of the Communist Party (Itoh, 1995). However, the socialist market economy in China is aimed at the effective coordination of the planned economy with market regulation. The growth-oriented new system can no longer guarantee every working age adult a job. Instead, it depends on supply and demand in the labour market, and allows employers to hire and dismiss employees in order to achieve economic goals (Dong, 1996).

The 15th Congress of the CCP, held in 1997, concluded that capital, technology and other productive factors were to be included in the distribution of revenues. It was decided that distribution according to labour and distribution according to productive factors should be joined together. By doing this, distribution according to productive factors was made clearer and more detailed. The income distribution policy would adhere to the principle of "efficiency comes first with consideration of fairness". State-owned enterprises were given the power to internally decide salary levels and distribution patterns.

The distribution principle "efficiency comes first with consideration of fairness" continued to be discussed at the following congress of the CCP, in 2002. Labour, capital, technology and management were basic productivity factors, while the positive impact of knowledge, resources, information and other productive factors on the creation of wealth was recognized. The congress declared that the distribution of productive factors should depend on contributions. The congress also gave clear answers about the relationship between efficiency and fairness. The initial distribution should emphasize efficiency and capitalize on the benefits of market reforms.

It was recognized that some people initially get rich legally through their hard work; and that re-distribution should focus on fairness. Therefore, the government should play an adjusting role in keeping the income distribution in order. In short, the initial distribution of income is rooted in the principle of efficiency while re-distribution addresses social justice concerns.

4. WIDENING INCOME GAP

4.1. Gini trend shows income inequality

Growth-oriented economic reform in China has greatly improved the overall income level. In fact, income levels continue to increase as the new leadership of the Chinese central government has launched an ambitious program that aims to double the annual income of both urban and rural residents by 2020 (State Council, 2015). The rise in income levels has improved many peoples' living conditions; however, the growing income gap between rich and poor continues to be a societal concern.

A study found that Gini coefficients in China had risen as high as 0.62 in year 2010 (Li, 2013), although the official data shows that the overall Gini coefficient began to decline in 2008 (see Figure 1). Yet, it remains at a level above 0.4. The overall official Gini coefficient reached its peak at 0.491 in 2008, an increase of 0.012 compared to 2003. Both rural and urban Gini coefficients have risen since 1978, with urban areas contributing more to the overall escalation (Cheng, 2007).

Although the proportion of both wealthiest households and poorest households has been reduced nationally between 2012 and 2014, the Gini coefficient in 2014 was still at the very high level of 0.7 in terms of household net property worth, indicating a large gap between the rich and the poor in China (Jin and

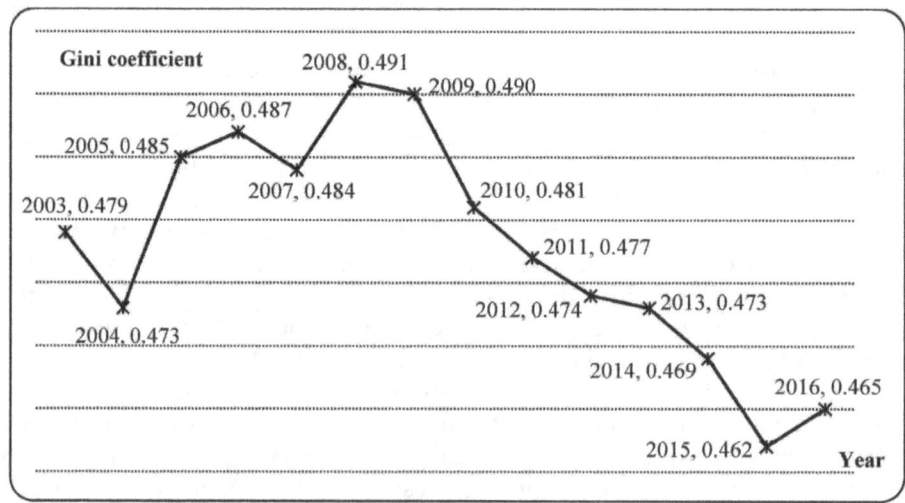

Figure 1. Gini coefficients, China, 2003-2016
Data source: Gini coefficients data are from two NBS reports. The data for the years 2003-2012 is from http://www.stats.gov.cn/tjgz/tjdt/201301/t20130118_17719.html, and for the other years from http://www.stats.gov.cn/tjsj/sjjd/201701/t20170120_1456268.html.

Xie, 2017:50-69). It is a warning to the government as well as the general public.

4.2. INCOME GAP BETWEEN RURAL AND URBAN RESIDENTS

Data from NBS indicates that disposable income per capita for urban residents was ¥6,280 in 2000; it increased steadily to ¥31,195 in 2015. The net income per capita for rural residents was ¥2,253 in 2000 and ¥11,422 in 2015 (NBS, 2016). Although the annual incomes of both urban and rural residents are rising, urban residents' annual incomes are growing much faster than those of rural residents. During these 16 years, the disposable income for urban residents per capita grew by approximately ¥25,000, compared to only about ¥9,000 for their rural counterparts.

The absolute difference between urban and rural income was only ¥4,000 in 2000, but it rose to ¥20,000 in 2015. Rural-urban disparity in both absolute income and growth rates are very serious societal issues. Xie and Zhou's study (2014) shows that China's income inequality has surpassed that of the United States by a large margin, and that China is among the world's most unequal nations, especially when compared with countries that have comparable or higher standards of living.

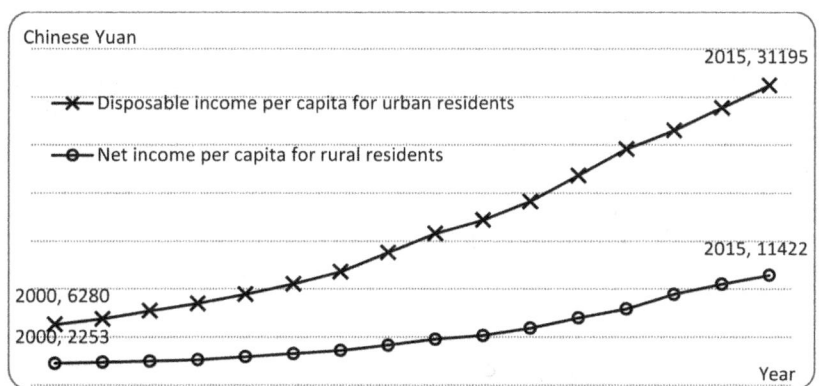

Figure 2. Annual income for urban and rural residents in China, 2000-2015.
Data Source: Official annual data from the website of NBS, http://data.stats.gov.cn/easyquery.htm?cn=C01.

4.3. INCOME GAPS AMONG DIFFERENT SECTORS AND OCCUPATIONS

Income gaps have increased among different sectors since China's transition to a "market economy" in recent decades. Based on the official data released from the NBS, the average wage of urban employees was ¥9,333 in 2000 and ¥62,029 in 2015; the average wage in state-owned enterprises was ¥9,441 in 2000 and ¥65,296 in 2015, an increase of over ¥55,000; the employees of urban collective sectors earned ¥6,241 on average in 2000 and ¥46,607 in 2015, an increase of ¥40,000; and the urban employees in other ownership workplaces earned ¥11,238 in 2000 and ¥60906 in 2015, an increase of nearly ¥50,000. The net wage growth in the state-owned enterprises was the largest compared to collective and other ownership types, while employees in urban collective sectors earned the lowest wages among all. The absolute wage difference between state-owned and collective-owned enterprises was ¥3,200 in 2000, but it increased to ¥18,689 in 2015 (NBS, 2016).

Income gaps among different occupations also increased dramatically. For instance, the average annual income in the financial sector was ¥114,777 in 2015, while it was only ¥48,886 for employees in the construction industry (NBS, 2016). At the end of 2012, a migrant worker could only earn ¥36,864 per year on average, with very limited growth of ¥2496 compared to the previous year (MHRSS, 2016). Lastly, government employees' income, benefits and job security are better or much better than that of most other sectors. Thus, each year's "Guokao"—National Civil Service Exam—attracts a million candidates, although their chances of landing a civil servant job are about 36 to 1 (BBC Trending, 2016).

Employees in non-agricultural sectors have on average much higher salaries than those in agriculture. Employees working in monopoly industries, such as electricity, gas, tobacco, railway, airline and telecom, usually have much higher incomes than those working in other areas. As China's reform in its domestic financial market deepens, the incomes in the financial sector became even higher.

4.4. Income gap between regions

In China, there are major regional income disparities. Workers in the east and southeast coastal regions have higher incomes than their inland and western region counterparts. There was a series of national development plans implemented for dealing with regional income gaps. The "new path to urbanization" is one of the most important such plans. Urbanization has been regarded by the Chinese leadership as one of the key strategies for sustainable economic development (Li, 2013), which means that the urbanization will continue to be an important stimulus of China's future economic growth.

The proposal of a "new path to urbanization" was designed to tackle issues China faces, with regional development imbalance being one of them. The "new path" concerns the development of rural areas and rural residents, especially rural-urban migrants. The proposals for migrants include helping rural migrant workers obtain more employment skills, equal access to urban public services and social welfare programs, and encouraging them to start businesses in their own hometowns (State Council, 2014). Such national plans aim to improve living conditions of low-income populations, such as rural migrants and residents in inland and western areas. The regional income difference had reduced to some extent after the efforts of some national development plans, which contributed to additional employment opportunities and improved income levels for rural, inland and western residents.

4.5. Tax policies help to balance income gaps

Personal income tax policies have helped to narrow the income gap between high-income and low-income groups. During the 1990s and 2000s, there were continuous modifications to the personal income tax laws. The tax exemption level for monthly personal income was ¥1600 in 2006; it rose to ¥2000 in 2008 and to ¥3500 in 2011, while the lowest tax rate decreased from 5 percent to 3 percent (People's Congress, 2011; MOF, 2011). Since 2007, the government has imposed additional taxes on people whose annual incomes exceed ¥120,000. The modification of the personal income tax laws demonstrates the government's intention to reduce the income gap.

4.6. OTHER ASPECTS OF THE INCOME GAP ISSUE
In order to have a comprehensive understanding of income disparity in China, three additional aspects of the issue should be explored.

First, the issue of aging is important when understanding the income gap in a long-term perspective. An aging population will be an ongoing and increasingly important social phenomenon in China (Peng, 2011). The elder generation will control more capital than the younger generation; meanwhile, the working-age population is taking on a heavier burden in caring for their own parents and grandparents as well as their own young children. The younger working-age population will become increasingly burdened and vulnerable. Generational social inequality will be significantly increased. As a result, an integrated package of public policies, as well as fundamental restructuring of the society and economy, is urgently required to deal with the aging problem and its consequences (Peng, 2013).

Second, attention needs to be paid to the developmental disparity between urban and rural areas. Addressing this issue is important as it relates to long-term social harmony. It also relates to the balance of urban and rural economic development. Narrowing income differences between rural and urban residents is an urgent matter. In order to achieve this, the income levels of rural residents, both rural farmers and urban-rural migrant workers, must be increased. As well, more policy protections should be put in place to help guarantee that rural residents receive a fair income.

Third, an improved personal income tax system is necessary to address income disparity. It has generally been thought that the personal income tax system is a useful policy tool to guarantee equal re-distribution of wealth between the rich and the poor. However, the current personal income tax system imposes too much pressure on the middle class, while taxation rules and regulations were not adequately enforced for those belonging to the high-income bracket. Many suspect that tax evasion is commonly practiced by the wealthy. Hence, necessary steps should be taken to better enforce taxation rules. Avoidance of tax should be strictly forbidden and any violation deserves punishment. Hidden and non-wage income should also receive closer scrutiny.

5. RECENT REFORMS OF INCOME DISTRIBUTION POLICY
Social equity has attracted the attention of the central government. In 2006, the Political Bureau of the CCP Central Committee held a meeting to discuss the existing income gap problem. It reached an agreement that social fairness should follow economic development. Soon after the meeting, the "Proposal on advancing the reform of income distribution policy" was drafted. Income

distribution reform was also emphasized in the Twelfth Five-Year Plan (the national plan for the five-year period 2011–2015). In February 2013, the State Council approved the "Proposal on deepening the reform of income distribution policy" (State Council, 2013).

The general requirements of this latest reform cover the following four aspects. The first general requirement is to comprehensively implement the spirit of the 18th Congress of the CCP held in 2012, especially "to let people enjoy the fruits of development equally". The second is to continue economic reform as the central development strategy. The government seems to aim for an equitable and just economic environment while its income distribution policy remains largely unchanged: distributing income according to work as a major method, with different kinds of co-existing methods. The government also called for equal attention to be paid to the policies of initial distribution and re-distribution, as well as for standardizing income distribution.

Four main goals are then set in the context of the general requirements. The first goal is to double the average income level of both urban and rural residents by the end of 2020 from 2010 levels, and especially to make the income levels of low-income and middle-income people rise more quickly than those in high-income group. The second goal aims at further narrowing the income gap and establishing an "olive-shape" distribution of wealth. The third goal is to protect legal income, to adjust high income, to outlaw hidden income, and to ban illegal income. The last goal is to raise the proportion of citizens' personal income in the overall distribution of national income.

The new income distribution policy will continue to improve the initial distribution mechanism, which is to distribute income according to work, capital, skills and management. In order to do this, the new policy aims to provide a more positive employment policy, to increase the income of labour participants, and to achieve high-quality employment. It is also mentioned in the reform process that the current wage system requires deeper reform. A market-determined system is useful to adjust the unreasonably high incomes of, for example, government and monopoly sector employees. To help shape such a system, the government should make sure that all companies and individuals use production factors equally, participate in fair market competition, and enjoy the protection of the law.

The new income distribution policy also sets out to improve the redistribution mechanism via policy tools such as taxes, social security and transfer payments. The adjustment power of taxation will be made stronger than ever before, using methods such as reform of the personal income tax system, improving property tax collection, and reducing the tax burdens of low-and-middle income individuals and small- and mini-scale enterprises. The government will work diligently to improve the quality of basic public services. Efforts will also be made to ensure that every rural and urban resident will enjoy social security. Standard social security cards will be issued nationwide regardless of urban or rural residency. An improved social insurance, social assistance and social welfare system will be built up in order to ensure social equality.

Both the initial distribution and redistribution policies were aimed to narrow income gaps between rural and urban residents.

It is worth noting that in the new stage of reform, the Chinese government is determined to establish a long-term system to stimulate rapid income growth among rural residents. To establish such a system, China needs to speed up the integration of urban and rural development, and promote an equal distribution of public resources between urban and rural areas. Moreover, the reform and restructuring of the Hukou system must be accelerated in order to improve the quality of lives of rural migrants.

In February 2013, the income distribution policy came under review for potential reform. During this round, new policy tools and targets of re-distribution were set to deal with the problem of income disparity. Particularly, the new policy aims at reducing the income gap between rural and urban residents by raising the income level of rural residents. The latest reform also promised a transparent and fair income distribution. The Chinese government is determined to modify and standardize the income distribution system through improving relevant laws and regulations.

6. POVERTY ALLEVIATION POLICIES

The international poverty line standard is set at 1.25 US dollars per day (PPP, Purchasing Power Parity). The World Bank uses another standard, US$2 per day (PPP), but US$1.25 per day (PPP) is more frequently employed. The Chinese poverty line is lower than either figure.

The Chinese government continues its efforts at poverty alleviation and eradication. China's poverty line standard rose significantly between 2011 and 2015, from ¥2,300 to ¥2,855 based on current prices (CPG, 2017). The Chinese government aims to build a moderately prosperous society in all aspects by the end of 2020. One of the most important milestones in achieving this goal is "no poverty". This is a political commitment made openly by the Chinese government to all (Hu and Hang, 2017).

China's national poverty alleviation policies have especially focused on rural poverty. "The National 'Eight Seven' Poverty Alleviation Program" was issued in 1994. The term "Eight Seven" is a reference to solving the problem of eighty million rural people living in poverty within a period of seven years (that is, from 1994 to 2000). The issuing of this policy marked the first time that the Chinese government implemented a large-scale, well-organized poverty reduction program (State Council, 1994). By the end of 2000, the program was completed and it was a success. The number of rural poor dropped to 32 million by the end of the program (NBS, 2002).

"The Rural China Poverty Reduction Outline (2000–2010)" issued in 2001 was the second essential act to accelerate the reduction of poverty. It aimed at alleviating poverty in rural China using two main measures: developing the rural economy, and improving rural production and living conditions. The number of rural poor fell to 26.9 million at the end of 2010 (NBS, 2011).

Other policies also contributed to the poverty alleviation process in rural China. Since 2005, agricultural taxes have been subject to exemption in over 26 provinces. The exemption of agricultural taxes removed the burden on farmers and promised them a potentially higher income. In addition to agricultural tax exemptions, agricultural subsidies are another way of increasing the income of rural residents.

In 2011, a follow-up to the Rural China Poverty Reduction Outline was issued, "The Rural China Poverty Reduction Outline (2011–2020)". The new outline is the third poverty alleviation policy initiated at the national level. It articulates the direction of poverty reduction over the next ten years. The first task is to consolidate the goals of the former outline, including achieving rural prosperity, improving the environment, and enhancing development capability. The challenges faced in the new round will be more complicated and difficult than in the previous round. As the country develops, absolute poverty will lessen, but relative poverty remains. It will be more difficult to deal with relative poverty than absolute poverty and may require the Chinese government to pay more attention to income gaps and relative income distribution issues.

The new outline is more target-based, with an explicit "three-in-one" framework, which combines "specific-project-based poverty reduction", "industrial poverty reduction" and "social poverty reduction" (SCIO, 2011). The framework calls for the combination of poverty alleviation projects and the rural minimum social security policy. Security policies are more effective in compensating for impediments to people's welfare caused by reform (Lin, 2011).

6.1. Security policies and the reduction of poverty

6.1.1. *Minimum wage security for employees*

Minimum wage security is provided to employees, with no distinction between rural or urban employees. However, the minimum wage varies from region to region and city to city. The minimum wage standard is adjusted frequently in order to keep pace with rapid economic growth and inflation. The provincial minimum standards usually have three to four different levels, from which each municipal government has the authority to choose according to its own economic and status.

For example, the highest level of the minimum wage in Jiangsu province was ¥1,770 per month in 2016 (see Table 2). Cities such as Nanjing and Suzhou, where economic growth was much faster than in other cities in Jiangsu Province, had the highest minimum wage standard.

Table 2. Provincial Minimum Wage Standards (Yuan ¥)

Province	Minimum wage/month	Minimum wage/hour	Effective date (D/M/Y)
Shanghai	2190	19	01/04/2016
Tianjin	1950	19.5	01/07/2016
Xinjiang	1670/1470/1390/1310	16.7/14.7/13.9/13.1	01/07/2015
Jiangsu	1770/1600/1400	15.5/14/12	01/01/2016
Shandong	1710/1550/1390	17.1/15.5/13.9	01/06/2016
Jilin	1480/1380/1280	13.5/12.5/11.5	01/12/2015
Ningxia	1480/1390/1320	14/11.5/12	01/07/2015
Liaoning	1530/1320/1200/1020	15/13/10.8/9.5	01/01/2016
Yunnan	1570/1400/1180	14/ 13/12	01/09/2015

Province	Minimum wage/month	Minimum wage/hour	Effective date (D/M/Y)
Anhui	1520/1350/1250/1150	16/14/13/12	01/11/2015
Jiangxi	1530/1430/1340/1180	15.3/14.3/13.4/11.8	01/10/2015
Gansu	1470/1420/1370/1320	15.5/15/14.4/13.9	01/04/2015
Sichuan	1500/1380/1260	15.7/14.4/13.2	01/07/2015
Guangxi	1400/1210/1085/1000	13.5/11.5/10.5/9.5	01/01/2015

Data source: MOHRSS (Ministry of Human Resources and Social Security, China), http://www.mohrss.gov.cn/SYrlzyhshbzb/gongzishourufenpei/fwyd/201612/t20161213_261789.html and http://www.mohrss.gov.cn/SYrlzyhshbzb/gongzishourufenpei/fwyd/201612/t20161213_261787.html.

The Labour Contract Law (2008 edition) protects the minimum wages of employees. Paying employees less than the local minimum wage standard is deemed a breach of contract. According to the eighty-fifth provision of the Labour Contract Law, the employer must compensate the employee with back wages within certain time limits (CPG, 2007).

6.1.2. *Minimum living security system for both urban and rural residents*
Urban residents were the first to enjoy the benefits of the minimum living security system. The "Regulations of minimum living security for urban residents" were implemented in October 1999. The original policy provided an important framework for the living security policy. There have been continuous amendments to the original policy since that time.

In order to solve the problem of poverty in rural China, the State Council decided to apply the minimum living security policy to rural areas in 2007. This includes the establishment and standardization of the system of subsistence allowances for poor rural residents, as well as improvements to the social assistance system. The rural minimum living security policy was designed for the rural poor, whose annual net income is below the local poverty cutoff. The main causes of poverty include disease, disability, and aging, all resulting in people no longer being able to work. After the minimum living security policy came into effect in rural areas, both urban and rural residents were able to enjoy the minimum living security subsidies. In 2008, the policy was renamed "the minimum living security system for urban and rural residents".

The current minimum living standards are calculated in the following two ways. The first is based on a calculation of the basic living expenditure, under which the urban and rural minimum living standard is set according to the realities of food and non-food expenditures. The necessary food expenditure is calculated according to the necessary food lists provided by the National Nutrition Institute. Non-food living necessities refers to necessary clothes, water and electricity, gas, transportation, and other daily expenditures. The second way is the Engel coefficient method, determined by the following formula:

$$\text{Minimum living standard} = \frac{\text{Necessary food consumption expenditure}}{\text{The Engel coefficient of the lowest household income in last year}}$$

Under such calculation methods, the national average minimum living standard has seen a steady rise during recent years. As reported by the Ministry of Civil Affairs of China (MCA), in 2013, the national average minimum living standard for urban residents was ¥330.1 per month/person, and ¥172.3 for rural residents (MCA, 2013). At the end of 2015, there were about 9.57 million urban households (about 17 million urban population) and 28.46 million rural households (about 49 million rural population) receiving minimum living security payments. The national averages for the minimum living standard for urban and rural residents were ¥451.1 and ¥264.8 per month per person respectively. The central government covers about 60 percent to 70 percent of the subsidy, with the rest would be covered by provincial and municipal governments. This coverage is expanding each year in order to help as many people as possible (MCA, 2016).

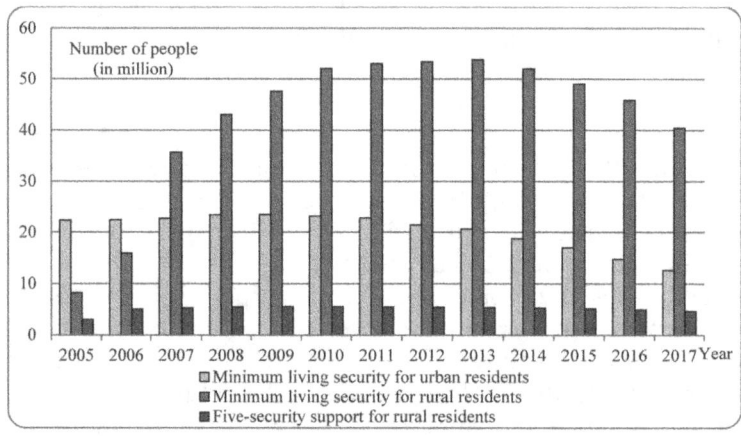

Figure 3. Number of recipients of the three major social security policies, 2005-2017

Data source: 2012 – 2017 statistical bulletin of social service development, Ministry of Civil Affairs of China (MCA). http://www.mca.gov.cn/article/sj/tjgb/.

In 2017, the national average urban minimum living standard was ¥540.6 per person/month, an increase of 9.3 percent over the previous year. As of the end of 2017, there were 7,415,000 households and 12,610,000 people eligible for urban subsistence allowances. In the year 2017, governments at all levels spent a total of ¥64.05 billion in urban subsistence allowances (MOC, 2018). In rural areas, there were 22,493,000 households and 40,452,000 people eligible for rural subsistence allowances in 2017. All levels of government spent a total of ¥105.18 billion in rural subsistence allowances. The national rural minimum living standard was ¥4,300.70 per person/year in 2017, an increase of 14.9 percent over the previous year (MOC, 2018).

6.1.3. The five-guarantees support for poor rural residents

The five-guarantees support is another living security policy designed to serve rural poor. The five guarantees include the guarantees of food, clothing, medical care, housing, and funeral expenses (and bringing up orphans). At the end of 2014, about 5.29 million rural people received the five-guarantees support. The total costs of the policy were about ¥18.98 billion in 2012 (MCA, 2015).

Rural poverty has been a serious challenge in China. Thus, the important poverty alleviation policies have all been focusing on addressing rural poverty issues. The two previous programs, namely the "Eight Seven Program" and the "Rural China Poverty Reduction Outline (2000–2010)", aimed to reduce absolute poverty among rural residents. After these two policies' implementation, China's rural poverty rate had dropped dramatically. The current poverty alleviation policy, the Rural China Poverty Reduction Outline (2011–2020), focuses on complicated poverty issues, such as poverty caused by the nation's economic reform.

Social security and the welfare system also play important roles in the alleviation of poverty. The minimum wage security and minimum living security programs cover all who are eligible, regardless their Hukou status. The difference is that the minimum wage security is for employees and the minimum living security program is for residents. Apart from these two security policies, the rural poor could also receive five-guarantees support if they qualify.

6.1.4. Housing security

The initial government proposal for addressing the low-income urban households' housing problem was issued in 2007. In the initial proposal, the government decided to address the issue mainly through the "low-rent home" policy, together with other multi-channel policy systems such as the "comfortable home" policy. It was aimed at improving the housing conditions of low-income households significantly by the end of 2010.

There are three main kinds of housing security provided by the government to urban residents: the low-rent home, comfortable home, and rent subsidy programs. Of the three, the comfortable home program is only available to low-income residents. If the resident is unable to afford a comfortable home, then he/she can apply for a low-rent home. Those who cannot afford to rent a low-rent home can obtain a rent subsidy from the government to help them afford a home rental.

The initial proposal also sought to improve the housing conditions of the urban poor and vulnerable population groups such as migrant workers. The improvement of shantytowns and old residences were both included in the plan. The government also required contractors to provide basic, clean, and safe living places for migrant workers.

At the end of 2007, the revised "Regulations on low-rent homes" came into effect. The regulations ensure that monetary and physical subsidies are combined to provide "low-rent home" security. The monetary subsidy requires tenants to rent homes, but also stipulates that local governments must provide rent subsidies to tenants, while the physical subsidy program requires local governments to provide low-rent apartment units for low-income tenants, with tenants paying their rents to the government.

In Shanghai, for example, the municipal government has issued relevant policies for the execution of the important social security measure. It also modifies relevant application and eligibility criteria each year. On December 20,

2017, the Shanghai municipal government issued its latest low-rent housing application eligibility criteria:

1. Members in the household must have legal relationships and be living together;
2. Members of the household must have permanent resident status in the city for three years, and have permanent resident status in the township where the application is submitted for one year;
3. The per capita living area of the applicant household is seven square meters or less;
4. The household's annual disposable income is ¥39,600 per person or less, and with a value of ¥120,000 or less in per capita property if it has three or more members; or annual disposable income of ¥43,560 or less and property of ¥132,000 or less per person if it has two or less members; and
5. The applicant household members did not sell or gift their own housing (within five years of the application), resulting in their housing problem.

A single person who meets the above criteria and who is 35 years of age or older, including those who are unmarried, widowed or divorced for three years, can apply independently (Shanghai Municipal Government Policy 2017–20).

According to the 2017 Shanghai New Policy on Low-Rent Housing Subsidy, the following households will be given priority if they wish to apply for low-rent housing:

1. Childless elders' households;
2. Moderate or severely disabled persons' households or households with grades 1–4 disabled soldiers;
3. Severely disease patients' households;
4. Households with members who are completely or mostly unable to work;
5. Households of a hero who sacrificed his/her life for others;
6. Households of someone who has been honoured as a Model Worker at or above the provincial (ministerial) level;
7. Households of someone who has been honoured as the March Eighth Red Flag Bearer at the national level (or twice at the provincial/ministerial level); and
8. Households that returned to China from overseas residency before the end of 1966 (http://shanghai.chashebao.com/gongjijin/17837.html).

6.2 Unemployment issues and unemployment insurance

Unemployment issues emerged in the wake of economic reform. It was a serious issue for the Chinese government between the mid-1990s and the mid-2000s. The reform of state-owned enterprises caused a massive number of workers to lose their jobs, most of them were middle-aged, between 40 and 50 years old. The issue became more serious during the late 1990s as the number of laid-off workers grew. Their income levels dropped significantly. By the end of 1994, 95 million were receiving unemployment insurance benefits (Dong, 1996). Between 1998 to 2000, about 21 million workers were laid off by state-owned enterprises. Compared to younger laid-off workers, laid-off workers aged 40 to 50 years have more difficulty finding new jobs, largely due to the difficulties of learning entirely new employment skills. Their reemployment was also particularly challenging because of the large numbers of young rural-urban migrants, who were willing to do virtually any kind of work.

After 1990, the restructuring of state-owned enterprises resulted in a great number of surplus personnel. The State Council issued the State-owned Enterprise Workers' Unemployment Insurance Regulations in 1993 to replace the 1986 Interim Provisions. However, the State-Owned Enterprise Workers Unemployment Insurance Regulations did not have a big impact and the limitations of the Interim Provisions persisted. Due to the rise in unemployment rates, the policy's implementation was not smooth and lagged behind the nation's economic development.

The State Council issued regulations in 1999 to improve the unemployment insurance system and strengthen the security function of unemployment insurance. These emphasized both the rights and obligations of the insured, reflecting the nature of unemployment insurance, safeguarding workers' legitimate rights and interests. The basic purpose of unemployment insurance is to ensure basic living standards for the unemployed and to promote reemployment. The scope of unemployment insurance extended to all types of enterprises and institutions in cities and towns. This new regulation established the three-party financing mechanism that includes contributions from the state, work-units, and employees. Unemployment insurance premiums would be in accordance with local minimum living standards but lower than local minimum wage standards. It strengthened the management of the unemployment insurance fund, including a designated banking account for the fund.

Unemployment among university graduates has become a major social concern in recent decades. Chinese colleges and universities began to expand their enrollments in 1999, with the number of graduates reaching new highs

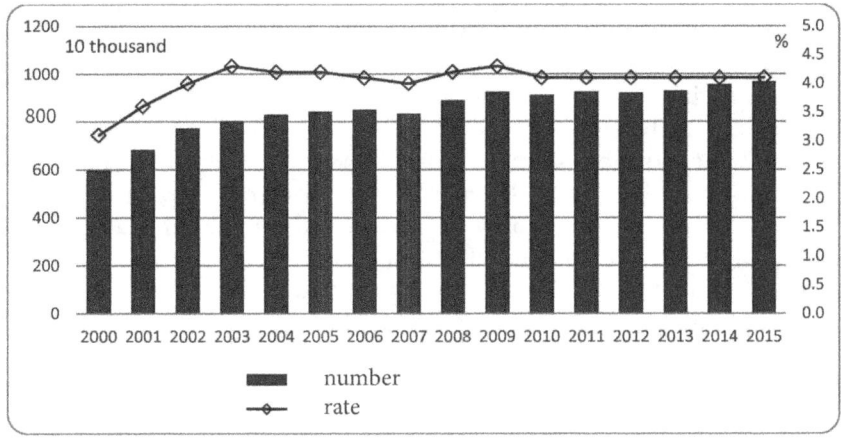

Figure 4. Urban registered unemployment, 2000-2015
Data source: Official annual data from the NBS website, http://data.stats.gov.cn/easyquery.htm?cn=C01

each year. According to official data from the NBS, the number of college graduates rose from 0.85 million in 1999 to 6.8 million in 2015 (NBS, 2016). As the overall economic growth rate has slowed in recent years, young graduates face fierce competition in finding a job. To deal with this pressing issue, the government has made every effort to provide more information about job openings through the media. There is an attempt to encourage graduates to find a job first and look for a better job later, and to encourage them to work in inland and western China. The unfavorable situation for college and university graduates will continue in coming years due to the number of university graduates and the scarcity of available positions.

By the end of 2015, there were 173.26 million people making contributions to the unemployment insurance fund, an increase of 2.83 million from the year before, and 2.27 million unemployed workers collected unemployment insurance (MHRSS, 2016). The official unemployment rate was 3.1 percent in 2000, and exceeded 4.0 percent in 2002 (NBS, 2016).

At the fifth session of the Twelfth National People's Congress held on March 5, 2017, Premier Li Keqiang delivered the 2017 Government Work Report. Li stressed that employment is the foundation of people's livelihood, and promoting employment and entrepreneurship is one of the leading priorities of the government. The Chinese government aims to improve employment policies, enhance employment training, and encourage flexible employment and new types of employment. Two specific groups are prioritized: university graduates and zero-employment families (i.e., no member in the household has a job). The number of university graduates reached 7.95 million in 2017. The Chinese government plans to promote multi-path employment and entrepreneurship to ensure new university graduates' employment. With regard to zero-employment families, the government wants to ensure that at least one family member has a secure and stable job (Li, 2017).

7. CONCLUSION

China's employment and income distribution policies began with an egalitarian model during Mao's era under a planned economic system. Economic reforms since 1978 have progressed through several phases. The first was from 1978 to 1983, during which China abandoned the old "equal distribution" principle and replaced it with "efficiency first with consideration of fairness". A major reform of the economic system occurred in 1987, during the second stage of development from 1984 to1991, when a transition from a planned economy to a planned commodity economy occurred. At the same time, a new income distribution policy was implemented, which aimed to distribute income according to the quantity and quality of one's work as the major method, with other kinds of distribution methods viewed as supplementary. Between 1992 and 2006, a socialist market economic system was established. Theoretically, this system is an integration of socialist ideology and market economy. During this third reform stage, income distribution policy was infused with new directives; for instance, productive factors such as capital and technology were allowed and encouraged in the income distribution.

Overall Gini coefficients in China have been remained above 0.4 for more than a decade, indicating an alarming impact on social equity. The income gap is still evident in many areas of society: between rural and urban residents, and among different sectors, occupations and regions. From the perspective of initial distribution, monopolies have been achieving very high revenues, which has greatly increased the income gap.

The current pay differences between migrant workers and native urban workers are mainly the result of job differences. Retraining workers can help them to obtain more highly skilled jobs, thus increasing their income. How to protect the rights of vulnerable social groups such as rural migrant workers is a serious challenge. Strict regulations should be in place to prohibit employers from delaying any worker's pay or denying anyone equal access to proper labour protection and work-related benefits.

The impact of the latest reform of income policy has not yet become apparent. Results will depend on the effectiveness of implementation. However, one thing is quite certain: the government is making efforts to let every resident enjoy the benefits of the nation's economic growth as well as to realize equity in society.

REFERENCES

BBC Trending (2016, December 1). The people who can't quite get a government job. http://www.bbc.com/news/blogs-trending-38151203.

Cheng, Y. (2007) China's overall Gini coefficient since reform and its decomposition by rural and urban Areas since reform and opening-up. *China Social Science* (4): 45-60.

CPG (Central People's Government, China) (2007). *Labour Contract Law of People's Republic of China (The 2008 Edition)*, http://www.gov.cn/ziliao/flfg/2007-06/29/content_669394.htm.

Dong, Weizhen (1996). *Urban Women's Employment and Unemployment in An Age of Transition*. Institute of Social Sciences, The Hague. WP No. 222.

Feuchtwang, Stephan, Athar Hussain, & Thierry Pairault (1988). *Transforming China's Economy in the Eighties*. Westview Press: Boulder, CO.

Hu, Angang and Hang, Chengzheng (2017). China promises to win the fight against poverty'. http://www.gov.cn/xinwen/2017-02/24/content_5170443.htm.

Itoh, Makoto (1995). *Political Economy for Socialism*. Macmillan: London.

Jin, Yongai and Xie Yu (2017). Household property. In Xie Yu et al. (eds.), *China Family Panel Studies 2016*, pp. 50-69. Beijing: Peking University Press.

Li, Gan (2013). Income inequality and consumption in China. http://international.uiowa.edu/sites/international.uiowa.edu/files/file_uploads/incomeinequalityinchina.pdf.

Li, K. (2013). The key essential of the 'new path to urbanization' is people, and the interests of farmers must be protected: Chinese Premier Li Keqiang answers questions from Chinese and foreign reporters after the 12th session of the NPC meeting. http://news.xinhuanet.com/2013l-h/2013-03/17/c_115053973.htm.

Li, Keqiang (2017). Report on the work of the government. Delivered at the Fifth Session of the 12th National People's Congress of the People's Republic of China on March 5, 2017. http://online.wsj.com/public/resources/documents/NPC2017_WorkReport_English.pdf.

Lin, H. (2011). *Interpretation of "The Rural China Poverty Reduction Outline (2011–2020)*. http://www.gov.cn/jrzg/2011-12/01/content_2008683.htm.

Majid, Momaan (2015). *The Great Employment Transformation in China*. International Labour Office Employment Working Paper No. 195

Mann, Jim (1986, September 3). China to end lifetime jobs for workers. *Los Angeles Times*. http://articles.latimes.com/1986-09-03/news/mn-13140_1_lifetime-job.

MCA (Ministry of Civil Affairs, China) (2011). Guidance on further standardizing the minimum living standard of urban and rural residents. http://www.mca.gov.cn/article/zwgk/fvfg/zdshbz/201105/20110500154356.shtml.

MCA (Ministry of Civil Affairs) (2013). The 2012 statistical bulletin of social service development. http://www.mca.gov.cn/article/sj/tjgb/201306/201306004747469.shtml.

MCA (Ministry of Civil Affairs) (2015). The 2014 statistical bulletin of social service development. http://www.mca.gov.cn/article/sj/tjgb/201506/201506008324399.shtml.

MCA (Ministry of Civil Affairs) (2016). The 2015 statistical bulletin of social service development. http://www.mca.gov.cn/article/sj/tjgb/201607/20160700001136.shtml.

MCA (Ministry Of Civil Affairs) (2018). 2017 Statistical Bulletin Of Social Services Development, p. 7. http://www.mca.gov.cn/article/sj/tjgb/.

MHRSS (Ministry of Human Resources and Social Security) (2016). The 2015 statistical bulletin of human resources and social security development. http://www.mohrss.gov.cn/SYrlzyhshbzb/zwgk/szrs/tjgb/201606/t20160601_241070.html.

MHRSS (Ministry of Human Resources and Social Security, China) (2016). Different Regions Minimum Wage Standard in the Country. http://www.mohrss.gov.cn/SYrlzyhshbzb/gongzishourufenpei/fwyd/201612/t20161213_261789.html and http://www.mohrss.gov.cn/SYrlzyhshbzb/gongzishourufenpei/fwyd/201612/t20161213_261787.html.

MOF (Ministry of Finance) (2011). Press Conference on the Adjustment of Personal Income Tax. http://www.mof.gov.cn/zhengwuxinxi/zhengcejiedu/2011zhengcejiedu/201104/t20110420_539060.html.

NBS (National Bureau of Statistics, China) (2002). Research on the "Hot Issues" of China's Rural Areas—2000. China Statistics Press, http://www.stats.gov.cn/tjzs/tjsj/tjcb/200204/t20020404_36141.html.

NBS (National Bureau of Statistics, China) (2011). The 2010 Statistical Bulletin of National Economy and Social Development of China. http://www.stats.gov.cn/tjsj/tjgb/ndtjgb/qgndtjgb/201102/t20110228_30025.html.

NBS (National Bureau of Statistics, China) (2012). National Data. http://data.stats.gov.cn/easyquery.htm?cn=C01.

NBS (National Bureau of Statistics, China) (2013). Ma Jiantang answers questions from reporters about the national economic operation situation of 2012. http://www.stats.gov.cn/tjgz/tjdt/201301/t20130118_17719.html.

NBS (National Bureau of Statistics, China) (2016). National Data. http://data.stats.gov.cn/easyquery.htm?cn=C01.

NBS (National Bureau of Statistics, China) (2017). Director of NBS answers questions from reporters about the national economic operation situation of 2016. http://www.stats.gov.cn/tjsj/sjjd/201701/t20170120_1456268.html.

NPC (National People's Congress, 1992). *Law of the People's Republic of China on the Protection of Rights and Interests of Women*. http://www.npc.gov.cn/englishnpc/Law/2007-12/12/content_1383859.htm

Peng, X. (2011). China's demographic history and future challenges. *Science*, 333(6042), 581–587.

Peng, X. (2013). China's demographic challenge requires an integrated coping strategy. *Journal of Policy Analysis and Management*, 32(2): 399–406.

People's Congress (2011). Decision of the Standing Committee of the National People's

Congress on amending the individual income tax law of the People's Republic of China. http://www.mof.gov.cn/zhengwuxinxi/caizhengxinwen/201107/t20110701_569185.htm.

People's Daily (2011, November 30). 'The Rising of Poverty Standard to ¥2300 (Policy Interpretation): Increasing 92% Compared to the 2009 Standard. http://politics.people.com.cn/GB/1026/16437873.html.

Piazza, Alan (2014). Poverty and Living Standards since 1949. *Chinese Studies*. http://www.oxfordbibliographies.com/view/document/obo-9780199920082/obo-9780199920082-0080.xml.

SCIO (The State Council Information Office, China) (2011). *New Progress in Development-oriented Poverty Reduction Program for Rural China*. http://www.scio.gov.cn/zfbps/ndhf/2011/Document/1048758/1048758.htm.

State Council (1994). *National Seven Eight Poverty Alleviation Program*. http://www.cpad.gov.cn/art/1994/12/30/art_46_51505.html.

State Council (2013, February 3). *Several Opinions on Deepening the Reform of the Income Distribution System*. http://www.gov.cn/zwgk/2013-02/05/content_2327531.htm.

State Council (2014). *National New Urbanization Plan (2014–2020)*. http://www.gov.cn/zhengce/2014-03/16/content_2640075.htm.

State Council (2015). China aims to double 2010 GDP, people's income by 2020. http://english.gov.cn/news/top_news/2015/10/29/content_281475222963544.htm.

Xie, Yu and Xiang Zhou (2014). Income inequality in today's China. *PNAS*, 111(19): 6926–6933. https://www.ncbi.nlm.nih.gov/pmc/articles/PMC4024912/pdf/pnas.201403158.pdf.

Chapter 9
Education Policy in China

Weizhen Dong, Lichun Qin, Zhennan Wang

ABSTRACT

Education forms a very important part of social policy in China, not only because China has a large population, but also because the Chinese people place a high priority on education, especially the education of children and youth. The government's education policy determines the nation's educational system's development, which also determines the quality of education.

The evolution of education policy in China can be divided into three stages: 1949–1966, 1966–1976, and from 1977 on. The period from 1949 to 1966 was the initial stage of setting up the socialist education system in new China, which was followed by the Cultural Revolution years. Since 1977, China has started to reconstruct its educational system and embrace market elements in the rapidly growing sector. Although these three periods seem to be disconnected, the development of China's educational system was actually a continuous process.

In recent decades, educational disparity has emerged as a great challenge. This includes regional and rural-urban disparities, disparities among different social groups, and disparities among different types of educational programs. As in other spheres of society, unequal access to social resources divides people, particularly when there are large income gaps, and affects the overall development of the country. The Chinese government needs to develop an effective education policy to ensure there is no financial burden for students from relatively poor families, and make sure that no student is turned away because they cannot afford tuition fees or boarding expenses. Students are the future of the country. The education level of the population is the key to the prosperity of the nation.

1. INTRODUCTION

In the process of the education system's development, there were hundreds of policies issued by the central government of China to ensure the successful implementation of relevant principles. This chapter examines the evolution of education policy during the 17 years in which a socialist educational system was constructed (1949–1966), the decade of the Cultural Revolution (1966–1976), and reforms carried out since 1977. It also discusses current issues such as disparities between urban and rural areas, across regions, among social groups, and among different educational programs. Educational equity, the financial burdens of education, and the future trajectory of the country's education policy are discussed as well.

2. EDUCATION POLICY DEVELOPMENT IN CHINA
2.1. Education in New China (1949–1966)

After the establishment of socialist New China in 1949, two important objectives were set for education: to increase Chinese citizens' access to education by promoting a universal education system, and through formalized and institutionalized education to supply society with talented workers for the purposes of modernization and national defense. The conflict between equality and efficiency in educational development was officially characterized at the time as the dilemma of choosing between universal and elite education. It was a challenge for the new government to adhere to the socialist value and revolutionary spirit of mass education while meeting the needs of the nation's modernization.

Equity was the main focus in the early years of the New China. The government stressed that education should be accessible to all, and particularly to workers and farmers. There were various popular and active programs for cadres' education, worker-farmer accelerated schools, etc. The New Democratic Education program (Ministry of Education, 1949), enacted in 1949, stipulated that education should incorporate both theory and practice, and that the purpose of education was to serve the people; high priority should be placed on the education of workers, farmers and soldiers. The guiding policy of education should be an appropriate combination of training the general public and the elites (National Institute of Education Sciences, 1984).

In the 1950s, China began to incorporate ideas from the Soviet Union in its education system. By 1955, the worker-farmer accelerated middle schools stopped recruiting new students. The formalization of education and the emphasis on education quality gradually replaced the previous focus on education equality (Yang, 2006).

The national education plan, especially in regard to higher education, aimed to directly promote economic, scientific and technological advance, and represented the pursuit of efficiency by the nation. The emphasis on the direct utilitarian value of education in promoting scientific, technological and economic development yielded knowledge and talent that could be put to use in economic modernization and national defense development during the 1950s and 1960s. But problems arose in terms of lack of resources and an imbalance in the allocation of education resources. Primary education, especially at the village level, remained underdeveloped.

The so-called *key school system* in primary and secondary education was a typical reflection of the emphasis on elite education. In May 1953, at a meeting of the Political Bureau of the Central Committee of the Communist Party, Chairman Mao Zedong decided to establish key middle schools, of which 194 were established across the country. In the early 1960s, the development of key schools was again on the agenda, as part of the process of adjusting and reorganizing primary education. By 1963, 487 key middle schools were operating in 27 provinces, cities and autonomous regions across China, accounting for 3.1 percent of all public middle schools (Ministry of Education, 2014). The primary function of these key schools was to train qualified new students to meet the requirements of higher education, and eventually to attend university (Yang, 2014).

In 1959, at the Second National People's Congress, Premier Zhou Enlai declared that the priority was "first, to concentrate our efforts on building a group of key schools, so as to train specialized talents with high quality for the country" (Ministry of Education, 2014). In 1962, the Ministry of Education issued a notice that required local governments to designate groups of key primary and secondary schools, the number and size of which should be proportional to recruitment by higher-level schools (Ministry of Education, 1962).

This system, however, resulted in tremendous adverse effects when put into practice. Key schools enjoyed advantages over regular schools in terms of allocation of teachers, facilities, and funding, etc. As a result, gaps were created between schools; in the process of training and selecting elite students, a large group of underdeveloped or poor quality schools were also created, which harmed the majority of students. Meanwhile, competition among key schools negatively affected the overall goal of basic education (Liu, 2014).

Matrix 1. Main Policies Issued (1949–1966)

Year	Policy Document Issued	Core of the Policy
1949	The Common Program of the Chinese People's Political Consultative Conference	Chinese education is new-democratic, national, scientific and public in nature.
1950	First National Conference on Education	The key principle of education is serving the workers, farmers and soldiers, and the needs of production and construction.
1957	On the Correct Handling of Contradictions among the People	The principle of education is to enable students to develop morally, intellectually, and physically, and to become educated workers who support socialism.
1958	Instructions on Educational Undertaking	The Communist Party's education policy is that education should serve the needs of proletariat politics, and education should be integrated with production.
1958	Provision to the Issue of Delegating Power to Lower Levels in Education Administration	Governance in education is decentralized to local governments.

Source: He Dongchang, *Important Educational Documents of the People's Republic of China: 1949–1975*, Hainan Press, 1998.

2.2. EDUCATION DURING THE CULTURAL REVOLUTION (1966–1976)

The Cultural Revolution was an unusual period in Chinese history. Its impact on education was enormous. Several education policies were issued at the beginning of the Cultural Revolution. The first such policy was the Decision on the Great Proletarian Cultural Revolution in 1966, which marked the start of the Cultural Revolution (Central Committee of the Chinese Communist Party, 1966). The Decision required that old education systems, policies and practices be reformed; education should serve the proletariat, be integrated with production, and train students morally, intellectually, and physically, so they would become educated workers who followed socialist ideals. Schooling programs should be short, coursework should be concise and the teaching materials should be completely reformed (Central Committee of the Chinese Communist Party, 1966).

The second policy was the Notice for Reforming Enrollment in Higher Education in 1966 (Central Committee of the Chinese Communist Party and State Council, 1966). It stipulated that new students enrolled in 1966 should accept the jobs assigned to them by the state; recruitment would be delegated to the provincial and municipal governments; and recruitment in higher education would be based on a combination of recommendation and selection, rather than examination alone (He, 1998a).

The third policy was the Report of Educational Department on Educational Conference of Work-Study in Cities Nationwide, approved and forwarded by the State Council in 1966 (Ministry of Education, 1966; He, 1998a). Its major provision was that schools should allow for part-time study by workers and farmers, integrating education with real life practice, universalizing middle-school education in cities, and mobilizing urban young intellectuals seeking work experience in rural areas. Slogans such as "Integrating work and study", "Learning through working", and "Go to the countryside"—these messages were related to education but sparked mass movements in the entire society. For example, countless urban school graduates went to live and work in rural and remote areas, following the government's call of "Up to the Mountains and Down to the Countryside".

Matrix 2. Main Policies Issued (1966–1976)

Year	Policy Document Issued	Core of the Policy
1966	Decision on the Great Proletarian Cultural Revolution of the Central Committee of the Chinese Communist Party	Education reform: reform the old education systems, policies and practices; education should serve the needs of proletarian politics, be integrated with production, and train students morally, intellectually, and physically, so they will become educated workers who follow socialist ideals; schooling should be short, the coursework should be concise and the teaching materials need to be completely reformed.
1966	Notice for Reforming Enrollment in Higher Education	New students enrolled in 1966 should accept the jobs assigned to them by the state; recruitment will be delegated to the provincial and municipal governments; recruitment in higher education will be based on a combination of recommendation and selection, rather than examination alone.
1966	Report of Educational Department on Educational Conference of Work-Study in Cities Nationwide, Approved and Forwarded by the State Council	The school should allow for workers and farmers' part-time study, integrate education with real life practices, universalize middle-school education in cities, and motivate urban young intellectuals in the city to seek work experience in rural areas.

Source: He Dongchang, *Important Educational Documents of the People's Republic of China: 1949–1975*, Hainan Press, 1998a.

2.3 Education in the New Era (1978–present)

Education policy since the beginning of economic reform and opening up has incorporated the lessons and experiences from the preceding two periods as well as the educational ideology of Mao Zedong. An in-depth understanding of past educational development enabled a balanced view towards education in the new era. However, the movement to emancipate the mind and bring order out of chaos in education was not immediately completed in the late 1970s, as it only restored the common sense perspective that education and knowledge were needed, but did not explore new ways of tackling higher-level issues such as what kind of education is better, and how to reform the educational system.

One important issue in education is funding for schools. Article 12 in the Compulsory Education Law of China issued in 1986 stipulates that "the State Council and local governments of different levels should finance the operational expenses and investments for essential construction required for the implementation of compulsory education. The rate increase in financial allocation on compulsory education should be higher than that of the national revenue, and education spending per student should increase gradually" (The NPC Standing Committee, 1986). Furthermore, "Different levels of local governments should collect funds for public education across towns, cities and counties in accordance with state regulations, and these funds should be primarily used for compulsory education. The government should subsidize those areas with financial difficulties for implementing compulsory education".

The Guidelines of China's Education Reform and Development issued in 1993 by the State Council clearly stipulated that the government should gradually increase the proportion of GDP spent on education to 4 percent at the end of the 20th century. However, this objective was not realized. In 2004, GDP was ¥15,987.8 billion, but spending on education only accounted for 2.787 percent, the same level as in 1999, but much lower than in 2002 and 2003 (Kong, 2006).

In order to address insufficient education funding from the government, Article 48 of the Compendium of China's Education Reform and Development stipulates an "increase in the tuition for students at the phase of non-compulsory education, and collection of incidental fees at the phase of compulsory education in accordance with different situations" (Central Committee of Chinese Communist Party and the State Council, 1993). This policy has resulted in arbitrary collection of fees, increasing special charges, high tuition fees for students outside of the recruitment plan and all kinds of arbitrarily labeled charges, such as donations for entering the school, sponsorship fees, joint construction fees, and incidental fees. Education, a nonprofit sector that aims to convey morals and knowledge and to clarify confusion, unexpectedly became one of the six areas where unreasonable charges were most frequently reported, the top target of complaint, and also one of the ten most profitable sectors (Wang, 2005).

By the end of the 20th century, the worldwide focus on education equity shifted from primary education to higher education. The first World Education Congress in October 1998 raised the point that, if the heavy burden of higher education is imposed on individual families, opportunities for receiving higher education will be more unequal. The World Declaration on Higher Education for the Twenty-First Century issued by UNESCO one year later emphasized that admission to higher education should be determined by individual merit rather than privileged social status.

On December 16, 2002, the Chinese National Development and Reform Commission announced that a nationwide investigation of arbitrary collection of fees had uncovered more than 12,600 cases, with illegal charges totalling ¥2.14 billion. Recently, education experts made a conservative estimate that, over the past ten years, arbitrary collection of fees in China's education system might have exceeded ¥200 billion.

Matrix 3. Main Policies Issued (1978–2010)

Year	Policy Document Issued	Core of the Policy
1981	Resolution on Certain Questions in the History of Our Party Since the Founding of the People's Republic of China	The policy that education should train students morally, intellectually, and physically, as well as to hold correct political views and gain professional knowledge, should be retained.
1982	Constitution of the People's Republic of China	The state promotes the all-round healthy development of children and youth, morally, intellectually and physically.
1985	Decision on Reform of Educational System by the Central Committee of the Chinese Communist Party	Education must serve the development of socialism, and the development of socialism must rely on education. Education should enable a supply of qualified intellectuals who meet the needs of modernization, the world and the future. All these intellectuals should be ambitious, with high morality, well-educated, disciplined, and passionate for socialism, and willing to sacrifice for the wealth of the nation and the people. They should constantly acquire new knowledge, seek truth, think independently and be innovative.
1990	Decision on the Ten-Year Plan and Fifth Five-Year Plan for National Economic and Social Development	Education must serve socialist modernization, must be integrated with production and real life practices, and provide society with socialist constructors and successors who are intellectually, morally and physically well trained.
1993	Compendium of China's Education Reform and Development	Education must serve socialist modernization, must be integrated with production and real life practices, and provide society with socialist constructors and successors that are intellectually, morally and physically developed.
1995	The Law of Education of the People's Republic of China	Education must serve socialist modernization. It must be integrated with production and real life practices, and provide society with socialist constructors and successors who are intellectually, morally and physically well developed.
1999	Decision on Deepening Educational Reform and Promoting Quality-Oriented Education by the Central Committee of the Chinese Communist Party and the State Council	The priority should be to deepen education system reform, promote quality education, and train new socialist constructors to meet the needs of modernization in the 21st century.

Year	Policy Document Issued	Core of the Policy
1999	Education Promotion Plan of Action for the 21st Century	The major goals of the Promotion Plan are to universalize basic education across the country, eliminate adult illiteracy, improve vocational and continuing education, and actively promote higher education.
2001	Decision on the Reform and Development of Basic Education by State Council	The Decision establishes the strategic role of basic education in socialist modernization, encourages prioritizing basic education, improves the education system, and promotes the sound and continuous development of compulsory education in rural areas.
2002	The Sixteenth National Congress of the Communist Party of China (CPC)	Education should serve the needs of modernization and the people, should be integrated with production and practices, and should train socialist constructors and successors in the all-around development of morality, intelligence, physique and aesthetics.
2004	Education Promotion Plan of Action for the 2003–2007 Period	The main contents include promotion of the development and reform of rural education and the construction of high-ranking universities and key disciplines; promotion of quality education, vocational education and training, higher education reform, employment of new graduates, the adoption of information technology in education, and the creation of a pool of highly qualified teachers and administrators; promotion of institutional innovation and management of education according to law; promotion of the sustainable, solid and rapid development of the private education system.
2010	Compendium of the National Program for Long- and Medium-Term Educational Reform and Development (2010–2020)	The essence of education reform is the reform of the responsibilities of and the establishment of educational institutions.

Source: He Dongchang, *Important Educational Documents of the People's Republic of China: 1976–1990*, Hainan Press, 1998b; He, Dongchang, *Important Educational Documents of the People's Republic of China: 1991–1997*, Hainan Press, 1998c.

3. EDUCATION SYSTEM REFORMS

The evolution of the Chinese education system has always been connected with national economic and political changes. Before 1978, education system reform was closely related to political reform; since then, education system reform has been driven by market needs as the focus of the Chinese government shifted from politics to the economy.

3.1. Education Reforms Led by Politics

In the early 1950s, the education policy of the new China held that education was national, scientific and universal in nature. It emphasized that the mission of the government was to improve people's literacy levels, groom talent for national development, and eliminate feudal, capitalist and fascist ideologies. This kind of reform was infused with political overtones. Local governments took over public and private schools, set up departments of education at various levels, and remolded the role of teachers in education. The socialist transformation of China's educational system was completed by the end of 1956.

In order to swiftly universalize elementary education, the Government Administration Council (now the State Council) issued the Decision on School System Reform in October 1951. This was the first document dealing with formal school systems since 1949, under the new socialist government. It clearly emphasized the significance of education equity. It noted that the biggest weakness of the previous school system was that cadre schools and continuing education and training programs for workers and farmers did not have a corresponding status in the educational system. The new system broke ground by integrating worker-farmer accelerated schools, literacy schools, and political schools and political training programs into the educational system, thus forming an education system with three pillars: worker-farmer accelerated education, adult amateur education, and formal education. In addition, the length of primary education was reduced from six to five years. However, due to the hastiness of the reforms, implementation of the new system was aborted after one year.

The second education reform program was the Great Leap Forward of Education, from 1958 to 1960. At that time, production in agriculture and industry increased dramatically, and the whole country was zealous in moving forward because of the successful implementation of the first five-year plan. There was a consensus worldwide that socialism was rising while capitalism was declining, after the Big Family of Socialists meeting was held in Moscow in 1957 and the first artificial satellite was launched by the Soviet Union (Yang, 2009). In 1957, Mao Zedong stated that China should make an effort to advance socialism at a higher speed and with better quality and lower cost. The Central Committee of the Chinese Communist Party and State Council pointed out the need to develop secondary and higher vocational education, with everyone eligible for higher education if they wished. Considerable progress was subsequently made (see Figures 1 and 2 on the next page). The number of middle schools increased from 11,096 in 1957 to 28,931 in 1958 and higher-level schools from 229 in 1957 to 1,289 in 1960 (Department of Planning and Finance of the Ministry of Education, 2013).

The third educational reform occurred during the Cultural Revolution. Learning from experiences during the Great Leap Forward in Education, the education system carried out the policy of "adjusting, consolidating, enriching and enhancing" articulated by the Chinese Party Central Committee and its leader Chairman Mao in 1960. The Cultural Revolution left behind several serious issues in education; namely, the principles of education had been changed radically, and educational institutions and their programs were disrupted or unstable. School-societal collaboration in education, however, became a welcome change. Figure 1 on the next page shows that the number of middle schools generally increased during these years, although the number of high education institutions decreased (see Figure 2).

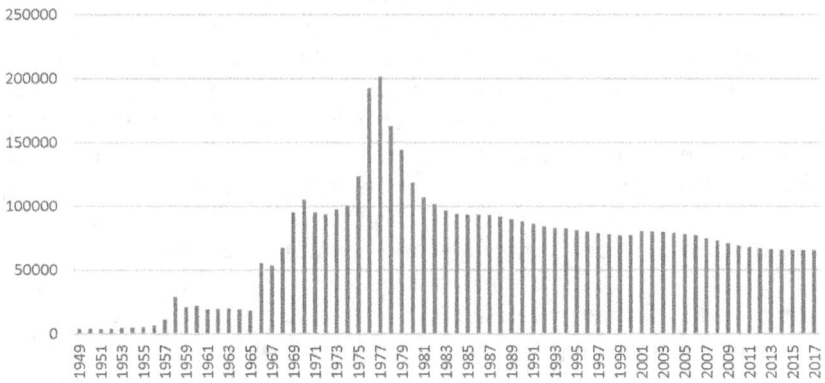

Figure 1. Number of Middle Schools (1949–2017)

Source: *Statistical Yearbook of China's Education*, 2017.

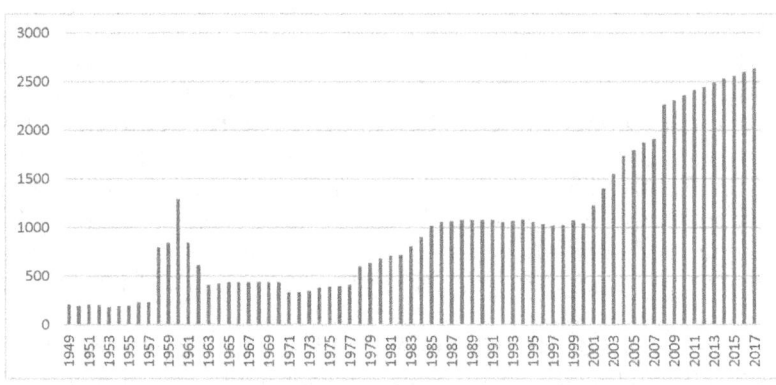

Figure 2. Number of Colleges/Universities in China (1949–2017)

Source: National Statistics Bureau, 2017.

3.2. Educational reform for economic development

Education in China got a new opportunity to develop after the government initiated economic reforms and the opening-up policy. The following are three key educational reforms that occurred in connection with the country's economic reforms.

First, the purpose of education shifted to serving socialist modernization. The 14th National Congress stated that the goal of reform was to establish a socialist market economy. Following the direction laid down for economic reform, the Guidelines for China's Education Reform and Development issued in 1993 stated that a new educational system that was consistent with the reform of the socialist market economy, political system and technological system should be established. The Guidelines set the direction for educational development. Educational reform was oriented towards a market-led education system, but increased disparities in education (Ministry of Education, 1993).

The second educational reform was reform in higher education, or the popularization of post-secondary education. In accordance with the principle of higher education popularization, enrollments in university and colleges started to increase in 1999. The Decision on Deepening Educational Reform and Promoting Quality-Oriented Education issued by the Central Committee of the Chinese Communist Party and the State Council in 1999 stated that it was important to increase the scale of middle and higher education, develop higher education in various forms, and increase the enrollment ratio of higher education from nine percent to 15 percent by 2010. As a result, the growth rate of enrollment in higher educational institutions was more than 42 percent in 1999 and 2000 (see Figure 3). This could be seen as an example of education serving the needs of economic reform. However, it led to issues such as declining quality in higher education, the irrational distribution of enrollment across various disciplines, and increased pressure on graduates in employment.

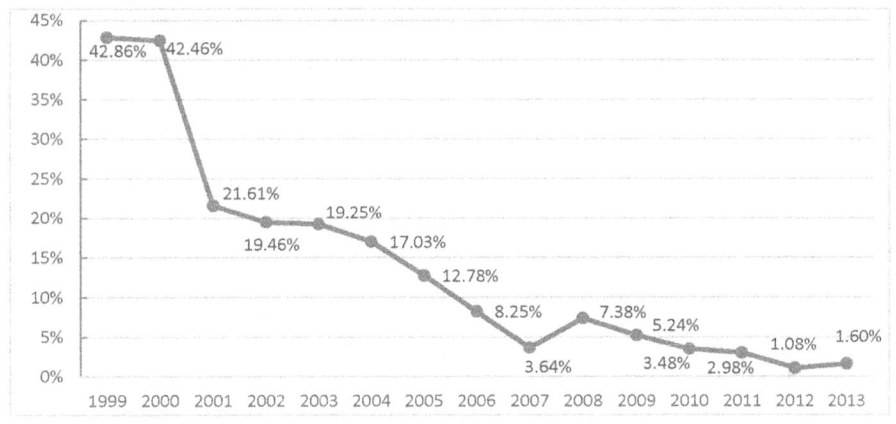

Figure 3. Growth Rate of Enrollment in General Institutions of Higher Education

Source: Statistical Yearbook of China's Education, 2014

The third education reform was the marketization of education. This process began as part of the development of the market economy in China, and was later embraced by Chinese authorities as a reality. There were some policy foundations for education marketization. In 1984, education was classified as part of the tertiary sector by the National Bureau of Statistics (Zhao and Zhang, 2004), implying that market forces were playing a role in education. The Decision on Accelerating Tertiary Sector Development by the Central Committee of the Chinese Communist Party and State Council in 1992 included education. In 1999, the Third State Conference on Education stated that education, as a knowledge sector, must be placed as a top priority on the development agenda (Chen, 2000).

3.3. Education Reform in Relation to Politics and Economic Growth

Sometimes it is difficult to distinguish whether an educational reform served political purposes or the needs of the economy. Following are two examples.

The first involved structural reform of higher education. The central government restructured universities and colleges in 1952 (Ministry of Education,

1952), adopting the same structure as the Soviet Union. After the restructuring, many high schools were closed; the number of engineering and polytechnic universities increased; the number of colleges in engineering, agriculture and forestry, as well as normal and medical schools, grew from 108 to 149 in 1952; the number of comprehensive universities decreased from 201 in 1952 to 181 in 1953 (Wang, 2009). The demands created by modernization of heavy industries were the main driver of educational reform, and disciplines related to economic development became the core focus of higher education. However, another motive of reform was to achieve political unity. The restructuring and reforms took away the autonomy of the institutions, reduced the number of students in disciplines in the humanities and social sciences such as sociology and politics, and eliminated private educational institutions.

The second example involved reform of the overall education system. In order to coordinate with decisions on economic reform and address the problems created by lack of skilled workers in key fields, the Central Committee of the Chinese Communist Party and the State Council issued the Decision on Reform of the Educational System in 1985. The Decision stated that educational institutions should be administered by different levels of government.

Specifically, high schools would be governed by the county-level governments, middle schools by township governments, and primary schools by village-level leadership. This new decentralized system shifted the responsibility and obligations from the central government to the wider public. It also increased disparities in education between urban and rural areas and between wealthy and poor regions. Meanwhile, local governments were authorized to charge extra fees, and were made responsible for developing educational programs and for implementing the nine-year compulsory education system.

4. DISCUSSION

Education policy in China has had a great impact on its citizens' lives, partly due to the great number of students enrolled in educational institutions, partly to the significant importance Chinese people deem education has in one's life. The overall prognosis for education in China is good, especially in terms of quality. There are severe disparities, however, that need to be tackled.

4.1. EDUCATION EQUITY

Education equity is the extension and embodiment of social equity in the field of education. As the basic value of modern education, equity has become one of the fundamental points of departure in formulating educational regulations and policies around the world. The pursuit of education equity dates back to ancient times. Confucius's declaration that education should be for all people without discrimination reflects this ideology. In Western philosophy, Plato was considered to be the first person to propose free elementary education, and Aristotle the first to recommend that the educational rights of free people should be protected by law.

John Rawls has proposed three principles of justice. First, each person is to have an equal right to the most extensive basic liberty compatible with a similar liberty for others; second, favorable treatment, offices, positions, and benefits should be open to any individual; third, when initial status in terms of distribution of income and wealth is unequal, the benefits of the least advantaged should be guaranteed by the method of "compensatory benefits". He illustrates two types of justice: one is egalitarian justice, which means equal treatment toward people with the same quality, a kind of horizontal and equal justice; the other is un-egalitarian justice, which means a vertical kind of justice. Meanwhile, he notes that the pursuit of social justice is to provide opportunities, benefits or compensations for disadvantaged groups in an unequal society (Yang, 2000).

Today, the right to equal education is viewed as a fundamental human right, one of the core values of modern education. The United Nations Universal Declaration of Human Rights proclaims that all children should have access to education regardless of social class, economic status, or parents' residence. In the wave of worldwide education reforms since the 1960s, education equity has become an issue of great concern. In 1960, the United Nations Educational, Scientific and Cultural Organization (UNESCO) elaborated on concepts such as equality of educational opportunity, which includes two components: elimination of discrimination and of inequality.

Discrimination refers to the phenomenon in which certain rights are denied, restricted or given only to people who are of a certain gender, race, ethnicity, and social class, or who speak a certain language, belong to a particular religion, or hold specific political opinions, with the purpose of eliminating or reducing equal treatment in areas such as education. It can be manifested in several ways: first, by depriving certain individuals or groups of opportunities of access to various levels of education; second, by restricting some individuals or groups to education at lower standards; third, by maintaining educational segregation for the benefit of some individuals or groups; and fourth, by placing some individuals or groups into situations that are not compatible with the dignity of a human being. On the other hand, inequality refers to unequal treatment among regions or groups not caused intentionally or formed on the basis of biases.

The traditional education system is beneficial to the privileged social class. Therefore, equality of educational opportunity, as the embodiment of a fundamental ideology of modern education, has a significant value orientation. The main task of modern education is to change the educational status of the disadvantaged social class; "the principle of equal opportunity means that all disadvantages, no matter [if they are] natural, economic, social or cultural, should be compensated from the education system per se" (Hummel, 1977). In the real world, education equity is always relative, and it grows gradually along with the process of economic development and social democratization. As a national public policy, education equity can be primarily achieved in several ways: implementing a compulsory education system and gradually achieving universal basic education; in terms of policy formulation and system arrangement, eliminating unfair restrictions based on biases, ideology or obtained benefits and establishing just and fair regulations; and arranging the allocation of education resources to promote the minimization of unfairness, correct the unequal distribution of education resources, and prioritize the most disadvantaged social classe' and groups' needs.

The Chinese government had been working toward education equity, especially in the early years of the new China. For instance, even during the most difficult periods in its development, activities for promoting mass education, such as teaching illiterate individuals to read and write, had never stopped. Literacy programs such as "couple learning words" demonstrated the happiness of farmers who acquired literacy during that period, something which became an important source of mass support for the Chinese communist party. At the Seventeenth National Congress of the Communist Party of China (17th NC-CPC), President Hu Jintao stressed that education is the cornerstone of national rejuvenation, and equal access to education provides an important underpinning for social equity (Hu, 2007). Moreover, he commented on the issues of education development in a great length. It has already become a common practice across countries to consider education as the fundamental condition for the realization of social equity, and as a primary goal in social development.

However, the basic premise of achieving education equity is to allocate educational resources evenly and ensure equal opportunity for everybody to access necessary education. This is precisely the problem facing education in China, one that has existed for a long time and has become increasingly severe. Unequal allocation of education resources was primarily evident in the great disparity in compulsory education between urban and rural areas; it extended to all phases and aspects of education.

The great disparity in compulsory education between urban and rural areas was inevitable, but the comprehensive education inequity of the 1990s was a result of government education policies. In other words, education policy, as a fundamental social policy, may have deviated from the right track since the 1990s. With the rapid economic and social development in China, income disparity between different regions and social groups grew quickly, and the issue of education inequality became more prominent as well.

4.2. Educational disparities in China
4.2.1. Urban-rural disparity

Urban-rural disparity is at the core of educational disparity. Urban-rural educational disparities are mainly in areas such as funding, human resources, equipment, and school buildings. The disparity in education funding, for example, is a direct indicator. From 1996 to 2002, the gap in education funding per student between urban and rural schools increased 1.80, 1.83, 1.86 and 1.82 times respectively. During the same period, the gap in education funding per student between urban and rural middle schools has increased from 1.59 times to 1.75, 1.97 and 1.94 times respectively. In fact the per-student education funding gap between urban and rural has always been in the range of 1.5 to 3 times per student (Zhang, 2009).

In terms of the three major indicators of education funding per student, budgetary education funding per student, and budgetary public funding per student, the gap between urban and rural education funding is obvious. For instance, in 2001, the average education funding per student in urban primary schools was ¥1,484 and in rural primary schools ¥798; the former was 1.86 times the latter. The average education funding per student in urban middle schools was ¥1,955, and ¥1,014 in rural middle schools; the former was 1.93 times the latter. The urban-rural gap in budgetary public funding was even larger. In 2001, the average budgetary public funding per student in urban primary schools was ¥95 and ¥28 in rural primary schools; the former was 3.39 times the latter. The average budgetary public funding per student in urban middle schools was ¥146, and ¥45 in rural middle schools; the former was 3.24 times the latter (Yuan, 2005a). Moreover, the overall qualifications of teachers in urban primary and middle schools were around 30 percent higher than those of teachers in rural schools, although the requirements for teacher's qualifications in China are relatively low. If the requirement were to go up one additional level, about 70 to 80 percent of schoolteachers in rural areas would be disqualified (Zhang et al., 2009).

Since the economic reforms took place at the end of 1970s, the enrollment rates at the three levels of education have increased from 90 percent, 60 percent and 20 percent to 99 percent, 90 percent and 53 percent respectively. In urban areas, nine-year compulsory education has been universalized, and the enrollment rate from primary school to middle school has already reached 98 percent. However, in rural areas, about 10 percent of the students were still unable or unwilling to enter middle school. The average enrollment rate of middle school across the nation was 53 percent in 2001. Enrollment rates in urban areas could be 70 percent, 80 percent or 90 percent, and in some cities the rate reached 100 percent. However, in some rural areas, the enrollment rates could be as low as 30 or 40 percent, and in those economically less developed areas, the rate could be less than 30 percent (Zhang et al., 2009).

It is a fact that students in rural areas tend to drop out of school. According to a study based on a selected sample of schools in rural areas, dropout rates varied considerably among 17 middle schools. The highest dropout rate was 74.37 percent, and the average dropout rate was about 43 percent. In many places, due to students' dropping out, there were merely three classes at the middle school level of first grade, two classes at second grade, and only one class at the third grade (Zhang et al., 2009).

Education is a key determinant of health and wellbeing. A recent study shows that education level has strong association with rural villagers' prevalence of chronic illness and their self-rated health. Lack of education resources has long-lasting consequence on rural China residents' education level and their health status, as well as their overall wellbeing (Mursal and Dong, 2018).

4.2.2. Disparity among regions
The average of all education funding indicators for basic education in eastern areas of China is about one to two times that in western areas. Among all the indicators, the gap in public education funding is the largest. Due to the implementation of the strategy of developing the western regions, education there has made good progress, but most indicators remain lowest in central China.

For example, in 2001, education funding per capita was ¥619 in the eastern region, ¥264 in the central region and ¥282 in the western regions. The top three cities in education per capita funding were Shanghai (¥1,160), Beijing (¥1,105) and Tianjin (¥722); the bottom three cities were in the provinces of Guizhou (¥176), Anhui (¥197) and Henan (¥203). The average of the top three was 5.2 times the average of the bottom three. In addition, large gaps among the eastern, central and western regions in terms of education funding per student, budgetary education funding per student and budgetary public funding per student were also evident (Yuan, 2005a).

Educational disparities within provinces are even greater than those between regions and provinces. Just as there are eastern, central and western regions in China, within each province, there are also eastern, central and western areas. In Shandong province, for example, total education investment per capita declines from east to west. The total education investment per capita in County E, a developed county in the east, is ¥440.74, but education investment per capita in County A in the west might only be ¥94.19. The former is 4.68 times the latter. In terms of compulsory education completion rate, the lowest rate was 76 percent in County A in the west, and the highest rate was 99 percent in County E in the east. The former was 23 percent less than the latter. In terms of the proportion of students enrolled in high school, the rate was only 52 percent in County A in the west, while it reached 88 percent in County E in the east (Yuan, 2005).

Due to the great economic development disparities between the eastern and western areas in Shandong Province, there is also a huge gap in teachers' salaries between the eastern and western regions. In rural primary schools, the lowest teacher's salary was ¥482 per month in County B in the west, while the highest was ¥1,771 in County E in the east. The latter is ¥1,289 higher than the former, or about 3.67 times as much. In rural middle schools, the lowest teacher's salary was ¥482 in County B in the west, and the highest was ¥1,653 in County E in the east. The latter is ¥1,171 higher than the former, or almost 3.43 times as much (Yuan, 2005a).

This type of regional disparity also exists in higher education. Since the economic reforms of the late 1970s, higher education in China has undergone tremendous transformation. By 2002, overall enrollment exceeded that in the United States. The higher education gross enrollment rate has increased from 3.4 percent in 1990 to 19 percent in 2004 (Yuan, 2005a), and to more than 40 percent in recent years (NBS, 2016). However, the popularization of higher education does not only mean the increase in the absolute number of people with higher education, but also a balanced development of higher education between regions, between towns and countries, and between social groups.

The reality, however, is that the gap among different regions in higher education development has in fact widened. Statistics relating to differences in higher education development among all provinces, cities and autonomous regions from 1978 to 2008 show that the standard deviation in the number of college students per 10,000 people across all provinces, cities and autonomous regions increased from 3 to 38.5 during that period. The number of college students per 10,000 people in Beijing, Shanghai and Tianjin was soaring, but such numbers in western provinces such as Tibet, Gansu, Qinghai, Ningxia and Guizhou were much lower than the national average. Indeed, the differences between these provinces and the national average in higher education are almost as wide as in 1953, and in some cases, they even exceed those in the year 1931 (Yuan, 2005a).

The regional disparity in higher education is also reflected in investment in education. In 2001, average spending on education funding per student among universities governed by the central government was ¥23,500.23. Among these universities, there were nine provincial level juristictions where average spending per student have reached or exceeded ¥20,000: Beijing, Tianjin, Shanghai, Jilin, Fujian, Shandong, Hubei and Guangdong. There were also 13 provinces where the average spending per student was lower than ¥20,000. Most of them located in central or western areas. The average spending per student among universities governed by local governments was ¥12,743.42. Among these universities, there were 24 provinces where the average spending per student reached or exceeded ¥10,000, and seven provinces whose average spending was lower than ¥10,000 (Shanxi, Inner Mongolia, Anhui, Jiangxi, Guizhou, Qinghai and Xinjiang), most of which were located in central or western areas of China (Yuan, 2005a).

4.2.3. Disparity among social groups
Advantaged social groups are privileged in enjoying high-quality educational resources. This is also true in China. It was estimated that more than 70 percent of students in key middle schools are from families of government officials or intellectuals, or families with high incomes. This pattern can also be observed in higher education. Father's occupation is an important factor that affects the opportunity for children to receive higher education.

According to a survey sponsored by the World Bank and the Ministry of Education of China, the proportion of university students from farmer family backgrounds declines as the ranking of the university goes up. Meanwhile, the proportion of university students from families of government officials, managers and technical staff rises as the ranking of the university goes up. This survey covered 70,000 students in 37 universities, from the enrollment years 1994 and 1997. It found that family background determines the likelihood of students entering universities.

For every student from a farming background, the families of 2.5 were workers, 17.8 were government officials, 12.8 were managers, and 9.4 were technical staff. In other words, government officials' children have the highest likelihood of attending higher education, followed by those of managers and technical personnel, while the children of farmers have the least likelihood of attending post secondary education, followed by their urban counterparts, workers' children. It also found that father's occupation not only affects the likelihood of children going on to higher education, it also influences the major that their children select. For instance, students whose families were government officials, managers or technical personnel were more likely to choose popular majors (Yuan, 2005a; National Office for Education Sciences Planning, 2006).

This disparity is caused by university tuition. Tuition for high-ranking universities and popular majors is particularly high. Tuition fees for higher education help to increase spending on educational resources and promote rapid educational development, but also present a new threat to education equity. Since 1994, universities in China have collected tuition fees. Before that, attending university was free of charge. In fact, the Chinese government used to pay living allowances to university students monthly. However, average households' incomes in China were not high, and the cost of higher education was much higher than the incomes of most households (Yuan, 2005a).

The cost of tuition inevitably affects relatively poor families' ability to support their children's higher education. In a study on the effects of tuition fees for higher education on the willingness of rural high school graduates to attend university, 53.6 percent of students surveyed indicated that tuition fees for higher education had a significant or major effect on their desire to pursue university degrees; 62 percent of female students indicated that tuition fees affected their motivation to attend university (Yuan, 2005b). National statistics from 2013 show that Ningxia rural residents with a per capita annual income of ¥6,000 cannot afford student tuition fees for arts programs, which are ¥8,000 annually. Although urban residents' per capita income in Ningxia was much higher than that of their rural counterparts—¥21,833—tuition of ¥8,000 accounts for 36.64 percent of annual income, which is obviously too high (NBS, 2015a).

The central government issued a policy regulating tuition fee practices nationwide, but it failed to contain tuition fees' increase. Although there are educational aid programs and scholarships available, poor families' children remain reluctant to attend university, leaving higher education to the children of families that can afford high tuitions.

4.2.4. Disparities among different types of education
Urban-rural disparities, regional disparities and disparities among social groups in relation to education are apparent, but disparities among different categories of education tend to be overlooked. In fact, the balanced development of different educational programs is an equally important issue in education.

4.2.4.1. Disparities between key and non-key schools
A consistent educational policy in China has been to build *key schools*. This policy has played a historical role in training talents by concentrating limited resources, but is seen as a double-edged sword. No matter the level of education, there are always differences between key and non-key schools. For instance, the difference in per student funding between key universities and non-key universities in the same location can range from ¥2,000 to over ¥7,000 (Yuan, 2005a).

Although there is no significant gap in education funding per student between key and non-key schools at the primary level, key schools also receive special funding, which is often several times the total amount of standard educational funding per student. These financial resources can improve the capability of key schools to charge fees and attract highly competent teachers.

4.2.4.2. Disparity between general and vocational education

According to research by the World Bank in 1988, the cost per student in vocational and technical schools in developing countries was about 153 percent higher than the cost in general schools. Some research finds that investment in good vocational education can be seven times that in general secondary education. However, investment in the best vocational schools is only equivalent to the investment in key secondary schools. Due to the comprehensive development of education at the high school level, the proportion of registered students in vocational schools to all registered students in the high school has been steadily declining each year since 1998. For instance, in 2003, 38.75 percent of high-school level students were enrolled in vocational schools, compared to 45.70 percent in 1990 (Yuan, 2005b). The fundamental cause for this issue lies in insufficient investment in vocational and technical education, resulting in vocational education being of inadequate quality.

4.2.4.3. Disparities between research and non-research universities

The job market demands nine engineers for every scientist, but higher education in China produces nine scientists for every engineer. This issue was raised as early as the 1980s, but has not been effectively addressed. In recent years, the Ministry of Education has reiterated that institutions for higher education should not all offer the same programs but, rather, develop their own characteristics and specialties. However, trends favoring the pursuit of higher academic qualifications and the creation and growth of research universities have continued to strengthen (Cheng and Wang, 2012).

4.2.4.4. Disparities between public and private schools

In 2003, China issued the Private Education Promotion Law, which legally defined the nature, status and function of private education. However, private education did not prosper at that time. With the subsequent rapid development of primary education, private education in China has made great progress, although the speed and strength of its progress trail that of public education and remain inadequate to meet society's needs. From 1996 to 2003, the number of registered students in public middle and high schools increased by 25,000,000, but at the same period, the number of registered students in private middle and high schools increased by over 2,500,000. In 1996, there were 21 private institutions for higher education and 1,011 public institutions in China. By April 2004, there were 1,607 institutions for higher education, of which 197 were private and 1,410 public. In 1996, the number of registered students in private institutions for higher education was 14,000, increasing to 810,000 in 2004; meanwhile, the number of registered students in public institutions increased from 3 million to 19 million. The growth in the number of registered students in public institutions was about 20 times that in private institutions (Yuan, 2005b, Cheng and Wang, 2012).

4.3. FINANCIAL BURDENS OF EDUCATION

In 1997, total education expenditures in China were ¥253.17 billion, but national fiscal spending on education, including grants from all levels of government, additional education fees, donations by enterprises, and tax reductions or exemptions for companies run by educational institutions, was only ¥186.25 billion (Ministry of Education, 1998). This means the individual student families paid a high cost for education—they effectively filled the gap between the available funding and total expenditure on education. Growth of national education funding was much slower than growth of national revenue in China. For instance, in 2000, the growth rate for the national education budget was 2.18 percentage points lower than that of national revenue. In 10 of the 12 years between 1993 and 2004, growth in national funding on education lagged growth in national revenue (Yuan, 2005b; Cheng and Wang, 2012).

In 2000, national education spending was ¥384.9 billion, including ¥91.99 billion on compulsory education in rural areas, which accounted for 23.9 percent of total education spending and 54.2 percent of total expenditures on compulsory education. However, there were 120 million students receiving compulsory education in rural areas (Kong, 2006). According to an investigation by the research center of the State Council, only two percent of education spending on compulsory education in rural areas was from the central government, while 11 percent of funding came from provincial or municipal governments, 9 percent from county-level governments, and 78 percent from township governments. Some believe that families of the rural students have been paying a high proportion of education spending (Lu, 2004).

While the Chinese education system is the fastest-growing one in the entire world, the proportion of government fiscal spending on education has not increased correspondingly. In 2005, fiscal spending on education was ¥395.159 billion, only 2.16 percent of GDP (Yuan, 2005b). It reached 4.15 percent in 2014, however (NBS, 2015b). Local governments have been using the key school system as a grey area financially. In fact arbitrary collection of fees by schools, especially in key schools, became a norm. Thus, the education expenditure burden on students' families is continually increasing. According to one survey, household expenditure on children's education exceeds that of pensions and housing, topping all family expenditures (Zhu, 2005).

4.4. Education policy trajectory
4.4.1. Education policies to date
In the early years of the New China, the education system was highly centralized. After the completion of the basic socialist transformation, the Political Bureau of the Central Committee of the Communist Party of China issued the Provision to the Issue of Delegating Power to Lower Levels in Education Authority in 1958. The decentralized system resulted in confusion in educational work and a decline in education quality, and thus the Chinese government turned to a system of centralized leadership and decentralized administration.

Since the economic reforms took place, especially after 1985, the education system's decision-making structure started to decentralize, along with a gradual reduction in funding transfers from the central government. A system of basic education based on county-level management emerged in 2001 and was completely implemented by 2006. Policy support for this system includes the following documents: the *Decision on Course Reform and Development in Basic*

Education by the State Council (2001), the *Notice on Completing the Compulsory Education Management System in Rural Areas by the State Council* (2002), the *Decision on Further Strengthening Rural Education* (2003), and the *Law on Compulsory Education* (2006). The most important educational policy issued in the 21st century is the *Compendium of the National Program for Long- and Medium-Term Educational Reform and Development* (2010–2020). The compendium stated that the core of educational reform should be the reform of the education system, since that system takes in all factors affecting the nation's education.

The decision makers in the central government have taken a balanced approach towards different levels of education so far. In some years, more policies were issued dealing with post-secondary education, while in other years there were more policies on primary education. The large number of policies reflected the desire of the central government to tackle emerging issues in a timely fashion. Government policy changes regarding primary education tend to be more complicated than ones concerning higher education, except during the initial period of higher education system reform and in 1999 when popularization of higher education took place (Xie and Chen, 2006).

The government's policy for popularization of higher education changed the landscape of Chinese education. In year 1949, the gross enrollment rate for higher education was only 0.26 percent; even before 1998, it was merely 3.4 percent. After the issuing of the policy on the expansion of university recruitment, both the admission rate and gross enrollment rate for higher education increased dramatically. The university admission rate is now over 40 percent. The number of newly recruited students is increasing each year. The total number of students in China's 2,852 higher education institutions has reached 37 million (Higher Education Evaluation Center of Ministry of Education, 2016). There is a high number of university graduates each year (see Figure 4). Finding jobs for the millions of new university graduates is a great challenge (Stapleton, 2017).

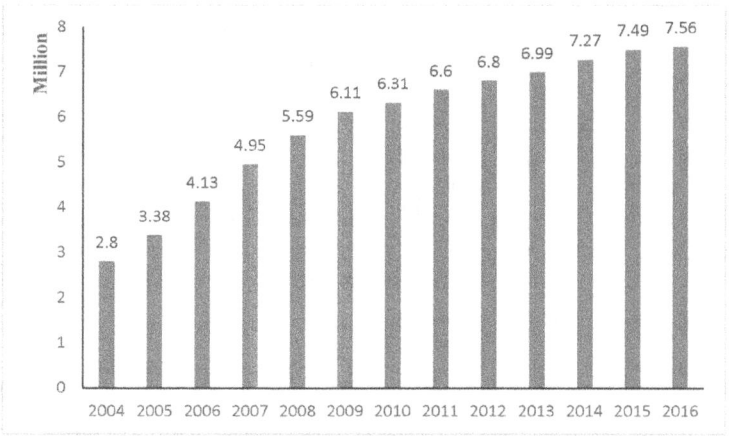

Figure 4. Graduates from Higher Education Institutions (2005–2016)

Source: National Statistics Bureau 2005–2017

4.4.2. The Future of Education in China

The latest government policy directives are set out in Premier Li Keqiang's report on March 5, 2017, when he noted the following policy areas and objectives.

First, the objective was set of making kindergarten available to all children. China will modernize its vocational education system, and the government will support the development of privately run educational institutions and ensure that they meet all standards.

Second, "families, schools, governments, and our society as a whole must together shoulder the responsibility of ensuring our children, our hope for tomorrow, are safe, healthy, and can grow up with the opportunity to reach their full potential". In particular, "education should promote the moral, intellectual, physical, and artistic development of students, and particular attention should be given to fostering all kinds of high-caliber creative talent".

Third, in order to ensure the quality of education, the government will improve the condition of poor areas' compulsory educational institutions. All schools that are providing compulsory education should comply with educational standards. The government will ensure more equal access to quality education. In particular, secondary education should be open to all.

Fourth, reform of the professional ranking system for teachers in elementary and secondary schools will be deepened.

Fifth, the average number of years of schooling received by China's working-age population will be increased to 10.8 years from the current 10.23 years. "Students from families with financial difficulties will be exempted from tuition and miscellaneous fees at regular senior high schools".

Sixth, mechanisms for funding compulsory education and improving conditions in boarding schools will be unified. A greater share of funds for public education will be allocated to the central and western regions and to remote and poor areas. The salaries and other benefits of teachers in rural areas will be increased.

Seventh, distance learning and the accessibility of quality educational resources will be expanded.

Finally, China will make efforts to develop more world-class universities and first-class programs in various academic disciplines, strengthening teaching and innovation capacity in institutions of higher learning.

From kindergarten to university and vocational education, the Chinese government has laid out a clear and promising plan for the future education system. Particularly encouraging is the attention that has been paid to education quality and equal access for all. Since education policy does not exist in a vacuum, the global trend of internationalization of education provides China both challenge and opportunity; therefore, other policy measures must be put in place to ensure these goals are achievable.

CONCLUSION

Education policy in China has gone through nearly seven decades of transformation and different phases of reform since 1949. From socialist transformation to Cultural Revolution and marketization and various reforms, the education system in China has witnessed a rapid development.

Different policies have been emphasized at different times. From the beginning of the 1980s to the end of the 20th century, the government and education agencies were more concerned with teaching activities. With the exception of only a few years, the number of policies dealing with teaching has always been much higher than the number of policies dealing with educational administration. This was a notable "Chinese characteristic" since government education departments tend to be more concerned with the overall education system and environment, and do not provide directives on teaching activities in the schools. It was a reflection of the historical characteristics of Chinese education policy that the Chinese government is seriously concerned with every aspect of education. After 1995, however, the number of policies on education administration has started to exceed those on teaching. The government has been paying more attention to macro-level educational system administration.

The total number of education policies issued each year, regardless of the subject, has fluctuated considerably over the years. There have been three peak periods for policy issuance since economic reform took place. The first peak occurred in the mid- to late 1980s, when universities were authorized to charge tuition and assign graduates to work after graduation; the second occurred in the middle 1990s, when education marketization reached its climax; the third happened at the beginning of this century, when the number of macro education policies exceeded that of teaching policies for the first time since the 1980s. This transformation clearly reflected the evolution of and changes in the Chinese government's focus regarding education issues. These three changes have had tremendous effects on the development of Chinese education, and the adverse effects of some policies, particularly those of the first two periods, still are felt today.

Education plays an important role in a society. In the human development index of the United Nations, education is a critical indicator in measuring the development of a country. In today's China, education has become a significant matter for students and their families, as well as the general public. Education disparity in China is a severe social issue deserving special attention. The consequences of education disparities are no less severe than those of income disparities. These disparities are also leading to greater social inequality. They seriously affect the entire population's wellbeing, which can impede the progress of societal advancement. In order to speed up the harmonious development of different regions and social groups, the realization of equity in education is essential.

REFERENCES

Central Committee of the Communist Party of China (1966). *The Decision on the Great Proletarian Cultural Revolution of Central Committee of the Chinese Communist Party.* Hong Qi, No. 10.

Cheng, Ying and Qi Wang (2012).Building world-class universities in Mainland China. *Journal of International Higher Education* 5(2): 67–69.

Department of Planning and Finance of Ministry of Education, China (2013). *China's Achievements in Education.* People's Press.

Dongchang, He (1998a). *Important Educational Documents of the People's Republic of China: 1949–1975.* Hainan Press.

Dongchang, He (1998b). *Important Educational Documents of the People's Republic of China: 1976–1990.* Hainan Press.

Dongchang, He (1998c). *Important Educational Documents of the People's Republic of China: 1991–1997.* Hainan Press.

Dongchang, He (2010). *Important Educational Documents of the People's Republic of China: 2003–2008.* New Century Press.

Higher Education Evaluation Center of Ministry of Education (2016, April 7). *Higher Education Quality Report.* http://www.moe.gov.cn/jyb_xwfb/xw_fbh/moe_2069/xwfbh_2016n/xwfb_160407/160407_sfcl/201604/t20160406_236891.html.

Hu Jintao (2007, October 25). *Report on the Seventeenth National Congress of the Communist Party of China.* http://www.huaxia.com/zt/tbgz/07-082/523727.html.

Hummel, Charles (1977). *Education Today for the World of Tomorrow.* UNESCO.

Kong, Shanguang (2006). Basic reason for more and more heavy burden of national education. *Guide for China's Society,* issue 6.

Li, H., et al. (2015). Unequal access to college in China: How far have poor, rural students been left behind? *The China Quarterly* 221: 185–207.

Liu, Minquan, Yu Jiantuo, Li Pengfei (2006). Analysis on issues of rising of tuition and equity of educational opportunity in higher education—based on structural and transitional vision. *Peking University Education Review,* issue 2.

Liu, Nianguo (2014). Four keywords on Mao Zedong's era: Education, medical treatment, income and housing. *Huasheng,* Vol. 1. http://hszz.voc.com.cn/view.php?tid=171&cid=8.

Lu, Xueyi (2004). Balance urban-rural development and resolve the three rural issues. *China Comment,* issue 4.

Ministry of Education of China (2014). *Case for China's Education Reform and Development.* http://www.moe.edu.cn/jyb_sjzl/moe_364/moe_902/moe_1002/tnull_9381.html.

Ministry of Education of China (2014). *China Education Yearbook, 2014,* pp.168–169.

Mursall, Adam & Weizhen Dong (2018). Education as a key determinant of health: A case study from rural Anhui, China. *Journal of Health and Social Sciences;* 3 (1): 59–74.

NBS (National Bureau of Statistics, 2015a). *2014 National Economic and Social Development Statistical Bulletin.* http://www.stats.gov.cn/tjsj/zxfb/201502/t20150226_685799.html.

NBS (National Bureau of Statistics, 2015b). *Statistics Report on the Performance of National Education Funds in 2014.* http://www.moe.edu.cn/srcsite/A05/s3040/201510/t20151013_213129.html.

NBS (National Bureau of Statistics, 2016). *Higher Education Statistics.* http://data.stats.gov.cn/.

National Institute of Education Sciences (1984). *Chronicle of Major Events Regarding Education in China (1949–1982).* Education Sciences Press.

National Office for Education Sciences Planning (2006). A review of studies on major policies regarding Chinese education in the transition period. *Forum on Contemporary Education*, issue 11.

Stapleton, Katherine (2017). China now produces twice as many graduates a year as the US. *World Education Forum*. https://www.weforum.org/agenda/2017/04/higher-education-in-china-has-boomed-in-the-last-decade.

The Standing Committee of the NPC (2006, March 3). *Compulsory Education Law of China (2006)*. http://www.edu.cn/jiao_yu_fa_lv_766/20060303/t20060303_165119.shtml.

UNESCO (1998). *World Declaration on Higher Education for The Twenty-First Century: Vision and Action*. http://www.unesco.org/education/educprog/wche/declaration_eng.htm.

Wang, Tiejun (2005). Three "red cards" in education. *China Distance Education* 3: 13–15.

Xie, Weihe & Chen Chao (2006). An analysis of the trend of policies regarding Chinese education reform and development: Research on the changes of number of policies regarding Chinese education since mid-1980s. *Research on Education, Tsinghua University*, issue 3.

Yang, Dongping (2000), Theory on education equity and its practice in China. *Oriental Culture*, issue 6.

Yang Dongping (2013). Basic feature of "seventeen-year education" in New China. *Tsinghua University's Educational Research*, issue 11.

Yuan, Zhenguo (2005a). *Balanced Development of Education: Basis for Constructing Harmonious Society, Research on Educational Development.*

Yuan, Zhenguo (2005b). Narrowing the gap: The important mission of Chinese education policy. *Journal of Beijing Normal University (Social Science Edition)*, issue 3.

Zhang, Ying, Bai Hua, & Ruan Zheng (2009). Research on regional difference of teacher's supplying in China's general high schools. Collected Papers for Colloquium of China's Educational Economics.

Zhao, Gongming, & Zhang Rongwei (2004). Reviewing and outlooking for marketization of China's education teachers. *Reading Extensively*, Issue 1.

Zhu, Liang (2005, October 31). A peasant needs 18 years' income to rear and support a college student. *Anhui Market Newspaper*.

Chapter 10
Healthcare Policy in Urban China

Weizhen Dong, Chun Chen, Li Shen

ABSTRACT

Healthcare policy in urban China since 1949 has undergone profound transformations over the years. During the first 30 years, the government took a "prevention first" approach: it built public health networks, emphasized grass-roots hygiene promotion, and provided universal healthcare coverage. The result of this approach was a miracle: it dramatically reduced mortality and rapidly increased life expectancy; it reduced or eliminated most infectious diseases, and effectively promoted social equity. Over the next 30-odd years, the government's healthcare policy changed to a market-centered approach. The government embraced market forces and started to withdraw its financial support for the healthcare system; and it began its cost-sharing strategy, which shifted the financial burden of disease to healthcare providers and individual healthcare service users. Thus, concerns that "seeking healthcare is expensive" and "seeking healthcare is difficult" became a major social issue. Of all the reforms that took place in China in the past several decades, healthcare reform has been the least successful. The Chinese public and the government are still looking for ways to improve the country's healthcare system. Hopefully, healthcare in urban China will be accessible and affordable to all in the near future.

1. INTRODUCTION

Healthcare policy is one of the most important social policies in a country. It reflects the country's key social values. The Chinese government has been issuing and implementing new healthcare policies since the founding of the People's Republic in 1949. The government has made great efforts to improve the Chinese healthcare system. Indeed, the Chinese government's policy on health and healthcare had a significant impact on the health of Chinese citizens within a short period of time, something which was hailed as a public health miracle. However, the dramatic social transformation in China that began by the end of 1970s shook the very foundation of its healthcare system. Different social groups experienced the government-led healthcare system reforms differently. The current Chinese healthcare system is still facing challenges such as cost escalation, a fragmented healthcare delivery system, and inequity in healthcare access. Obviously, the outcomes of the recent decades' healthcare reform policies are far from ideal.

This chapter provides an overview of the development of healthcare policy in urban China. It first presents a brief description of China's healthcare system during Mao's era. Then it introduces and analyzes the various stages of China's urban healthcare reforms, from 1979 to 2002 and from 2003 to 2016 respectively. The last section of the chapter discusses the challenges the Chinese urban healthcare system faces presently.

2. URBAN CHINA'S HEALTHCARE POLICY DURING MAO'S ERA (1949-1978)

2.1. Background

At the beginning of the People's Republic of China in 1949, under Mao Zedong's leadership, the Chinese socialist government viewed equity and equality as the core value of its social policy. At the First National Health Conference (1950), the Chinese government promulgated the general healthcare guidelines as "serving workers, peasants, and soldiers; prevention first; and developing both western and traditional Chinese medicine" (He, 1951). At that time, more than 85 percent of the Chinese population resided in the rural areas. It was not surprising that the guidelines emphasized the need to serve rural residents along with urban citizens. However, prior to 1965, healthcare resources had been disproportionately distributed between urban and rural China. Only 23 percent to 30 percent of the healthcare budget was allocated to rural areas, and only 20 percent to 40 percent of physicians were actively practicing in rural China (World Health Organization, 2015). Therefore, in 1965, Mao called upon the Ministry of Health to make rigorous efforts to improve the rural population's health status by training personnel and developing "barefoot doctor" programs in rural China (Zhang et al., 2003).

Planned and organized by the central government, the Chinese healthcare delivery system was established in a very short period of time. After about 20 years' development, a relatively complete healthcare system was established. The rural population gained access to basic healthcare services through cooperative medical systems (CMS) run by People's Communes, while the urban population was covered by employment-based healthcare insurance schemes, namely the Labor Insurance Scheme (LIS, *laodong baoxian*) since 1951, and the Government Insurance Scheme (GIS, *gongfei yiliao*) since 1952.

2.2. Healthcare coverage: GIS and LIS

These employment based publicly financed healthcare insurance schemes, which were established in 1951 and 1952 respectively, covered almost all urban residents. The Government Insurance Scheme (GIS), funded by the government, covered medical care expenditures for government employees (including the retired), and university students and teachers. The Labor Insurance Scheme (LIS) was funded by state-owned enterprises (SOE) and collectively owned enterprises and provided free healthcare services to enterprise employees and staff members. Moreover, family members of those covered by the LIS were entitled to at least 50 percent coverage of their total medical expenses. Since China implemented a full employment and lifetime employment policy during Mao's era, the employment-based healthcare insurance schemes covered all urban residents.

2.3. Healthcare delivery

The urban healthcare system was delivered through a four-level network that involved middle- and large-sized SOEs and urban hospitals. Middle-sized SOEs usually had their own clinics to provide free medical care, while large scale SOEs (those with more than 1,000 workers) had their own hospitals capable of providing in-patient care. Urban hospitals were responsible for the inpatient services required by employees of the middle-sized SOEs and for all services required by workers of small-sized SOEs and other urban dwellers who were not affiliated with SOEs. Operating costs, such as the salaries of healthcare personnel, were directly or indirectly funded by the government. These healthcare providers were also allowed to charge minor fees for each service to increase revenues. The below-cost fees charged for healthcare services and medicines by the healthcare providers were set under the government guidelines to ensure that healthcare services were affordable for people with low incomes. The government subsidized the hospitals' losses through financial transfers.

Matrix 1 is an example of Shanghai employees' healthcare insurance coverage. Each work unit would set aside a certain percentage of total wages as a welfare fund annually to finance healthcare expenditures incurred by the work unit's LIS beneficiaries (Dong, 2003).

Matrix 1. Shanghai employees' healthcare insurance prior to reform

Ownership	Work Unit	Healthcare Coverage	Coverage for Beneficiary	Coverage for Dependents
State	State-Owned Enterprise	Labor Insurance Scheme (LIS). Since 1951	Unlimited including prescription drugs	Yes (50%)
	State Institution	Government Insurance Scheme (GIS). Since 1952	Unlimited including prescription drugs	No
Local collective	Large-scale Enterprise/ Local Institution	Work Unit Labor Insurance Scheme	Unlimited including prescription drugs	Yes (50%)/ No (or depends on employer's financial ability)
	Small-scale Enterprise	Cooperative Healthcare	Limited before referral. Including prescription drugs	No

Source: Dong, 2003

2.4. Achievements and challenges

During this period, the Chinese people had access to preventative and basic healthcare services, which significantly improved China's national health. For example, life expectancy almost doubled (from 35 to 67.9 years), and infant mortality was slashed from 200 deaths to 34.7 deaths for every 1,000 live births. Additionally, China's maternal mortality rate dropped from 15,000 to 947 per one million births (Mai, 2009).

The establishment of the four-level public health delivery network—namely, neighborhood sanitation station and clinics, street community (*jiedao*) clinics and hospitals, district and city-level hospitals—as well as large-scale public health campaigns also played an important role in disease prevention and the improvement of the overall health of the population. The GIS and LIS effectively ensured urban employees' equal access to healthcare services.

3. URBAN CHINA'S HEALTHCARE POLICY IN THE INITIAL STAGE OF REFORMS AND OPENING-UP (1979–2002)

3.1. Background

The Third Plenary Session of the 11th Central Committee of the Communist Party of China declared Chinese society's transition from a planned economy to a socialist market economy. Subsequently, the Chinese government welcomed the market to play a role in the healthcare sector.

Aimed at tackling inefficiencies in healthcare delivery under the planned economy and to meet the healthcare demands of the public at an improved standard, the Chinese government issued a series of healthcare reform policies, which included the following measures.

First, some public healthcare facilities were privatized after the central government implemented the policy entitled "The Opinions of the Pilot Work on Strengthening Hospital Financial Management" (April 1979). After implementation of *The Report on Allowing Healthcare Practitioners to Open Their Private Medical Practice* (*guanyu yunxu geti kaiye xingyi wenti de qingshi baogao*) (August 1980), private ownership of healthcare facilities and private healthcare clinics was allowed. Private investment in new hospitals was promoted by letting private facilities charge much higher fees than those of publicly owned hospitals. Therefore, the number of healthcare institutions (and of beds in them) increased rapidly (see Figure 1).

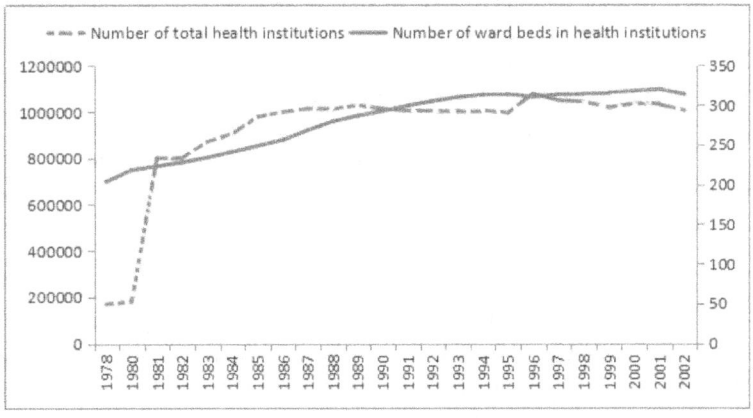

Figure 1. Healthcare institutions and beds in China, 1978–2002

Source: National Health and Family Planning Commission of the People's Republic of China, 2016

Second, the Chinese government changed its compensation mechanisms, price policies and the medical fee schedules of healthcare institutions. In 1985, the Ministry of Health issued *Report on Policy Issues in Healthcare Reform*, which emphasized decentralization. It centered on reducing the central government's funding to the healthcare sector and increasing the financial autonomy of public hospitals. Since then, the government has limited public funds for healthcare, and government financing for hospitals declined dramatically. In 1978, total health expenditure was 3.02 percent of China's GDP (National Health and Family Planning Commission of the People's Republic of China,

2016), covering only basic personnel wages and new capital investments, or about 25 percent to 30 percent of hospital expenditures (Dong, 2001). Additionally, most medical service fee schedules (e.g., physician fees and bed fees) set by the government remained low, with some being less than the actual cost of the service provided. To compensate for the financial loss in providing these services, the State Council issued *Opinions on Several Issues Related to Expanding Healthcare Services* in 1989, which allowed hospitals to charge higher prices for certain new and technology intensive procedures and, more importantly, impose a 15 percent or higher markup on the sale of prescription drugs (Chen et al., 2014). In 1992, the central government further emphasized that healthcare facilities should "rely on government subsidies for capital investment, but rely on user charges and drug sale markups for operational activities" (Ministry of Health, 1992). Therefore, drug price markups became vital for hospitals to survive financially. These policies led to a rapid increase in patients' medical expenditures.

Meanwhile, due to industrial restructuring and the reform of the employment system, many SOEs closed. Thus, many urban residents lost their jobs and healthcare insurance that attached to their jobs. The medical care coverage of the population declined sharply.

3.2. Healthcare coverage: UEBMI

In 1998, the Chinese government launched a salary-based medical savings account scheme, which is called Urban Employees' Basic Medical Insurance (UEBMI). UEBMI is a government-run mandatory program replacing LIS and GIS (Dong, 2003). The UEBMI was piloted in 1994 in Zhenjiang of Jiangsu Province and Jiujiang of Jiangxi Province (Lu, 2007). In 1996, the UEBMI expanded to 57 cities in 27 provinces (Dong, 2003), and further expanded to most cities of China in 2002, covering 69.3 million urban workers at the end of 2002 (Ministry of Labor and Social Security, 2006).

Similar to the GIS and LIS, UEBMI is an employment-based scheme. All work units (including state-owned enterprises, collective-owned enterprises, foreign-invested enterprises, private enterprises, etc.) or organizations (including government agencies, public institutions, social organizations, and private-non-profit agencies) registered in cities and municipalities must join the UEBMI scheme. The UEBMI is a medical savings account (MSA) that emulates the Singaporean healthcare system (Dong, 2006). Like the scheme in Singapore, the Chinese UEBMI is primarily financed by payroll deductions. The government mandates a fixed rate for annual premiums for the UEBMI, for example, 8 percent of payroll: employers pay 6 percent and 2 percent is deducted from employees' monthly pay. Of this 8 percent, 3.8 percent is assigned to individual medical savings accounts and 4.2 percent to a social pooling account (SPA). Risk pooling occurs at the municipal level, as opposed to the MSA, where it occurred at the work-unit level.

3.3. Healthcare delivery

The UEBMI has a deductible and also a ceiling based on the insured person's income level and age. Once the amount is exhausted, the insured person has to pay out of pocket for medical care services. The SPA is primarily used for inpatient care services and some special cases of outpatient services for catastrophic illnesses. When the out-of-pocket spending reaches 5 percent of the local average employees' annual wage, the SPA starts to cover the extra expenses until this amount reaches at a cap that is four times the local average employee's annual wage. Meanwhile, the insured patients must co-pay about 20 to 30 percent of medical care expenses.

Besides the UEBMI, China promoted a complementary employer healthcare insurance for employees, which is mainly run by private commercial healthcare insurance companies or large enterprises themselves. Additionally, government employees were covered by supplementary government insurance that deals with the situation when the UEBMI coverage cap is reached. Veterans, retired high-level cadres, and university students were still covered by GIS during this period (Liu, 2006).

3.4. ACHIEVEMENTS AND CHALLENGES

Above all, the results of healthcare reform during this period represented two sides of the same coin.

On the one hand, the reform mobilized more resources from users of healthcare services, increased overall capacity for medical care delivery, improved working conditions of the healthcare sector, and improved the efficiency of the Chinese healthcare system. The UEBMI provided the highest level of coverage extension, compared with all other social insurance schemes operating in the country (Liu & Darimont, 2013). Additionally, as a cost-sharing healthcare-insurance scheme, the UEBMI was effective in awakening users' cost awareness, which significantly reduced healthcare spending, especially during the early stage of the implementation of the new scheme.

On the other hand, neither healthcare providers nor the general public were satisfied with the new healthcare system.

The first reason was lack of government monitoring. Fee-for-service-based healthcare delivery with the markup policy described above resulted in a rapid increase in patients' medical care expenditures, and Chinese hospitals were increasingly profit-oriented in this period (Chen et al., 2014). The second reason was the weak risk-pooling capacity of the Chinese healthcare security system. Urban formal employees can enroll in UEBMI, which covered 24.5 percent of the urban population in 2015 (National Bureau of Statistics of the People's Republic of China, 2016). The low participation rate was due largely to the fact that some enterprises cannot afford or unwilling to pay their share of the UEBMI premiums, while many privately owned and foreign-invested enterprises were reluctant to pay premiums for their young employees.

Additionally, UEBMI had a negative impact on equity in healthcare service access. Usually poorer people have a higher risk of ill-health and greater healthcare needs; however, the cost-sharing level of UEBMI is the same for everyone regardless of income (Dong, 2003). Further, the different healthcare needs of different populations were covered by the medical savings accounts (MSAs) under the UEBMI. In Shanghai in 2001 it required about three working persons' healthcare insurance fund payments to cover one retiree's healthcare costs in 2001 (Dong, 2006). Because of lack of risk pooling, the MSAs were more like bank accounts specifically designated for enrollees' medical care costs than an insurance scheme (Dong, 2008).

Moreover, different social groups receive different healthcare insurance benefits, and some groups are privileged over other groups. Matrix 2 illustrates the different public healthcare programs during this period in Wenzhou City, Zhejiang Province.

Matrix 2. Wenzhou's healthcare insurance programs/scheme

Social groups	Healthcare insurance programs/schemes	Benefit package
Bureau-chief-and-higher-ranking officials and retirees from these posts, and revolutionary veterans	Government Insurance Scheme (GIS)	Unlimited coverage of 100 percent medical care expenditures including prescription drugs, and it covers 80 percent of medical care expenditures of their dependents who do not have regular incomes
University and college students	University and college students Insurance Scheme	Covers 80 percent of medical care expenditures
Full-time employees in standard employment situations	Urban Employees' Basic Medical Care Insurance (UEBMI)	It covers 75 percent to 92 percent of medical care expenditures ranging from ¥10,000 to ¥40,000
Retirees	Urban Employees' Basic Medical Insurance (UEBMI)	It covers 87.5 percent to 96 percent of medical care expenditures ranging from ¥10,000 to ¥40,000
Employees in non-standard employment arrangements	None	No medical care coverage by any social healthcare insurance programs/scheme
Rural-urban migrants	None	No medical care coverage by any city-based social healthcare insurance programs/scheme

Source: The Wenzhou Municipal Labor and Social Security Bureau.
Note: All the above insurance programs were to be implemented in the designated medical care institutions.

The above-mentioned reasons together caused the burden of out-of-pocket payments to increase significantly. Out-of-pocket payments rose from 20.4 percent of total healthcare expenditures in 1978 to reach a historic high of 60 percent in 2001. Meantime, in 2001 the government's share accounted for only 16 percent of total health expenditures (National Health and Family Planning Commission of the People's Republic of China, 2016). Therefore, unaffordable medical care costs and heavy financial burdens caused by disease became a major social issue.

Obviously, the healthcare reform in this period had exacerbated healthcare access disparities among different social groups.

4. URBAN CHINA'S HEALTHCARE POLICY IN THE PERIOD OF DEEPENING REFORM (2003–)

4.1. Background

The past two decades have witnessed China's economic take-off; however, the Chinese healthcare system has not kept pace with economic development (Yu, 2015). The turning point came in 2003, with the outbreak of severe acute respiratory syndrome (SARS), when the central government not only started to tackle the challenge of public health emergencies, but also became aware of the overall urgency of healthcare issues. Healthcare access no longer was seen as simply an individual issue. The Chinese government began to make efforts to resolve the problems caused by its healthcare policies and reforms, such as the unclear roles of the market and the government, uneven distribution of healthcare resources between urban and rural areas, inequality in healthcare access between different social groups, and low levels of healthcare awareness.

In 2005, Ge and colleagues from the State Council published a research report on China's healthcare reforms, which declared bluntly that they had been a failure (Ge et al., 2005). This was not the first publication to criticize healthcare reforms in China, as Dong had done a study and drew the same conclusion on this topic earlier (Dong, 2003; Dong 2004); but Ge et al.'s report carried much heavier weight, since the authors work with the State Council. This report attracted special attention and helped to push forward new actions around healthcare reform. In September 2006, the central government established a multi-ministerial coordinating team to promote a new round of healthcare reform (Chen, 2006). In October 2008, proposals for new healthcare reform were publicly released through the internet to elicit comments and suggestions (Chinese Health Reform Coordinating Team, 2008).

In March 2009, the Chinese central government issued documents setting out detailed policies for new urban healthcare system reforms (see Box 1). Of these, "Opinions on Deepening Health System Reform," issued by the Central Committee of the CPC and the State Council, set the aim of establishing universal health coverage by 2020 (The State Council, 2009). As this policy document stressed, the basic healthcare delivering system must be clearly defined as a public good that should be equally accessible to all Chinese citizens. Since then, a ¥850 billion (about US$125 billion) reform plan has been launched. Additionally, this policy document clarified the reform measures, including expanding healthcare insurance coverage, strengthening the capacity of the delivery system, establishing an essential medicine system, expanding public healthcare services, and reforming the public hospitals.

In February 2010, the State Council promulgated "Guiding Opinions on Pilot Public Hospitals Reform" (The State Council, 2010). Public hospitals in China have been facing great challenges in recent decades, have been consuming the majority of healthcare resources, and they drive the rising of medical care expenditures high in recent decades.

In March and October of 2012, the State Council successively issued the "Implementing Plan of Deepening the Healthcare Reform in the 12th Five-Year Plan Period" (The State Council, 2012a) and "The 12th Five-Year Plan for Healthcare Sector Development" (The State Council, 2012b). It proposed a

> Box 1. Recent Policies on Urban Healthcare System Reform
>
> 1. Opinions on Deepening Healthcare System Reform, The State Council (Zhongfa) [2009] No. 6, March 17, 2009
>
> 2. Implementation Plan of Main Areas of Healthcare System Reform in the Near Future (2009–2011), The State Council (Guofa) [2009] No. 12, March 18, 2009
>
> 3. Guiding Opinions on Pilot Public Hospitals Reform, The General Office of the State Council (Guobanfa) [2010] No. 6, February 11, 2010
>
> 4. Guiding Opinions on Establishing a General Practitioner System, The State Council (Guofa) [2011] No. 23, November 27, 2011
>
> 5. Implementing Plan of Deepening the Healthcare Reform in the 12th Five-Year Plan period, The State Council (Guofa) [2012] No. 11, March 14, 2012
>
> 6. Opinions on Consolidating and Improving Essential Medicine System and New Operating Mechanism, The General Office of the State Council (Guobanfa) [2013] No. 14, August 21, 2013
>
> 7. Some Opinions on Promoting Healthcare Service Industry, The State Council (Guofa) [2013] No. 40, September 28, 2013
>
> 8. Guiding Opinions on Pilot Comprehensive Reform of Urban Public Hospitals, The General Office of the State Council (Guobanfa) [2015] No. 38, May 17, 2015
>
> 9. Some Opinions on Integrating the Urban and Rural Residents Basic Medical Insurance System, The State Council (Guofa) [2016] No. 3, January 12, 2016
>
> 10. The Nation's 13th Five-Year Plan on Deepening the Medical and Healthcare System Reform, The State Council (Guofa) [2016] No. 78, December 27, 2016

series of milestones to be reached by the end of the five-year period, namely: to establish and improve the basic healthcare system covering urban and rural residents; to realize universal coverage for basic health insurance; to significantly improve the accessibility, quality, efficiency of healthcare service and to significantly increase patients' satisfaction; to significantly reduce the economic burden on patients receiving healthcare services; to gradually narrow the gaps in the distribution of regional healthcare resources and population health status; and to increase life expectancy by one year.

In May 2015, the "Guiding Opinions on Pilot Comprehensive Reform of Urban Public Hospitals" was issued by the General Office of the State Council (The State Council, 2015a). This policy document provides directions for the ongoing urban public hospital reform, including: replacement of the current profit-driven model, reduction of patients' medical care expenditures, achievement of independent and effective hospital management, establishment of appropriate remuneration mechanisms to motivate medical care staff, and mitigation of the unequal distribution of medical care resources.

This reform clarified the government's role in healthcare, especially in the provision of public goods and in promotion of equity. The Chinese government adopted various integrated strategies to achieving its goals, such as increasing the public funding of healthcare expenditures to 30 percent.

4.2. HEALTHCARE INSURANCE SCHEMES: URBMI, UEBMI, MFA, AND CMS

Due to the complexity of the Chinese healthcare system, government think tanks from the Research Centre of State Council for Development suggested building two complementary systems together: a basic healthcare system and social healthcare insurance system. The purpose of the basic healthcare system is to add healthcare insurance and medical care assistance to the existing healthcare system. The aim of social healthcare insurance is to cover severe, cost-intensive illnesses, the expense of which will not be covered by the basic care system.

Then a new vision of a three-tier healthcare system was put forward during this period (Chen et al., 2015). The first tier is the Social Medical Assistance System. It was designed to build a safety net for rural and urban vulnerable groups who lack labor power, family support, or other income sources. Under this system these vulnerable individuals can partly delay or forgo payments for medical procedures through the support of state and local authorities.

The second tier is the Social Basic Health Insurance System. It was designed to guarantee basic medical care services for the vast majority of people covered by different standardized tax-funded basic healthcare insurance schemes (including URBMI, UEBMI and NRCMS).

The third tier is the Supplementary Medical Security System. It was designed to meet higher-level medical care needs (including commercial or private healthcare insurance and other forms of supplementary medical care insurance).

Among urban Chinese residents, the healthcare system would encompass the medical care financial assistance program (belonging to the first tier), URBMI and UEBMI basic healthcare insurance for urban residents and employees (belonging to the second tier), and catastrophic medical care schemes (belonging to the third tier).

This "Multi-level Healthcare Security System with Chinese Characteristics" is represented graphically in Figure 2.

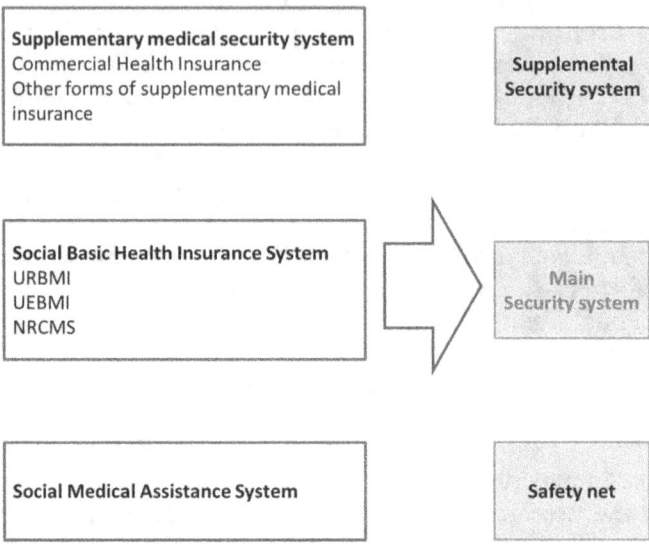

Figure 2. Multi-level Healthcare System with Chinese Characteristics

4.2.1. Urban Resident Basic Medical Insurance (URBMI)

In July 2007 the central government conducted the pilot of the URBMI program in 79 cities, and continued to expand the pilot in 2008. In 2009, more than 80 percent of cities in China had implemented the URBMI, and it was promoted and implemented nationwide in 2010. The launch of URBMI was a crucial step in closing China's medical care insurance coverage gap. University/college students, pre-school/primary/secondary school students, as well as the unemployed and disabled were all eligible to enroll in the URBMI, and the enrollment is voluntary.

According to data from the National Health and Family Planning Commission of the People's Republic of China (2016), the participation rate in URBMI in 2010 had reached 32.26 percent. By the end of 2015, 665.70 million or 48.43 percent of the urban residents participated in URBMI (see Matrix 3).

The funding of the URBMI is covered by both the enrollee and by government subsidies (including central and local governments' subsidies) on a 30 percent/70 percent split (He & Wu, 2016). During the pilot phase in 2007, the insured person received an annual subsidy of at least ¥40 from the government. The subsidy was doubled in 2008. According to data from the Office of the State Council, subsidies from central and local government budgets amount to ¥240 per capita; and between 2013 and 2016, the subsidies from central and local government budgets reached ¥280, ¥320, ¥380, and ¥420 respectively. Certain groups, such as children and students with severe diseases or disabilities, urban poor aged 60 years and over, and residents living in poverty-stricken areas can receive additional subsidies from local and the central governments. It is a pay-as-you-go based insurance. There are no URBMI individual medical savings accounts, and the URBMI's coverage is much lower than that of Urban Employees' Basic Medical Insurance (UEBMI).

Matrix 3. 2010–2015 Medical Insurance Participation among Urban Residents (million)

Insurance Type	2010		2011		2012	
	No.	%	No.	%	No.	%
URBMI	432.63	32.26	473.43	35.14	536.41	39.62
UEBMI	237.35	17.70	252.27	18.72	264.86	19.56
Total	669.98	49.96	725.70	53.86	801.27	59.18

Insurance Type	2013		2014		2015	
	No.	%	No.	%	No.	%
URBMI	570.73	41.94	597.47	43.68	665.70	48.43
UEBMI	274.43	20.17	283.25	20.71	288.93	21.02
Total	845.16	62.11	880.72	64.39	954.63	69.45

Local governments determine the annual upper and lower limits for URBMI, according to the principle that "spending is based on revenue (*Yi Shou Ding Zhi*)". A majority of URBMI benefit packages cover only a proportion of cost for inpatient care, while an increasing number of Chinese cities and counties have expanded their benefit packages to include outpatient care, although in most cases these are outpatient treatments for specific chronic illnesses or severe diseases.

4.2.2. Urban Employees' Basic Medical Insurance (UEBMI)
As in the earlier stage of reform period, the UEBMI continues to cover urban employees and retirees. According to the National Health and Family Planning Commission of the People's Republic of China, by the end of 2015, UEBMI covered 288.93 million urban employees, accounting for about 37.5 percent of total urban population (National Health and Family Planning Commission of the People's Republic of China, 2016).

4.2.3. Medical Financial Assistant Program (MFA)
Besides the URBMI and UEBMI, Medical Financial Assistance program (MFA) emerged for the poor in rural and urban areas in Shanghai in early 2001. The medical assistance schemes piloted in Shanghai covered poor households, and its financing was shared by various levels of government. The governments' civil affairs department administers the schemes. Eligibility was limited to those who are living under poverty while having a major illness such as uremia, mental illness or cancer, and having difficulty paying their medical expenses (Xu et al., 2008).

The goal of the MFA was broadly defined as protecting poor households from getting poorer because of the burden of illness. In urban areas, those who do not participate in the UEBMI and have difficulty paying for healthcare, as well as those living in poverty or other difficult situations, can apply for assistance from MFA (Liu & Darimont, 2013). Additionally, the MFA also funds premiums for vulnerable groups, enabling them to enroll in the NRCMS (rural) or URBMI (urban). With the help of MFA, 12.8 million poor residents accessed URBMI by the end of 2009 (Barber & Yao, 2010).

4.2.4. Catastrophic Medical Scheme (CMS)

In June 2014, a national healthcare working conference held by the Ministry of Health announced that upcoming healthcare reform would focus on insurance for catastrophic illness. The pilot program for urban residents' catastrophic illness insurance has developed very rapidly since 2013. It is estimated that at least 50 percent of medical care expenditure should be covered by this scheme, and the number of catastrophic illnesses covered will be expanded gradually. Unlike the NRCMS and the URBMI schemes that are administered by the government, commercial insurance companies manage the catastrophic medical care scheme. The catastrophic medical scheme has been piloted since August 2015 (State Council, 2015b).

4.3. Healthcare delivery

The compensation plan of the URBMI differs substantially across various cities in China, largely depending on the financial capacity of the local government. Here we take Wenzhou in Zhejiang Province as an example to illustrate the provisions of the URBMI scheme in 2015.

1. Eligibility: 1) Unemployed urban residents age over 18; 2) Severely disabled residents aged 18 and over; 3) Residents aged 18 and under but not attending school; and 4) Primary and middle school students.
2. Financing: Subsidies from central and local government budgets amount to ¥850 per capita, and individual participants pay ¥850 per year.
3. Benefit package (see Matrix 4):

Matrix 4. Benefit package of URBMI in Wenzhou, Zhejiang Province in 2015

Level of Hospital	Outpatient	Inpatient / Outpatient for chronic or severe disease	
	Compensation rate (%)	Deductible (Yuan)	Compensation rate (%)
Primary hospital	50	300	90
Secondary hospital	40	400	80
Tertiary hospital	35	700	75
Ceiling (Yuan)	1500	200000	–

Source: Wenzhou Municipal Labor and Social Security Bureau

5. DISCUSSION

An aging population, environmental and lifestyle changes, medicalization of society and healthcare services' high costs have led to rising healthcare expenditures. How to make full use of national, societal, and individual resources to optimize the healthcare insurance system, and how to make the healthcare security system sustainable, are the challenges facing the Chinese government. In order to meet these challenges, from 2003 onward, the Ministry of Health formulated a series of healthcare reform policies. Some policies have been proven effective, in particular the achievement of universal healthcare insurance coverage in 2011(Yu, 2015), as well as gradually establishing a national essential medicines system, advancing public hospital reform, improving the primary care system, and increasing equal access to and availability of public healthcare services (World Bank Group, World Health Organization, & National Health and Family Planning Commission of the People's Republic of China, 2016). However, China still faces daunting issues in healthcare. Meanwhile, the effectiveness of most of the healthcare reforms has been questioned.

5.1. EQUAL ACCESS FOR ALL

A well-rounded social security system guarantees equal access to healthcare for all. At the end of 2014, basic medical insurance coverage was provided to more than 95 percent of urban and rural residents (Information Office of the State Council, 2015). However, healthcare access inequality is still China's social reality, because different social groups are eligible for different healthcare insurance schemes—with full coverage for retired and on-the-post high-ranking officials and different levels of limited coverage for other groups (Dong, 2008). The Chinese healthcare system needs to address inequality in healthcare access.

First, because of regional segmentation, China's healthcare insurance system differs between urban and rural areas. Usually premiums for UEBMI are about 10 times higher than for URBMI and NRCMS (Yip et al., 2012). Therefore, despite increasingly broad healthcare insurance coverage, the Chinese government is still concerned about imbalances in fairness, accessibility and affordability of healthcare services between urban and rural residents (Wang et al., 2014). Since 2016, China's central government has taken steps to gradually integrate the URBMI and the NRCMS with the goal of establishing a unified healthcare insurance system (The State Council, 2016b). Furthermore, China's central government is making efforts to unify basic healthcare insurance at the provincial level and provide reimbursement for insured patients at levels of up to 75 percent, according to the nation's 13th Five-Year Plan on Deepening Medical and Healthcare System Reform (The State Council, 2016a). It is expected to set up a new integrated healthcare insurance system by 2020; prior to that, equality of benefit coverage across different insurance programs cannot be easily addressed.

Second, in the context of rapid urbanization and large-scale migration, improving portability of insurance coverage for the rural-urban migrant population is an urgent issue that needs to be resolved. China had approximately 286.52 million migrant workers at the end of 2017 (The State Council, 2018), most of them enrolled in NRCMS, which has much lower coverage than do URBMI and UEBMI. Migrant workers have to seek healthcare in the city, then go back to their home town or home village to get reimbursement. Because of the low reimbursement rate, many cannot afford the relatively high cost of healthcare in the cities they reside, which significantlys affect the accessibility and affordability of healthcare services for them. Aiming to tackle this problem, cities like Shenzhen have been experimenting with a pilot measure that allows migrant workers to enroll in either URBMI or UEBMI (Shenzhen Human Rresources and Social Security Bureau, 2015).

5.2. Improving the Effectiveness of the Healthcare System

In China, the structure and function of the healthcare delivery system have not changed much, even though the healthcare needs have changed over time. The imbalanced healthcare resource distribution among different regions and different levels of healthcare facilities is a severe issue in China, which affects healthcare access of citizens. Due to the availability of resources, most residents do not trust primary healthcare institutions—for example, the lowest level hospitals—and instead seek care in large, tertiary-level hospitals. This causes crowding and long waiting times in the large hospitals, and results in the resources of big hospitals being wasted in treating minor ailments. Without a high-quality and cost-effective network of community healthcare institutions, healthcare costs and the cost of healthcare insurance will continue to increase.

In order to effectively allocate healthcare resources, the government needs to transfer more funds into the public healthcare sector. Most importantly, the government should further reform the hierarchical management of healthcare resources and especially encourage quality improvement in primary healthcare institutions. Meanwhile, the healthcare insurance schemes should establish effective incentive mechanisms to promote primary healthcare utilization. An improved healthcare insurance system can encourage rational healthcare-seeking behavior in patients as well.

5.3. Controlling Cost and Improving Efficiency

One of the aims of recent healthcare reforms has been to establish universal medical care coverage in China. With the advent of universal medical insurance coverage, controlling the rapid increase in medical care costs is becoming a key issue. Although a number of relevant policies such as the "zero-profit policy" have been launched to address this issue, the effects of reform are so far not obvious. An increasing number of studies advise Chinese policymakers to use healthcare insurance schemes as a powerful tool to control healthcare expenditures, on the grounds of improving healthcare quality and efficiency (Chen et al., 2016; Yu, 2015).

Cost containment is a particularly challenging issue for the Chinese healthcare system as it currently stands. Chinese local or municipal governments usually hold the power to formulate their local healthcare policy and push forward reforms, which has created differing management measures for healthcare insurance funds among different local governments. All these lead to disparities in allocating regional healthcare funds. Challenges such as how to protect high-risk populations, how to control healthcare expenditure, how to gradually merge different types of health insurance plans and payments, how to implement unified and standard operational processes, and how to improve the efficiency with which funds are used—all need to continue to be addressed by the Chinese government in the years ahead.

6. CONCLUSION

China is experiencing rapid economic growth and also rapid reforms and innovations in its healthcare system. However, issues such as population aging and high prevalence of chronic disease have become more acute. At the same time, once the Chinese healthcare system became market-oriented in recent decades, the healthcare sector devoted more attention and resources to high-tech medical treatments than preventive care. Therefore, the cost of medical care continuously increases. Eventually, hospitals implemented measures to generate profits from patient care, which greatly diminished people's confidence in the public healthcare delivery system.

The core values for Chinese healthcare policy are protecting people's right to healthcare, ensuring social equality, and making sure the healthcare system is sustainable. The government needs to clearly identify the responsibility and accountability of the government itself as well as public hospitals and physicians, and make the public interest and its population's wellbeing a high priority. Since the central government provides the principal guidelines of the new policy for the local provinces and municipalities to design their own policy measures depending on their own situation and their local healthcare policy goals, the central government should therefore find a way to control the significant regional differences and gaps. New healthcare policy must take a comprehensive view of all elements, not only financial support, theoretical foundations, and specific reform plans, but also the overall management of healthcare delivery including drug price and drug supply. The road ahead for Chinese healthcare system reform remains long and difficult, but we expect a nation with a glorious past in public health and healthcare will learn from its setbacks and continue to improve its healthcare system.

REFERENCES

Barber, S. L. & Yao, L. (2010). Health insurance systems in China: a briefing note. *World Health Report*.

Chen, C., et al. (2016). Effect of the new maternity insurance scheme on medical expenditures for caesarean delivery in Wuxi, China: A retrospective pre/post-reform case study. *Frontiers of Medicine*: 1–8.

Chen, C., et al. (2014). Is the prescribing behavior of Chinese physicians driven by financial incentives? *Social Science & Medicine* 120: 40–48.

Chen, X. (2006). Chinese health reform coordinating team: Establish and run. *China's Health Industry* 12: 47.

Chen, Y. (2009). The implementation of the "three vertical and three horizontal" medical security system in China. Retrieved from http://theory.people.com.cn/GB/49154/49156/9094750.html.

Chinese Health Reform Coordinating Team (2008, October 14). Draft Proposal of Deepening Health System Reform.

Dong, W. (2003). Healthcare-financing reforms in transitional society: A Shanghai experience. *Journal of Health, Population and Nutrition*, 223-234.

Dong, W. (2004). Reform of the health care financing system in Shanghai. *China Health Economics* 8: 27-30.

Dong, W. (2006). Can health care financing policy be emulated? The Singaporean medical savings accounts model and its Shanghai replica. *Journal of Public Health* 28(3): 209-214.

Dong, W. (2008). Cost containment and access to care: The Shanghai health care financing model. *The Singapore Economic Review* 53(1): 27-41.

Ge, Y., et al. (2005). Reflections on Chinese healthcare system reforms. *China's Development Review* (A01): 1-14.

He, A. J. & Wu S. (2016). Towards universal health coverage via social health insurance in China: Systemic fragmentation, reform imperatives, and policy alternatives. *Applied Health Economics and Health Policy*: 1-10.

He, C. (1951). The summary report of the First National Health Conference. *Journal of Traditional Chinese Medicine* (1): 8-15.

Information Office of the State Council (2015). *White Paper: Progress in China's Human Rights in 2014*. http://www.china.org.cn/chinese/2015-06/08/content_35765892.htm.

Liu, D. & Darimont B. (2013). The health care system of the People's Republic of China: Between privatization and public health care. *International Social Security Review* 66(1): 97-116.

Liu, T. (2006). The corner which is forgotten by healthcare reform. *Med J Chin People Health* 18(6): 224-226.

Lu, X. (2007). *Social Construction: The World's Experiences and the Chinese Road*. Shanghai: Shanghai People's Publishing House.

Mai, Q. (2009). *1949-1978 Traditional Chinese Healthcare Mode*. http://www.china.com.cn/news/zhuanti/09dlms/2009-09/30/content_18636976.htm.

Meng, Q., et al. (2015). Consolidating the social health insurance schemes in China: Towards an equitable and efficient health system. *The Lancet* 386(10002): 1484-1492.

Ministry of Health (1992, September 23). *Opinions on Deepening Health System Reform*. chinalawedu.

Ministry of Labor and Social Security (2006). *China Labor and Social Security Yearbook, 2006*. Beijing: China Statistics Press.

National Bureau of Statistics of the People's Republic of China (2016). *China Statistical Yearbook, 2015*. Beijing: China Statistics Press.

National Health and Family Planning Commission of the People's Republic of China (2016). *Chinese Yearbook of Health Statistics, 2015*. Beijing: People's Health Press.

Shenzhen Human Rresources and Social Security Bureau (2015). *Implementing Plan of New Migrant Workers' Medical Insurance Policies*. http://www.xingyao5.com/yiliaobaoxian/20150924/4908.html.

The State Council (2009). *Opinions on Deepening Health System Reform*. http://www.gov.cn/test/2009-04/08/content_1280069.htm.

The State Council (2010). *Guiding Opinions on Pilot Public Hospitals Reform*. http://www.gov.cn/ztzl/ygzt/content_1661148.htm.

The State Council (2012a). *Implementing Plan of Deepening the Healthcare Reform in the 12th Five-Year Plan Period*. http://www.gov.cn/zwgk/2012-03/21/content_2096671.htm.

The State Council (2012b). *The 12th Five-Year Plan for Health Sector Development*. http://www.gov.cn/xxgk/pub/govpublic/mrlm/201210/t20121019_65645.html.

The State Council (2015a). *Guiding Opinions on Pilot Comprehensive Reform of Urban Public Hospitals*. http://www.gov.cn/zhengce/content/2015-05/17/content_9776.htm.

The State Council (2015b). *Opinions on the Implementation of Urban and Rural Catastrophic Medical Scheme*. http://www.gov.cn/zhengce/content/2015-08/02/content_10041.htm.

The State Council (2016a). *The Nation's 13th Five-Year Plan on Deepening the Medical and Healthcare System Reform*. http://www.gov.cn/zhengce/content/2017-01/09/content_5158053.htm?gs_ws=weixin_636195785413303350&from=timeline&isappinstalled=0.

The State Council (2016b). *Opinions on Integrated Urban and Rural Medical Assistance System*. http://www.gov.cn/zhengce/content/2016-01/12/content_10582.htm

Wang, X., et al. (2014). Integration of rural and urban healthcare insurance schemes in China: An empirical research. *BMC Health Services Research* 14 (1): 1.

World Bank Group, World Health Organization, & National Health and Family Planning Commission of the People's Republic of China (2016). *Deepening Health Reform in China: Building High-Quality and Value-Based Service Delivery*. World Bank Publications.

World Health Organization (2015). *People's Republic of China Health System Review*. Manila: WHO Regional Office for the Western Pacific.

Xu, Y., et al. (2008). Medical financial assistance in rural China: Policy design and implementation. *Studies in Health Services Organization & Policy* 23: 295–317.

Yip, W. C.-M. et al. (2012). Early appraisal of China's huge and complex health-care reforms. *The Lancet* 379(9818): 833–842.

Yu, H. (2015). Universal health insurance coverage for 1.3 billion people: What accounts for China's success? *Health Policy* 119(9): 1145–1152.

Zhang, J., et al. (2003). The development, status and legislative suggestions of rural doctors. *Chinese Health Management* 179(5): 299–300.

Chapter 11
Healthcare Policy in Rural China

Weizhen Dong, Qicheng Jiang, Shanfa Yang, Lidan Wang, Zehan Pan

ABSTRACT

This chapter reviews the development of healthcare in rural China and illustrates the evolution of the Chinese rural healthcare system since the establishment of the People's Republic of China in 1949. Rural China's successful three-tier healthcare network and its numerous "barefoot doctors" were recognized as public health miracles in a period of limited resources and vast population. The system deteriorated rapidly after China began its economic reform in 1978. Privatization of land made public services a thing of the past in rural China.

In recent years, government-led healthcare reforms aimed to improve healthcare access and make the healthcare system more effective. However, there are many challenges facing rural residents as well as their healthcare providers, including aging villagers' healthcare and overall wellbeing, especially that of elders living alone; availability of healthcare resources—human resources and resources allocated to village- and township-level primary care in particular; and healthcare accessibility and affordability for all. Healthcare reforms in Anhui Province in central China are presented as an example.

1. INTRODUCTION

China has a large proportion of its population living in rural areas. Even after decades of massive rural-urban migration, in 2017, 576.61 million people were rural residents, which was 41.48 percent of the nation's total population. Therefore, healthcare reform and healthcare access is very important for rural China. In fact, the Chinese healthcare system has changed greatly since the establishment of the People's Republic of China in 1949. As in many other countries, healthcare in rural areas remains a major challenge. During Mao's years, grassroots "barefoot doctors" made a tremendous difference in improving China's rural residents' health status. Market reforms and major social transformations including changes in demographics and household structures have created challenges for rural healthcare reform.

The historical development of the Chinese rural healthcare system can be divided into three stages: from 1949 until the beginning of economic reform in 1978; from 1978 to the new healthcare reform in 2009; and from 2009 to the present. This chapter examines the evolution of the Chinese healthcare system, its main policies and reforms. Anhui Province's experiences and lessons are presented for a better understanding of regional and local scenarios.

2. HEALTHCARE POLICY DEVELOPMENT IN RURAL CHINA (1949–1978)

Before the establishment of the People's Republic of China in 1949, there were few healthcare institutions in rural China. Only a few local healthcare workers schooled in traditional Chinese medicine were serving rural residents. After

1949, the new Chinese government made enormous efforts to improve the health status of the its people and achieved great progress in building the rural healthcare system. Many healthcare institutions were established, even in rural towns and villages, and nearly all highly prevalent infectious diseases were eliminated or brought under control. Programs for hygiene and health protection were introduced even in the most remote areas. The communes in rural China provided healthcare through a three-tier network that was managed and financed by the local governments.

The cooperative medical system (CMS), which was part of the people's commune system and was financed by the commune's welfare funds, organized the well-known "barefoot doctors" and provided medical care services to the rural population.

On June 26, 1965, Minister of Health Qian Xinzhong reported to Mao Zedong on his work. He said that there were more than 1.4 million healthcare workers in China, but 80 percent of senior medical care personnel were working in urban areas, 70 percent of them in big cities; 20 percent in counties and townships; and only 10 percent in rural areas. Meanwhile, rural areas accounted for only 25 percent of healthcare expenditures, urban areas for 75 percent. Mao was outraged after learning these figures; he told Minister Qian: "The focus of our healthcare mission should be put in the countryside! ... We should train a large number of medical doctors who our rural regions can afford, and they will serve our rural residents."

Subsequently, Mao advocated short-term training programs in primary care and public health, such as antiviral treatmens and prenatal care, to meet the demands of rural areas, especially poor areas. The number of barefoot doctors educated in these short-term programs grew rapidly. In the summer of 1968, Shanghai Wenhuibao published an article entitled "The Direction of Medical Education Revolution from the Growth of Barefoot Doctors." Later that year, *Red Flag* magazine and *People's Daily* reprinted this article. Mao declared in the *People's Daily* on September 14, 1968: "Barefoot doctors are good." After that, "barefoot doctor" became a specific name for rural healthcare workers who were part agricultural and part medical workers.

The rise of barefoot doctors was closely related to the rural cooperative medical system, which was widespread in China at that time. Barefoot doctors were faithful practitioners of the cooperative medical system. The CMS served as a supplier and a collector of insurance funds for the farmers to pay for the minor cost of their healthcare. By 1980, healthcare institutions were established and a large number of healthcare personnel had been trained. Indicators of improvement were the decline in the annual mortality rate from about 17 per 1,000 in 1952 to 6.34 per 1,000 in 1980, and the increase in life expectancy from 40.8 years in the early 1950s to 65.3 years in the late 1970s (Chow, 2006).

Figure 1 on the next page shows the rapid development of the CMS. The proportion of villages covered by the CMS was only 10 percent in 1958; but by the year 1962, 46 percent of villages were covered. Although the CMS' operational system was not properly monitored during the late 1960s, it returned to normal and continued to develop in the 1970s. By 1976, 90 percent of the villages in China were covered by the CMS (Zhou, 1994).

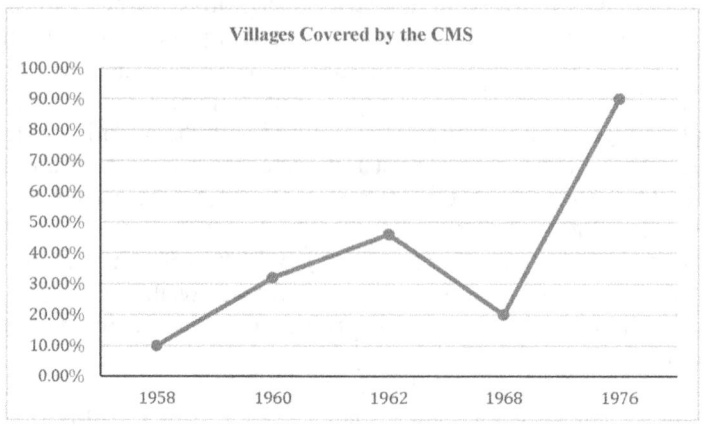

Figure 1. Development of the CMS in China (1958–1976)

Source: Shouqi Zhou, Research of the Chinese CMS development, *Journal of the Chinese Rural Healthcare Administration*, 1994 (9): 7–11.

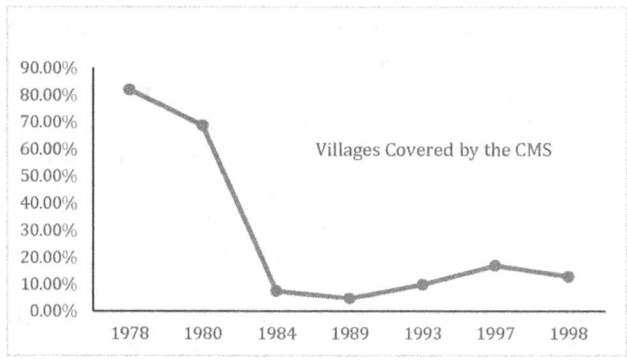

Figure 2. Decline of the CMS in China from 1978 to 1998

Source: Data for 1978–1989 is from *China Statistical Yearbook 1978–1989*; data for 1979 from Zhenjiang Ma (2000), On rural primary healthcare system construction with Chinese characteristics, *Journal of Chinese Health Economics* (9): 51–52

2. RURAL HEALTHCARE POLICY EVOLUTION FROM 1978 TO 2008

China's economic reform transformed its centrally planned healthcare system into a market-driven system. It moved from a system that provided prevention and affordable basic healthcare to all residents, to one in which many people—especially rural residents—cannot afford even basic healthcare. Many families were driven into poverty by medical expenses in this market-driven system. China did not develop a comprehensive health insurance system when it started its economic reform in 1978. As a result, households had to bear a large share of medical expenses once collective farming shifted to private household farming; the disappearance of the commune welfare fund that had supported the CMS led to the collapse of the CMS, which had been the pillar of healthcare security for 900 million rural residents until then. Publicly provided healthcare became the responsibility of local governments. Poor regions, where the financial resources from taxation were not adequate to cover healthcare costs, nonetheless were responsible for providing healthcare.

The facilities and services in rural China deteriorated rapidly. "Barefoot doctors" found it more profitable to work full-time in farming or to set up private practices outside the healthcare system. As a result, 90 percent of all rural residents were left uninsured (Hsiao, 2007), and some 700 million rural Chinese were required to pay out of pocket for virtually all healthcare costs. Although the Chinese government tried to establish a healthcare insurance system to replace the CMS several times, its effect was very limited. The rapid decline of the CMS can be seen in Figure 2.

During the economic transition—marketization, privatization, and de-centralization—the Chinese government experienced a drastic reduction in revenue. The government reduced funding for disease prevention and public health, along with subsidies for public healthcare facilities. Government subsidies made up only 10 percent of such facilities' total revenues by the early 1990s, forcing public healthcare facilities to rely on patients' out-of-pocket payments. Meanwhile, the government established an irrational pricing policy that set service prices below the actual costs, but it allowed profit margins for drugs and new high-tech diagnostic services to offset the losses incurred by public healthcare facilities. In 2002, per capita consumption expenditures of the middle income group among urban households were ¥5452.94, far more than their rural counterparts earned (¥645.04). The ratio of the mean of the net urban income per capita of ¥7730.30 to the rural income per capita of ¥2476 in 2002 was 3.11 (National Statistics Bureau, 2005). As a result, the rural population could afford much less healthcare than the urban population, and this became a serious social problem during the reform process (Dong, 2016).

The SARS outbreak at the end of 2002 and the beginning of 2003 severely affected China's development, economically and otherwise. It was a big shock to both the Chinese government and its general public. President Hu Jintao, Premier Wen Jiabao, and other leaders of the Politburo worked to address the relevant issues. Since reforming the financing and delivery of healthcare were the Chinese government's top priorities, it decided to promote New Rural Co-operative Medical System (NRCMS) initiatives for rural residents with public funds.

Table 1. Government policies on the New Rural Cooperative Medical Scheme

Time	Issuing Government Agency	Policy
2003-01-16	Ministries of Health, Finance, and Agriculture	Notice On The Establishment Of New Rural Cooperative Medical Scheme
2003-03-24	General Office of The Ministry Of Health	Notice On The Pilot Work Of New Rural Cooperative Medical Care Scheme
2003-08-25	Ministry of Finance Ministry of Health	Notice On The Issues Concerning The Central Government's Financial Assistance For The Farmers In The Central And Western Regions To Participate In The New Rural Cooperative Medical Scheme

Time	Issuing Government Agency	Policy
2004-01-13	Ministries of Health, Finance, Agriculture, Education, and Personnel; Development and Reform Commission, Population and Family Planning Commission, Food and Drug Administration, Bureau of Poverty Alleviation	Notice On The Advices For Further Strengthening The Experiment Of The New Rural Cooperative Medical Scheme
2004-06-21	Ministry of Finance Ministry of Health	Notice On The Issues Concerning Improve The Ways Of The Central Government Funds' Transfer For The New Rural Cooperative Medical Scheme
2004-08-09	General Office of The State Council	Notice On The Pilot Work Of The New Rural Cooperative Medical Scheme In The Second Half Of 2004
2004-10-22	Ministry of Finance, Ministry Of Health	Opinions On The Establishment Of New Rural Cooperative Medical Scheme Risk Fund
2005-05-31	General Office of The Ministry Of Health	Notice On Printing And Distributing The Basic Regulations Of The New Rural Cooperative Medical Information System (For Trial)
2005-06-22	General Office of The Ministry of Health	Notice On The Establishment Of The New Rural Cooperative Medical Research Center In The Ministry Of Health
2005-08-10	Ministry of Health, Ministry of Finance	otice On The Trial Of New Rural Cooperative Medical Scheme
2005-09-13	Wu Yi, Vice Premier	Make Great Efforts To Speed Up The Progress And Overcome The Difficulties, Actively Promote The Healthy Development Of The New Rural Cooperative Medical System (Speech By Vice Premier Wu Yi In The Pilot Work Of The New Rural Cooperative Medical System)
2005-09-29	Ministry of Health, National Bureau of Traditional Chinese Medicine	Opinions On Allowing The Traditional Chinese Medicine Playing A Great Role In The Pilot Work Of The New Rural Cooperative Medical Scheme
2005-10-26	China Insurance Regulatory Commission	Some Suggestions On Improving The Pilot Work On Insurance Sector's Participation Of The New Rural Cooperative Medical System
2006-01-10	Ministry of Health, National Development and Reform Commission, Ministry of Civil Affairs, Ministries of Finance and Agriculture, National Food And Drug Administration, National Bureau of Traditional Chinese Medicine	Notice On Accelerating The Pilot Work Of The New Rural Cooperative Medical Scheme
2006-01-25	Ministry of Health Ministry of Finance	Notice On Strengthening The Management Of New Rural Cooperative Medical Care
2006-03-23	General Office of The Ministry Of Health	Notice On Carrying Out The Evaluation Of New Rural Cooperative Medical Scheme Pilot Work
2006-11-22	Ministry of Health	Guiding Opinions On The Construction Of The New Rural Cooperative Medical Care Information System

Time	Issuing Government Agency	Policy
2007-01-31	Ministry of Finance Ministry of Health	Notice On Issues Concerning The Modification Of The Central Government's Fund Transfer Methods For The New Rural Cooperative Medical System
2007-03-02	Ministry of Health Ministry of Finance	Notice On Improving The New Rural Cooperative Medical Service In 2007
2007-09-10	Ministries of Health snd Finance, National Bureau of Traditional Chinese Medicine	Guiding Opinions On Improving The New Rural Cooperative Medical Scheme's Compensation Plan
2008-03-13	Ministry of Health Ministry of Finance	Notice On Provide Better New Rural Cooperative Medical Care Service In 2008
2008-12-04	Ministry of Health	Guiding Opinions On Regulating The New Rural Cooperative Medical Scheme's Secondary Compensations
2009-07-02	Ministries of Health, Civil Affairs, Finance, and Agriculture; National Bureau Of Traditional Chinese Medicine	Opinions On Consolidating And Developing The New Rural Cooperative Medical System
2009-09-29	Ministry of Health	Opinions On Adjusting And Formulating The Reimbursable Drugs' List For The New Rural Cooperative Medical Scheme
2010-04-06	General Office of The Ministry of Health	Notice On Regulating The Usage And The Management Of The New Rural Cooperative Medical Care Funds
2011-04-06	Ministries of Health, Civil Affairs, and Finance	Notice On The New Rural Cooperative Medical Care System's Tasks In 2011
2011-05-25	Ministry of Health Ministry of Finance	Opinions On Further Strengthening The Management Of The New Rural Cooperative Medical Care Fund
2011-12-13	General Office of The Ministry of Health	Notice On Carrying Out The Pilot Work Of An Information Platform Construction For The New Rural Cooperative Medical
2012-04-11	Ministry of Health, China Insurance Regulatory Commission, Ministry of Finance, Office of Health Care System Reform Advisory Group of The State Council	Guiding Opinions On Commercial Insurance Company's Participation In The Operation Of The New Rural Cooperative Medical Schemes
2012-05-15	Ministry of Health, National Development and Reform Commission, Ministry of Finance	Guiding Opinions On Promoting The Reform Of Payment Methods Of The New Rural Cooperative Medical Scheme
2012-09-19	General Office of the Ministry of Health	Notice On Promoting The Construction Of An Information Platform For New Rural Cooperative Medicine
2013-06-17	General Office of National Health and Family Planning Commission	Notice On Printing And Distributing The Technical Blueprint Of The New Rural Cooperative Medical Information Platform Unicom (Trial)
2013-09-05	National Health and Family Planning Commission, Ministry of Finance	Notice Of The New Rural Cooperative Medical Service In 2013
2014-05-04	National Health and Family Planning	2013 NRCMS Progress And Focus Of Work In 2014

Time	Issuing Government Agency	Policy
2014-07-08	General Office of National Health And Family Planning	Notice On Several Key Tasks Of New Rural Co-operative Medical System
2015-01-23	National Health and Family Planning Commission, Ministry of Finance	Notice Of The New Rural Cooperative Medical Service In 2015
2015-02-27	National Health And Family Planning Commission, Ministry Of Finance	Guiding Opinions On The New Rural Cooperative Medical Scheme For Inter-Provincial Medical Expenses' Verification And Reporting
2015-10-26	General Office of National Health and Family Planning	Notice On Comprehensively Promoting The Construction Of Nationwide New Rural Cooperative Medical Information Platform
2015-11-23	Ministry of Finance, Ministry of Human Resources and Social Security, National Health and Family Planning Commission	Notice On Modifying The Measures Of Payment Of The Central Financial Subsidy Funds For Urban Residents' Basic Healthcare Insurance And The New Rural Cooperative Medical Scheme
2016-04-29	National Health and Family Planning Commission, Ministry of Finance	Notice Of The New Rural Cooperative Medical Care Service In 2016
2016-06-08	National Health and Family Planning	Notice On Issuing The Implementation Plan Of National New Rural Cooperative Medical Care Network For Reporting Medical Treatment In Different Places
2016-09-07	General Office of National Health and Family Planning Commission	Notice On Issuing The New Rural Cooperative Medical System For Inter-Provincial Medical Treatment, Networks, Referral And Referral Procedures And Information Exchange Operational Standards (Trial)
2016-09-30	General Office of National Health and Family Planning Commission, General Office of Ministry of Finance	Notice On The Convergence Of National Negotiation Drugs And New Rural Cooperative Medical Scheme's Reimbursement Policy
2017-04-13	Ministry of Finance, National Health and Family Planning Commission	Notice on the Work of New Rural Cooperative Medical System
2018-03-05	Ministry of Finance, National Health and Family Planning Commission, Ministry of Human Resources and Social Security, National Development and Reform Commission, State Administration of Traditional Chinese Medicine Medical Reform Office of the State Council	Notice on Consolidating the Achievements of Eliminating the Practice of Using Drug Mark-up Sells' Profits to Mend Medical Service Income Loss (Yi Yao Bu Yi) and Continuously Deepening the Comprehensive Reform of Public Hospitals

Table 2 shows that the NRCMS premium rate increased rapidly from ¥10 in 2005 to ¥180 in 2017. Although the governments' co-pay had also been increased from ¥20 to ¥450 in the same period, individual rural residents still feel premiums as a growing burden.

Table 2. NRCMS premiums and governments' share (2003–2018) (Unit: Yuan ¥)

Year	Rural Resident	Central Government	Local Government	Total (per year)
2003	10	10	10	30
2005	10	20	20	50
2008	20	40	40	100
2009	20	40	40	100
2010	30	60	60	150
2011	50	200		250
2012	60	240		300
2013	70	280		350
2014	90	320		410
2015	120	380		500
2016	150	420		570
2017	180	450		630
2018	180	490		670

Source: NRCMS Information Platform, http://www.xnh.org.cn; Yang, Shanfa, *Study on the Evolution of the Chinese CMS*, Nanjing University Press, 2012: 198; Chen Xu & Li Xue (2018, December 11), *One of the New Medical Reform series: Anhui broke through in the medical reform and personal health expenditure dropped 10% in the past 10 years*; National Health Commission of the People's Republic of China (2017, April 19), *Policy Interpretation: The National Health and Family Planning Commission and the Ministry of Finance Deploy the New Rural Cooperative Medical System in 2017*.

3. NEW HEALTHCARE POLICY REFORM AFTER 2009

In April 2009, during the global financial crisis, the Chinese government made an important decision to deepen healthcare reform by officially promulgating "Opinions on Deepening the Healthcare System Reform". The hope was to solve social problems such as access to medical care and to promote economic development. The new healthcare reform aimed at providing basic healthcare to all Chinese citizens by the year 2020, focusing on basic healthcare in rural districts and local healthcare reform. However, the new reforms were hard to implement, especially at local government level, since they were closely related to the interests of different sectors, institutions and populations. Thus, seven months after the implementation of "Deepening the Healthcare System Reform", almost all provinces of China were still at the stage of considering and formulating relevant policies.

Table 3 shows how China's healthcare expenditures have increased, especially in per capita terms. The expenditure in 2014 was nearly 6.6 times that in 2001. Complaints that "It is too difficult to get medical care" and "It is too expensive to receive medical care" became a major social issue in China. Since coverage provided by the government programs was quite limited, out-of-pocket expenditures were too great for many patients. Public outcry was nationwide, but rural residents were most affected.

Table 3. Healthcare expenditure in China (2001–2017)

Year	Total healthcare expenditure (hundred million Yuan ¥)	Healthcare expenditure per capita (Yuan ¥)	Healthcare share of GDP (%)
2001	5025.93	393.80	4.56
2002	5790.03	450.75	4.79
2003	6584.10	509.50	4.82
2004	7590.29	583.92	4.72
2005	8659.91	662.30	4.66
2006	9843.34	748.84	4.52
2007	11573.97	875.96	4.32
2008	14535.40	1094.52	4.59
2009	17541.92	1314.26	5.08
2010	19980.39	1490.06	4.89
2011	24345.91	1806.95	5.03
2012	28119.00	2076.67	5.26
2013	31668.95	2327.37	5.39
2014	35312.40	2581.66	5.55
2015	40974.64	2980.80	5.95
2016	46344.88	3351.74	6.23
2017	52598.28	3783.83	6.36

Source: National Bureau of Statistics of the People's Republic of China, http://www.stats.gov.cn/.

Meanwhile, Anhui Province took the lead in launching comprehensive local healthcare reform in its 32 pilot counties. It chose an essential medicine system as its starting point and created a series of comprehensive healthcare reform policies, such as management, personnel, incentives and security system reform. In November 2009, the government of Anhui Province issued "Comprehensive plan of local medical system reform", together with three other affiliated policy documents and five collaborative implementation plans. This series of nine policy documents coordinated and supported one another and formed a comprehensive local healthcare reform policy system. Soon after that, local healthcare system reform was implemented in its 32 pilot counties. The implementation process went smoothly, achieving success and attracting wide attention. In September 2010, the whole province began to implement comprehensive healthcare reform after carefully analyzing the experiences of the 32 pilot counties.

In the course of this process, comprehensive local healthcare reform in Anhui has made significant progress. This was affirmed by then vice premier of the State Council, Li Keqiang, who was responsible for the new healthcare system reform. He stressed that China would make new breakthroughs in improving the national health insurance system, improve the essential drug system, promote the reform of public hospitals, and coordinate the related supporting reforms (Li, 2010). What Anhui Province has done became a significant part of nationwide reforms and has been termed the "Anhui Model".

4. RURAL HEALTHCARE REFORM IN ANHUI

Rural healthcare reform in Anhui has been going on for several years. This section aims to probe into the process of healthcare reform and the effect of new policies in rural Anhui province.

4.1. Social, economic and population features of Anhui Province

Anhui Province is located in the southeast of China, where the economy is primarily based on agriculture. The province makes up 1.45 percent of China's land area. At the end of 2017, the total population was 62,550,000 of which 50.85 percent were rural residents. The GDP per year is ¥2,701.8 billion, and the GDP per capita is ¥43,401. Disposable income per capita of urban residents was ¥31,640 in 2017, while the net income of rural residents was ¥12,758 per capita for the whole year, rising by 8.9 percent compared to the previous year (Anhui Provincial Bureau of Statistics, 2018).

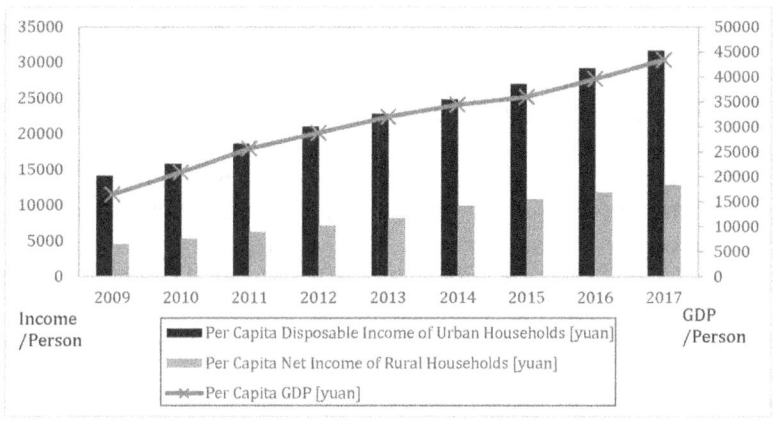

Figure 3. Anhui Provincial GDP and Per Capita GDP (2009–2017)

Source: Anhui Statistical Yearbook, 2010–2018.

From 2001 to 2016, the total expenditure on healthcare (TEH) in Anhui Province increased from ¥11,694 million to ¥164,329 million; the figure per capita rose from ¥190.84 to ¥2,652.17. The proportion of the TEH in GDP increased steadily from 3.60 percent to 6.73 percent (Table 5). On the whole, the TEH increased a little faster than the size of the economy (Tang, 2013).

Table 4. Healthcare expenditure in Anhui (2001–2016)

Year	Total healthcare expenditure (hundred million Yuan ¥)	Healthcare expenditure per capita (Yuan ¥)	Healthcare share of GDP (%)
2001	116.94	190.84	3.60
2002	147.34	239.82	4.19
2003	168.52	273.44	4.30
2004	198.52	318.76	4.12
2005	241.11	394.35	4.51

Year	Total healthcare expenditure (hundred million Yuan ¥)	Healthcare expenditure per capita (Yuan ¥)	Healthcare share of GDP (%)
2006	293.97	481.12	4.81
2007	399.10	652.34	5.42
2008	468.09	762.98	5.29
2009	607.76	991.30	6.04
2010	718.50	1206.14	5.81
2011	891.65	1494.04	5.83
2012	112.02	1857.08	6.46
2013	1221.50	2025.71	6.42
2014	1321.64	2172.67	6.34
2015	1460.42	2376.98	6.64
2016	1643.29	2652.17	6.73

Source: National Health Commission of the People's Republic of China (2018), China Health Statistics Yearbook Publishing House.

5. HEALTHCARE REFORM IN RURAL ANHUI
5.1. Healthcare reform policies in rural Anhui

The recent round of healthcare reforms in Anhui, which began in 2009, includes five parts: healthcare insurance, essential drug policy, the system of primary medical care institutions, equalization of primary public healthcare, and reform of public hospitals. The reform of primary medical care institutions is comprehensive, and includes organization, management, personnel, distribution, medicine, and insurance systems. Specific aspects of the reforms are as follows:

1. Primary healthcare institutions should fulfill a public purpose, mainly providing basic public healthcare and medical care services.
2. All staff members of primary healthcare institutions should compete for their posts.
3. Job performance assessment should be implemented and wages determined by the assessment and position.
4. All primary healthcare institutions only have the right to use national essential drugs and provincial complementary medicines, of which procurement, price-setting and delivery are unified at the provincial level, and all these medicines are sold by the primary care institutions without any profit—the so-called "two-envelope system".
5. Governments will subsidize those institutions participating in healthcare reform for infrastructure construction, personnel expenditures, the cost of delivering basic public healthcare, and the loss of profit due to the essential drug policy.

The Anhui Model can be summed up as follows: through the "two-envelope system", enterprises that offer high quality medical products at a reasonable price can win the provincial bidding. Local financial agencies will compensate those medical institutions for the loss of profit caused by the "zero mark-up" drug policy. The function of medical institutions has been redefined, and a policy of separation between revenues and expenditures implemented; the wage distribution mode shifts from relying on prescriptions to being associated with performance (Dai and Wang, 2011).

Matrix 1. Process of Anhui healthcare reform

2009	Pilot comprehensive reform of primary medical care system in Anhui, including management, personnel, distribution, medicine, insurance and other supporting reform practices.
2010	Comprehensive reform of primary medical care system in full swing
2011	30 complementary healthcare reform policies implemented, including the compensation mechanism, personnel training in primary medical care institutions, insurance system for village doctors, public hospital reform, and measures to safeguard the achievements of the reform.
2012	County public hospitals implement new systems for budget and management. The local hospital visit rate would increase to over 90 percent by 2015, which means patients with serious diseases could be treated in local hospitals without needing to leave their local county for treatment. Healthcare service price reforms in county level public hospitals are required.
2013	The compensation management system for county public hospitals begins. The Anhui NRCMS Reimbursement Scheme was issued, and both the funds raised in the current year and accumulated surpluses are combined in the fund pool, enhancing the range and strength of the medical aid program; guidelines for the NRCMS reimbursement rate for county public hospitals' outpatients and examination fees were issued.
2014	10 reform practices including medical care capacity building in township hospitals, personnel management, information services in county hospitals.
2017	The Provincial Healthcare Insurance Management Committee and its Office in Anhui was established. Anhui Province also required three cities, Hefei, Bengbu and Chuzhou, to undertake the pilot reform.
2018	Anhui Provincial Healthcare Insurance Office, Provincial Human Resources Social Security Department, Provincial Health and Family Planning Commission and Provincial Price Control Department jointly promulgated the "Catalogue of Basic Healthcare Insurance Covered Drugs in Anhui Province" and the "Catalogue of Basic Medical Service Items in Anhui Province".

As new problems emerge during the process of healthcare reform, the Anhui provincial government continues to develop new policies and measures for tackling them (Matrix 1). In 2014, ten main healthcare reforms were launched, which include improvement of service in primary medical care institutions in rural areas, integration of rural healthcare institutions, standardization of outpatient prescriptions in primary healthcare institutions, exploration of ways to make urban primary care institutions the watchdogs of healthcare service, reinforcement of the management of medical staffs, implementation of annual score assessment, reform of clinic professional title evaluation, establishment of "supervising information platforms" for public hospitals at the county level, and creation of medical care service platforms for the public.

5.2. RURAL HEALTHCARE REFORM IMPLEMENTATION

Since September 1, 2010, all public primary healthcare institutions have implemented the "zero mark-up" drug policy. At the end of 2012, about 144 county level public hospitals in Anhui had implemented this policy. According to data provided by the Anhui healthcare reform office, after the implementation of this policy, when the essential drugs were procured at the provincial level, the bid prices of national essential drugs decreased by 53.2 percent on average, compared with the national guided prices. In addition, the drug prices in county public hospitals decreased by 36.6 percent on average. Since 2010, all levels of government have invested a total of 8.8 billion RMB into primary healthcare institutions, with investment increasing at a rate of 32 percent per year. In 2013, the ¥960 million profits the county hospitals lost because of the "zero mark-up" drug policy were offset by subsidies from both the provincial government (25 percent) and the healthcare insurance fund (75 percent).

By 2009, the NRCMS had covered all of the rural areas in Anhui province (Anhui Provincial Bureau of Statistics, 2011), and by the end of 2010, the New CMS actual reimbursement ratio for inpatient care was on average 46 percent. In the province, all of the medical care institutions that provide inpatient care services have been integrated into the New CMS Information System (Lu, 2009). Meanwhile, aid to provide rural medical care for the needy has increased annually. For example, from 2010 to 2017 the aid fund expenditure increased from 6.3 billion to 27.5 billion RMB, which helped around 97.7 million patients (Figure 4).

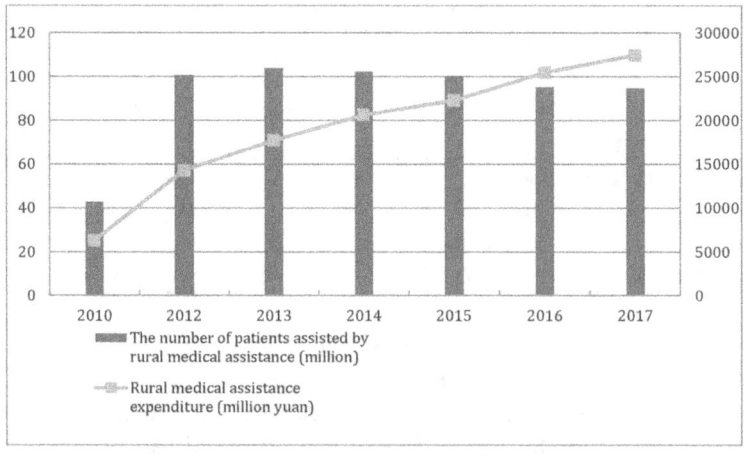

Figure 4. Medical Aid Expenditures in Anhui (2010–2017)

Source: Anhui Statistical Yearbook, 2010–2018.

A 2011 survey shows that about 21,000 healthcare personnel were laid off in Anhui either because of lack of qualifications or due to long absences from their jobs (Wang, 2013). In 2014, data from the 32 pilot counties in Anhui showed that among those who secured their jobs through job market competition, about 75 percent were the original permanent staff members who also accounted for about 61.3 percent of the fired personnel ("Anhui: Urban and Rural Medical Assistance", 2012). Recently, professionals in the primary medical care institutions account for about 87.2 percent of the total number of healthcare workers, which has increased 10 percent since the healthcare reforms began. Today, each village clinic has one medical doctor for 1,000 rural residents (Tian & Shao, 2011).

5.3. CURRENT RURAL MEDICAL CARE SITUATION

Anhui Province's average life expectancy increased from 71.85 years of age in 2000 to 76 in 2015, which was above the national average ("Last Year Per Capita Life Expectancy", 2013). From 2000 to 2015, the provincial infant mortality rate decreased from 28.98 to 4.54 per 1,000 live births, and the mortality rate of children under 5 years of age decreased from 34.43 to 6.85 per 1,000 live births. The mortality rate for pregnant women was 17.26 per 100,000 which was below the national figure of 20.1 per 100,000 (People's Government of Anhui Province, 2015). Prevalence of moderate and severe malnutrition in children under 5 years old in Anhui decreased from 3.1 percent in 2000 to 1.14 percent in 2013 and the breastfeeding rate for infants under 6 months of age decreased from 80.8 percent to 63.7 percent (Anhui Provincial Bureau of Statistics, 2014; The National Health and Family Planning Commission of the People's Republic of China, 2014), which was much higher than the national level of 30 percent (Anhui Provincial Bureau of Health and Family Planning, 2014).

The number of people in the province older than 60 reached 11 million at the end of 2016, accounting for 15.61 percent of the total population of the province (Anhui Provincial Bureau of Statistics, 2017). The population of Anhui Province is aging rapidly, and the problem of aging in rural areas is most serious. According to data provided by the Anhui provincial fifth NHSS 2013, children 0–5 years old accounted for 6.8 percent of the total provincial population, while the elderly (65 years old and above) accounted for 16.2 percent. Both figures were higher than the average urban level (5.6 percent and 14.6 percent). The sex ratio in rural areas was 0.97, which was lower than the 0.98 found in cities, although men numbered fewer than women in both areas. This is consistent with other research findings (Liu, 2013). Meanwhile, the survey also showed that the rural two-week morbidity rate is 21.5 percent, and the two-week chronic disease morbidity rate is 28.5 percent, both lower than the urban rates (24.0 percent and 30.2 percent). The two-week outpatient rate is 8.3 percent, and the two-week rate of those who were sick but did not receive medical care is 15.3 percent, both lower than the urban rates of 10.0 percent and 15.4 percent respectively (Anhui Provincial Bureau of Health and Family Planning & Anhui Medical University, unpublished).

According to the 2011 medical care utilization report for rural Anhui's three-level medical institutions, during the three-year implementation of the reforms, outpatient and inpatient rates increased by 7.62 percent and 4.72 percent respectively. For example, more villagers chose village clinics for medical care: the rate increased from 27.7 percent in 2008 to 36.22 percent in 2011; fewer patients visited township hospitals, and county hospital visits also decreased from 18.46 percent to 17.27 percent. The inpatient rate for township hospitals decreased from 38.37 percent in 2008 to 21.76 percent in 2011, while the proportion of county hospitals increased from 25.82 percent to 33.74 percent (Anhui Provincial Bureau of Health and Family Planning, 2011).

Researchers found that the morbidity rates of circulatory system diseases and malignant tumors were still high (Tan et al., 2009; Niu et al., 2010). Wang and other researchers found that malignant tumors became the most severe threat to the rural population's health and economic status (Wang, 2008). The surveys carried out by Y. Wang and colleagues (2013) show that the Anhui rural population's hypertension morbidity rate was 12.06 percent (lower than the national average figure of 26.6 percent), and that the male morbidity rate (12.39 percent) is higher than that of females (11.71 percent) (Chen et al. 2008; Ma & Li, 2010). The implementation and improvement of NRCMS, on one hand, facilitated healthcare access for the Anhui rural population, especially access to inpatient medical care (Zhu, 2010). On the other hand, the reform has also improved the utilization rate of healthcare service in rural areas (Wang, 2008; Lin & Du, 2008). However, another survey shows that about 54.2 percent of rural residents have no knowledge of the specific nature of healthcare reform in primary medical care institutions, about 84.2 percent of the respondents were satisfied with the healthcare reform, and 79.6 percent of them were satisfied with the new essential drug policy (Zhu, 2011).

A recent study on social determinants of health in rural Anhui sponsored by the Lupina Foundation found elders' wellbeing a crucial issue in rural society. In particular, many of them have medical debt.

Table 5. Debt and household structure in different counties

Household Structure	Have debt (%)				Have medical debt if have debt (%)			
	County 1	County 2	County 3	Total	County 1	County 2	County 3	Total
Elders living alone	7.14	12.86	18.60	27.45	33.33	33.33	43.75	39.29
Elders living with spouse	21.98	22.02	37.85	38.33	26.83	35.71	40.74	35.96
Elders living with grandchildren	31.18	35.82	44.29	37.36	31.03	20.83	26.98	26.72
Elders living with children	37.96	26.67	59.38	37.09	24.69	25.00	22.81	24.23
Three generations living together	30.93	31.44	57.14	34.38	28.89	22.22	25.00	25.60
Young couples living alone	44.44	27.78	40.00	33.01	0.00	0.00	0.00	0.00
Couples living with own children	17.19	26.12	50.45	16.67	9.09	17.65	16.07	15.84
Other	33.33	0.00	20.00	31.71	0.00	0.00	0.00	0.00
Total	27.70	25.34	43.32	27.45	26.16	26.51	30.11	27.94

Source: Dong, Weizhen. "Social Determinants of Health in Rural Anhui". Presentation at the International Sociological Association's Forum, University of Vienna, Vienna, Austria, July 13, 2016.

Table 5 presents the financial status of rural Anhui residents in our study's sample villages in County 1, County 2 and County 3. They represent different financial and physical environments in Anhui; County 3 is the poorest, and County 1 is the wealthiest. While household debt usually includes loans for house construction and for medical care, County 3 had the highest number of households that have all three kinds of debt. While elders' households in County 3 have the highest prevalence of medical care debt, households of elders living with grandchildren, even in County 1, also had high incidences of medical debt (Dong, 2016).

Evidently, old age is the determining factor in predicting medical debt, since only young couples living alone do not have any medical debt. How to develop a healthcare system that can ease the burden of disease for the elderly, particularly those with chronic illness, is an urgent task. Poor—sick—poorer—sicker is a vicious cycle. It is more so in rural areas. Elders, the chronically ill, as well as persons with disabilities are especially vulnerable.

5.4. Debates on Anhui rural healthcare reform

There are two opinions about the impact of the Anhui healthcare reforms. Some people appreciate Anhui's practices, especially the effect of price reduction through bidding procurement. Others believe the reform weakens the effectiveness of primary medical care institutions and affects doctors' work motivation. They also think government financial support is insufficient (Wu, 2010). Some scholars say that because the new system is not yet completed, more time is needed for the reforms to show their positive effects (Wang, 2013). The public and the media expressed doubts about the new essential drug bidding procedure, especially the "two-envelope" system. They believe corruption is likely to occur during the process of drug bidding. Moreover, the essential drugs' reduced costs may not necessary translate into reduced medical care expenditures for patients.

In terms of the adjustment of reform policies, including the complementary essential drug list, some scholars regard them as a reform in reverse gear. Some scholars analyzed the Anhui healthcare reform from the perspective of health economics, and think it is a real reform that reflects the public's interests and provides guidance for other provinces (Zheng et al., 2012). Some senior government officers consider the achievements of Anhui healthcare reform significant, and believe that other regions in the nation should follow suit (Fu & Zheng, 2012).

Xu (2014) claims that the medical care capability in township hospitals has sharply declined, despite significantly increased government financial support. Peng (2013) states that the most important factor in grassroots-level healthcare reform is budget. According to the requirements of the 2001 No. 61 document of the Anhui Provincial Government, both public health spending and basic expenditures of every grassroots-level healthcare institution should be funded annually (and in a timely fashion). Subsidies for public health and the "zero mark-up" drug policy lag considerably behind the timetable, however. Some counties even used public health funds and township hospital revenues to pay for medical personnel. Zhang (2009) also points out that the NRCMS has not yet been affected by delayed payments because it has a surplus fund that accumulated yearly; however, this will directly result in delaying the adjustment with the NRCMS payment system. In the long term, if the government cannot subsidize funding fully and in a timely fashion, the sustainability of the system will be affected.

Studies found rural Anhui residents' relatively lower overall education attainment is affecting their health status (Mursal and Dong, 2018); and that the education level of the township hospitals' healthcare providers is not satisfactory, since only 20 percent of them have received training from a college or university (Chen et al., 2010). Zhang and colleagues (2014) point out that fewer qualified medical doctors want to work in grassroots-level healthcare institutions. At the same time, medical school graduates do not want to start their career in rural areas. Some of them choose to work in township hospitals because they guarantee better salaries.

6. DISCUSSION AND POLICY DEVELOPMENT

Some provinces began healthcare reform with an essential drug policy or a "zero mark-up" drug policy, but Anhui implemented comprehensive reforms. These reforms in Anhui were unprecedented, and they changed the healthcare management system, especially the personnel management system in township hospitals. Anhui's provincial and local governments made great efforts in enacting the reforms.

Anhui Province played a role as a pioneer in the new healthcare reform and as one of the first pilot provinces, developing a reform model known as the "Anhui model". Reforms have now entered a critical stage, since a great number of issues have emerged. There are still many tough issues that need to be tackled. For example, a shortage of healthcare professionals in primary healthcare institutions and inadequate government funding affect the sustainability of the healthcare system as well as reform of the system. The service capacity of primary medical care institutions is limited due to the shortage of professionals, making it difficult for patients to get timely and effective treatment, which in turn is causing problems in the doctor-patient relationship.

As a large country with a high proportion of its citizens residing in rural areas, China needs to emphasize local governance of its healthcare system reform. Relevant institutions and mechanisms must be carefully designed and formulated. More importantly, local governance in rural healthcare reform should focus on strategies that can be adapted in different circumstances, and create innovative local capabilities among managers. Similar suggestions were made by Cheung (2009), encouraging different regions to design their own regulations and plans while having the nation's healthcare system reform blueprint in mind. Based on different local experiences, a sound rural healthcare system reform plan could then be chosen and recommended to other regions.

Premier Li Keqiang said in his 2017 work report: "We will ensure the full protection of the rights and interests of women, children, and people with disabilities, and strengthen support and services provided to the children, women, and elderly who remain in rural areas while their family members work away in the cities." He also promised more financial support to rural community healthcare services. Specifically, he stressed that the government "will advance the coordinated reform of medical services, healthcare insurance, and the pharmaceutical industry. Health is at the root of happiness. This year, we aim to realize full coverage of the severe disease insurance scheme, and government funding for the scheme will be increased to reduce the financial burdens of those who suffering from severe diseases". And the central government "will allocate ¥16 billion to be used in both rural and urban areas for healthcare assistance and subsidies, an increase of 9.6 percent over last year. We will merge the basic healthcare insurance systems for rural and non-working urban residents, and increase government subsidies for the scheme from ¥380 to ¥420 per capita per year. We will reform the ways for making healthcare insurance payouts and expedite the building of a nationwide network for basic healthcare insurance so that medical expenses can be settled where they are incurred via basic healthcare insurance accounts" (Li, 2017).

Li then further stated that "we will see that more cities participate in piloting comprehensive public hospital reform; move forward in a coordinated way with medical service pricing reform and reform in medicine distribution; and deepen the reform of the evaluation and approval systems for medicines and medical equipment. We will move faster to train general practitioners and pediatricians". This will help to ease the human resources shortage in healthcare, and improve the conditions for medical service. The government will also "carry out trials for tiered medical services in around 70 percent of prefecture-level cities, increase basic annual per capita government subsidies for public health services from ¥40 to ¥45, and see that more medical resources are channeled toward the community level in urban areas and toward rural areas. We will encourage the development of privately run hospitals". Finally, Li said that the government "will promote the development of traditional Chinese medicine and the medical traditions of ethnic minorities. We will establish human resources and wage systems suited to the medical sector to motivate medical practitioners and protect their enthusiasm" (Li, 2017).

Premier Li's policy directives provide hope that both rural residents' health status and their access to healthcare will be improved significantly in the future.

On October 11, 2017, the government of Anhui Province issued the "Announcement on the Establishment of Provincial Healthcare Insurance Management Committee and its Office". The announcement said that in order to smooth the healthcare insurance management system, unify the administrative functions of basic healthcare insurance, coordinate and guide the healthcare insurance work of the whole province, and promote the "three medical linkages", Anhui Province had decided to set up the Provincial Healthcare Insurance Management Committee and its Office, which were responsible for coordinating the healthcare insurance policy and organizing the implementation of the reform of the healthcare insurance management system. The executive deputy governor of the provincial government was concurrently appointed as the director of the Healthcare Insurance Committee. The deputy governor of the provincial government in charge of the medical and health fields was concurrently appointed as the first deputy director. The deputy secretary-general of the provincial government related to the medical and health fields, the governor of the provincial Health and Family Planning Commission and the governor of the provincial Human Resources and Social Security Department were concurrently appointed as the other deputy directors. The Healthcare Insurance Office was to be responsible for the daily work of the Provincial Healthcare Insurance Commission, which would be established in the provincial government office and maintain a relatively independent operation.

Anhui Province also required three cities, Hefei, Bengbu and Chuzhou, to undertake the pilot healthcare insurance reform. Specifically, the pilot cities should establish municipal medical reform commissions, start the integration of the urban residents' healthcare insurance and the new rural cooperative medical scheme, unify the management functions of the basic healthcare insurance for urban and rural residents, gradually unify other relevant healthcare insurance management functions, and thus achieve the "three insurances in one" objective in the healthcare insurance system. Drawing on the experience of Sanming City in Fujian Province and combining it with the local features, the pilot cities were encouraged and supported to centralize the medical and healthcare management and to transfer relevant management functions from the various departments to the Municipal Healthcare Reform Office. These include the management functions of urban workers' basic healthcare insurance and urban and rural residents' maternity insurance in the Human Resources and Social Security Department, the management functions of the centralized procurement and distribution of medicines and devices in the Health and Family Planning Department, the management functions of urban and rural medical assistance in the Civil Affairs Department, and the management functions of the medical service and the drug prices in the Price Control Department.

In September 2018, Anhui Provincial Healthcare Insurance Office, Provincial Human Resources Social Security Department, Provincial Health and Family Planning Commission and Provincial Price Control Department jointly promulgated the "Catalogue of Basic Healthcare Insurance Drugs in Anhui Province" and the "Catalogue of Basic Medical Service Items in Anhui Province". The new versions of the drug catalogue and the medical service catalogue were officially implemented on January 1, 2019. The scope of application covers workers' healthcare insurance, urban and rural residents' healthcare insurance, work-related injury insurance, maternity insurance and so on. The new version of the medical service catalogue contains 4,666 medical service items. The new version of the drug catalogue contains 2,885 reimbursable drugs, of which 1,588 were added to the medication offerings for rural insured residents, an increase of 122.5 percent, and 48 were added to the medication offerings for urban insured residents, an increase of 1.7 percent. The leader of the Anhui Provincial Healthcare Insurance Department stated that the differences in the drug and medical service catalogues among workers' healthcare insurance, urban residents' healthcare insurance, and the new rural cooperative medical scheme resulted in inequality in healthcare insurance coverage. The "three-in-one" of the healthcare insurance catalogue was conducive to a more equitable healthcare insurance, and was also a key step in the reform of "three insurances in one" in Anhui Province.

On January 1, 2019, Anhui Province started to implement the new versions of the healthcare insurance catalogues, which also marked the implementation of a unified catalogue of drugs and medical services for employees, urban residents and new rural cooperative medical scheme in the province. After the implementation of the new catalogue, the benefits of insured patients were further expanded.

7. CONCLUSION

Healthcare policies for rural China have undergone several waves of reforms since the 1950s. The health of the rural population has been a great concern of the Chinese government since the early days of the socialist regime. In fact, early on China achieved its most impressive accomplishments in healthcare in its rural areas. Mao's "Prevention First" policy and the campaign for the eradication of infectious diseases improved rural residents' health status, while "barefoot doctors" provided necessary primary care in rural villages, increasing villagers' life expectancy. The sharp decline of mortality rates testified to the success of the government's "Prevention First" policy.

The impact of economic reforms on the rural healthcare system was enormous. Although there were differences between regions, Anhui Province's experience was representative of a general picture. In the early years of the economic reforms, rural village and township enterprises emerged to employ surplus rural labour. Once rural-urban migration gained momentum, rural economic development slowed down. Income disparities between rural and urban regions continued to widen, and rural poverty became a social issue.

Government attention to rural health will make a big difference. The development of the New Rural Cooperative Medical Scheme has slightly eased the financial burden for some villagers who were trapped in the sick—poor—sicker—poorer vicious circle, since it covers part of the medical care cost for the patients. The gradual increase in funding and coverage and negotiated lower drug prices are expected to make the scheme more effective. The recent integration of urban and rural health care systems is a positive development. It is particularly beneficial to rural-urban migrants.

New measures need to be put in place to provide rural residents with better healthcare access, including more affordable care and higher quality care. Attention needs to be paid to primary care providers, financing of hospitals and healthcare centers, and village clinics, as well as drug prices. Rural elders' wellbeing also requires special attention. Care for elders by their families is no longer a given, once able-bodied rural residents migrate to the cities to seek opportunities. Innovative strategies to safeguard the wellbeing of the high percentage of rural elders living apart from their children are much needed. Overall, healthcare reform in rural China in recent decades has not been markedly successful.

REFERENCES

Anhui Provincial Bureau of Health and Family Planning (2011). *Health service utilization report of rural three-level medical institutions in Anhui province in 2011.*

Anhui Provincial Bureau of Health and Family Planning (2014). *Work summary in 2013 and plan for 2014 of maternal and child health, community health, health education in Anhui province.*

Anhui Provincial Bureau of Health and Family Planning & Anhui Medical University (n.d.). *The fifth health services survey in Anhui province* (Working paper, Anhui Medical University).

Anhui Provincial Bureau of Statistics (2011, February 10). The new rural cooperative medical work made new achievements in Anhui. *Official Website of Anhui Provincial Bureau of Statistics.* http://www.ahyg.gov.cn/showNews.asp?classifyID=0&newsID=1851.

Anhui Provincial Bureau of Statistics (2014, August 14). *Child development status report in Anhui province in 2013.*

Anhui Provincial Bureau of Statistics (2015). Anhui elders over ten million, 54 to every one hundred working age persons. http://www.renkou.org.cn/china/anhui/2015/2767.html.

Chen, B., & Ai, L. (2010). Construction and improvement of the new rural cooperative medical insurance system: A case study of Anhui. *Journal of Anhui Radio and TV University* (1): 5–8.

Chen, C. M., et al. (2008). The role of dietary factors in chronic disease control in china. *Obesity Reviews* 9(1): 100–103.

Cheung, S. N. S. (2009). Record of climbing up during many disasters: Financial crisis and China's future. *Beijing: China Critic Press,* 359.

Chen, X, & Li, X. (2018) *One of the New Medical Reform series: Anhui broke through in the medical reform and personal health expenditure dropped 10% in the past 10 years.* https://www.sohu.com/a/281031827_100189947.

China News Network. (2016, July 11). Ministry of Civil Affairs: In 2015, 66.347 million people were supported to participate in basic medical insurance. http://news.cctv.com/2016/07/11/ARTIvbBiyQV0h3h2lBrLZ6H8160711.shtml.

Chow, G. (2006, August). *An economic analysis of healthcare in China.* Princeton University, CEPS Working Paper No. 132.

Dai, L., & Wang, C. (2011, December 27). The most thorough health reform sample: Anhui model is difficult to continue. *Caijing.* http://news.qq.com/a/20111227/000436.htm.

Dong, W. (2016). Social determinants of health in rural Anhui. Presentation at the International Sociological Association's Forum, University of Vienna, Vienna, Austria, July 13, 2016.

Feng, M. (2012, June 18). Anhui: Urban and rural medical assistance benefit the needy. *Chinaacc.* http://www.chinaacc.com/new/184_900_201206/18zh522741688.shtml.

Fu, Y., & Zheng, J. (2012, March 6). Zhu Chen: The achievements of health care reform in Anhui province is recognized as worthy of national promotion. *Ifeng.* http://news.ifeng.com/gundong/detail_2012_03/06/13000297_0.shtml.

Hsiao, W.C. (2007). The political economy of Chinese health reform. *Health Economics, Policy and Law, 2007* (2): 241–249.

Last year per capita life expectancy of Anhui is over 75 years old, above the national average (2013, October 21). http://news.ifeng.com/gundong/detail_2013_10/21/30512614_0.shtml.

Li, J., & Cui D. (2015, May 21). Ministry of Civil Affairs: 102 million people spent 25.4 billion on medical aid in 2014. http://society.people.com.cn/n/2015/0521/c1008-27035325.html.

Li, K. (2010). Ensuring the basics, strengthening the locals and constructing the mechanisms are the focus of health reform. *Public Administration Reform, 2010* (9): 4–10.

Lin, B., & Du, Y. (2008). Progress in application of disease burden study in accessibility assessment of health services. *Chinese General Practice,* 11(15): 1375–1377.

Liu, J. (2013). *Research on structural changes of rural population and related policy in Anhui Province* (Doctoral dissertation). Anhui Agricultural University, Hefei, Anhui Province.

Lu, X. (2009, April 21). Anhui Provincial Bureau of Health and Family Planning interpretation of the effectiveness of health care reform in Anhui. *Xinmin.* http://news.xinmin.cn/rollnews/2009/04/21/1851006.html.

Ma, W., & Li, J. (2010). Status survey of prevalence and risk factors of hypertension. *Internal Medicine of China,* 5(2): 173–176.

Ministry of Civil Affairs of China. (2014, September 29). An analysis report on the operation of medical aid in China in 2013. http://cva.mca.gov.cn/article/yw/shjz/llyj/201409/201409007075699.shtml.

Ministry of Civil Affairs of China (2017). In 2016, 87.204 million medical aid cases were implemented nationwide. http://www.xinhuanet.com/politics/2017-02/21/c_129488174.htm.

Mursal, A. and Dong, W. (2018). Education as a key determinant of health: A case study from rural Anhui, China. *J Health Soc Sci.* 3(1): 59-74.

National Statistics Bureau (2005). *2004 China Statistical Yearbook.* China Statistics Press.

National Health Commission of the People's Republic of China. (2017, April 19) Policy Interpretation: The National Health and Family Planning Commission and the Ministry of Finance deploy the New Rural Cooperative Medical System in 2017. http://www.moh.gov.cn/zwgk/jdjd/201704/b2c9d5b058f84cf2ae079bbac13c7cb2.shtml.

National Statistical Office. http://www.stats.gov.cn/.

National Health Commission of the People's Republic of China. (2018). China Health Statistics Yearbook Publishing House.

Niu, T., et al. (2010). The study on the status of the utilization of the health services of the Shandong Province rural elders and its influencing factors. *Chinese Primary Health Care* 24(5): 7–8.

Peng, J. (2013). Problems and suggestions for Anhui health care reform in rural area. *The Chinese Health Service Management* 30(12): 884–885.

People's Government of Anhui Province (2011). *Child development outline in Anhui province (2011-2020).* Wan Zheng, No. 113.

Tan, L., et al. (2009). Cross-sectional survey of health status of urban and rural residents in Sichuan. *Modern Preventive Medicine,* 36(22): 4252–4256.

Tang, F. (2013). *The research on financing and resource allocation of the total health expenditure in Anhui Province* (Doctoral dissertation). Anhui Medical University, Hefei, Anhui Province.

The National Health and Family Planning Commission of the People's Republic of China. (2014, February 26). *The statistical bulletin of health and family planning career development in China in 2013.*

Tian, H., & Shao, B. (2011, July 28). "One down two liters" is beneficial to the people, and rural integration management in Yi Xian promotes the equalization of public health. *Official website of Government of Huangshan.* http://www.huangshan.gov.cn/News/NewsDetails.Aspx?ArticleId=37348.

Wang, G. (2008). *Research on economic burden of disease of rural residents in Henan Province* (Doctoral dissertation). Huazhong University of Science and Technology, Wuhan, Hubei Province.

Wang, H. (2013, December 27). Anhui province started a new round of counterpart support for urban and rural hospitals. *Anhui News.* http://ah.anhuinews.com/system/2013/12/27/006247206.shtml.

Wang, W. (2008). *A comparative study on the health services utilization before and after enforcing the new-type rural cooperative medical system* (Doctoral dissertation). Zhejiang University, Hangzhou, Zhejiang Province.

Wang, Y., et al. (2013). Investigation of epidemic characters of hypertensive disease of rural residents in Anhui province. *Journal of Bengbu Medical College,* 38(3): 321–323.

Wu, Y. (2010, February 1). "One-stop service" in Huaibei city, Anhui province has simplified examination and approval procedures for medical treatment. *ChinaNews.* Retrieved from http://www.chinanews.com/jk/jk-zcdt/news/2010/02-01/2102810.shtml.

Xu, J. (2014). Opinions on health care reform in rural Anhui. *Chinese Rural Health Service Administration,* 34(2): 121–123.

Yue, X., & Tang, J. (2012, June 18). Elderly people over 60 has nearly ten million in our province. *Anhui News.* http://ah.anhuinews.com/qmt/system/2010/12/28/003613436.shtml.

Zhang, L. (2009). *Empirical research on improving financing and payment system of the new cooperative medical scheme* (Doctoral dissertation). Fudan University, Shanghai, China.

Zhang, Z., & Zhao, J. (2014). Situation, problems and suggestions of village doctors in Anhui Province. *Journal of Anqing Teachers College (Natural Science Edition)* (1): 78–82.

Zheng, A., Ju, Z., & Wang, X. (2012). Interpretation of Anhui "new medical reform" from the perspective of health economics. *China Medical Engineering,* 20(11): 181–182.

Zhou, S. (1994). Research of the Chinese CMS development. *Journal of the Chinese Rural Healthcare Administration* (9): 7–11.

Zhu, J. (2010). *The influence of new rural cooperative medical system to health use and benefit distribution of different groups* (Doctoral dissertation). Shandong University, Jinan, Shandong Province.

Zhu, M. (2011). Research on rural residents' satisfaction of local health system reform in Anhui Province (Master's thesis). Anhui Medical University, Hefei, Anhui Province.

Chapter 12
Healthcare Policy and Reforms in Hong Kong

Alex Jingwei He

ABSTRACT
Hong Kong, a special administrative region of the People's Republic of China, is one of the healthiest places in the world, in terms of major population health indicators. Behind the outstanding achievements is a well-built health system that ensures equal access and high quality of care. The dominance of public financing and highly subsidized inpatient care in the public sector are the key features of Hong Kong's healthcare system. This system is, however, not immune from global healthcare policy challenges, especially the consequences of an aging population and rapid escalation of costs. This chapter presents a survey of healthcare policy in Hong Kong and analyzes the challenges as well as new reform initiatives. As an aging post-industrial society, Hong Kong offers an excellent example of the daunting challenges to healthcare policies and potential remedies.

1. INTRODUCTION

Hong Kong, a former British colony, has been a special administrative region (SAR) of the People's Republic of China since the transfer of sovereignty in 1997. Known as one of the so-called "Asian tigers", this small territory (1,104 square kilometers or 426 square miles) experienced extraordinary economic growth from the 1960s to the 1990s with the relocation of labor-intensive industries from the West to East Asia. Between 1961 and 1997, Hong Kong's GDP grew 180 times while GDP per capita increased almost 90 times (Yeung, 2008). Despite a slowdown in economic growth in recent years, it is still one of the most affluent economies in the world. With a per capita GDP of US$61,540 in 2017, Hong Kong ranks in the top ten wealthiest economies of the world (World Bank, 2018).

Healthcare policy in Hong Kong has undergone significant transformation since the end of colonial rule. Having produced outstanding performance, the system is widely commended for equal access and high quality of care. This chapter presents an overview of Hong Kong's healthcare policy and its recent reforms. It will first introduce the historical background and evolution of healthcare policy in Hong Kong. The governance framework in which the healthcare system is embedded will also be outlined. The body of this chapter will examine the arrangements and key features of Hong Kong's healthcare service provision and financing, as well as critical policy challenges and reform initiatives.

2. POLICY BACKGROUND

Though part of China, Hong Kong enjoys a high degree of autonomy in all aspects except defense and foreign affairs, under the principle of "One Country, Two Systems." The principle of "big market, small government" and the spirit of the rule of law created a low-taxation, investment-friendly and free-trade environment that is conducive to economic prosperity (Cheung, 2000). Hong Kong's capitalist economy has remained unchanged since the handover. It ranks as the third most important international financial center, after London and New York City (Long Finance, 2014).

Hong Kong's population was 7.39 million at the end of 2017, predominantly Chinese. It is one of the most densely populated regions in the world. Thanks to its high living standard and well-functioning healthcare system, the health of Hong Kong's population is among the world's best across most indicators, outperforming many other affluent Asian peers (Table 1). The healthcare system underpinning these enviable achievements is a typical tax-funded and public-dominated one, resembling the model of the old colonial master. The current system, however, did not take shape until the 1960s when the British colonial administration began to pay serious attention to demands from the grassroots (R. Gauld, 1998).

Table 1. Key population health and health financing indicators of selected economies, 2014

	Life expectancy at birth (total) 2013	Infant mortality rate (per 1,000 live births) 2013	Total expenditure on healthcare as share of GDP 2014
Singapore	82.64	1.8	4.9%
Hong Kong	83.74	1.7	5.7%
South Korea	81.43	3.0	7.4%
Taiwan	79.26	3.9	6.2%
Japan	83.31	2.1	10.2%
US	78.88	6.0	17.1%
UK	80.45	3.8	9.1%
Germany	80.66	3.3	11.3%

Source: Health expenditure data from Global Health Expenditure Database, the World Health Organization. Infant mortality rate data from OECD Statistics. Life expectancy data from United Nations Department of Economics and Social Affairs, *World Population Prospects*, 2015 Revision.

In the early decades of colonial rule, limited provision of health services funded by the government was almost exclusively reserved to the British whereas the local population had to mainly rely on traditional Chinese medicine (TCM) practitioners. The vast unmet demand for inpatient services was later mitigated by charitable organizations, e.g., the Tung Wah Hospital. The period from the 1930s to the 1960s saw increased government involvement in healthcare, but it remained inadequate, largely owing to the government's *laissez faire* attitude. Efforts were mainly devoted to providing primary care and quarantine services to combat epidemics and high mortality rates (Chu, 1994).

The year 1964 marked a new chapter in Hong Kong's healthcare policy. The colonial administration published its first White Paper on health titled *De-*

velopment of Medical Services in Hong Kong, which for the first time officially declared that "the policy of government is to provide, directly or indirectly, low cost or free medical and personal health services to that large section of the community which is unable to seek medical attention from other sources" (cited in D. Gauld, 2006). The critically pressing issue then was to increase the supply of hospital beds to tackle mounting needs for curative care. (The historical background to this issue was the influx of mainland refugees in the 1960s, striving to escape famine and political struggles. Loose immigration control at that time led to a drastic increase in Hong Kong's population.) The new healthcare policy responded with a commitment to increase the physical capacity of hospitals and clinics (R. Gauld, 2004).

Rapid economic growth and improved living standards in the 1960s and 1970s accelerated the epidemiological shift from infectious diseases to non-infectious degenerative ones such as cancers and cardiovascular diseases. This prompted the government to review the appropriateness of its strategic emphasis on primary care and take significant measures to provide more hospital-centered curative services (Ramesh, 2004). The goal of a substantially increased number of hospital beds and improved inpatient facilities was largely met with the help of funding generated by a booming economy. While the public healthcare system expanded remarkably in scale, the financial burden placed on patients did not increase proportionately as the government still played a key role in financing. A tax-financed public healthcare system providing low-cost inpatient care without means-testing, similar to the National Health Service in the UK, took shape and remains largely unchanged to this day (Liu and Yue, 1998).

3. GOVERNANCE STRUCTURE

The constitutional structure of the Hong Kong SAR is characterized by the domination of the executive branch. The Chief Executive, head of the SAR government, is assisted by three principal secretaries, each supervising several bureaus (equivalent to ministries) that formulate public policies. This structure is further extended to policy implementation; each policy bureau oversees a number of executive departments whose main duties are policy execution and law enforcement. After several rounds of administrative restructuring and changes of name, the Food and Health Bureau has since 2007 been the central body formulating health policies and overseeing their implementation. Figure 1 on the next page depicts the structure of Hong Kong's healthcare system. Subordinate to the Bureau are the Department of Health, the Food and Environmental Hygiene Department, the Agriculture, Fisheries and Conservation Department and the Government Laboratory.

There is a clear line of division between the health bureau and the health department in Hong Kong with the latter answerable to the former. The Department of Health has a wide range of functions including health promotion and disease control, and, more importantly, it also directly participates in service delivery by providing subsidized healthcare services through its centers and clinics. In the aftermath of the SARS (severe acute respiratory syndrome) epidemic, the government launched the Center for Health Protection by consolidating public health functions—especially those related to disease surveil-

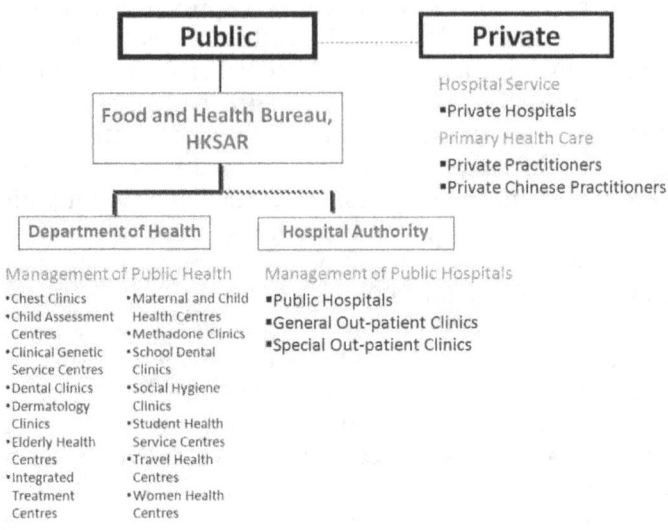

Figure 1. The Structure of the Healthcare System in Hong Kong

Source: Hong Kong SAR Government, retrieved from http://www.gov.hk/en/residents/health/hosp/overview.htm.

lance, management of public health crises and epidemiology—in the newly established Center. Preventive services such as immunizations for children and influenza vaccinations for the elderly are provided free of charge at government-run general outpatient clinics and maternal and child care centers.

What makes Hong Kong's healthcare system unique in the region is that public hospitals as the main provider of secondary and tertiary services are managed by neither the Bureau nor the Department, but a corporatized organization called the Hospital Authority (HA), in keeping with the government's vision of modernizing public healthcare governance (Cheung, 2002).

While public facilities dominate the provision of health services, there is also a substantial presence of private providers. It must be stressed that while public hospitals as a whole dominate the inpatient sector (90 percent of hospital inpatient days), the bulk of outpatient consultations (70 percent) are actually provided by private clinics (Food and Health Bureau, 2008). The private health sector in general enjoys a high degree of autonomy and the government does not intervene unless laws or professional regulations are violated.

4. HEALTH SERVICE PROVISION

The salient feature of Hong Kong's healthcare delivery system is the large number of independent providers, each working in its own market niche (R. Gauld, 2004). There are about 15,000 registered medical practitioners in Hong Kong—the majority are graduates of two local medical schools, the La Ka Shing Faculty of Medicine of the University of Hong Kong and the Faculty of Medicine of the Chinese University of Hong Kong—with roughly half of all practitioners working in the private sector. The medical doctor to population ratio was 1:519 as of 2017 (Department of Health, 2018).

The concept of the family doctor remains largely unaccepted by ordinary Hong Kong people who generally prefer to shop around in the private market for episodic care instead of developing ongoing relationships with doctors (Leung and Bacon-Shone, 2006). Most private outpatient clinics are located in residential areas and cater to the basic needs of the neighborhood. More established doctors, particularly specialists, locate their clinics in commercial areas as their patient base is not necessarily defined by geographic boundaries. Constrained by tight space and high housing prices, private clinics are usually equipped with only basic diagnostic equipment; if more sophisticated clinical tests and technologies are required, patients will be referred to specialized centers nearby which serve multiple clinics.

Fees and charges for general outpatient visits at private clinics typically range from HK$150 to HK$500 exclusive of drug costs, much higher than fees charged by their public counterparts. The payment system in the private sector, including private hospitals, is generally based on fee-for-service. Fee schedules are set by individual practitioners and are not subject to government regulation or guidance (Wong et al., 2010). Residents who consult private practitioners do so mainly for convenience given the crowding of public outpatient clinics. With the increased popularity of "contract medicine" and staff medical benefit schemes (corporate group insurance) in Hong Kong, enrollees in the schemes have become an important source of patients for private outpatient clinics. The public system looks after those who cannot afford private care. The government runs 73 public general outpatient clinics providing subsidized medical services.

The overarching principle of Hong Kong's public healthcare system is that "no one should be prevented, through lack of means, from obtaining adequate medical treatment". Providing highly subsidized services in public hospitals and clinics ensures that no citizen is left out. Hong Kong citizens (including non-permanent work visa and student visa holders) are all defined as eligible persons entitled to the low level of fees and charges set out in Table 2.

Table 2. Fees and charges for healthcare services in Hong Kong's public hospitals and clinics

Service	Fees
Accident and emergency	$180 per visit
In-patient (general acute beds)	$75 admission fee, plus $120 per day
Specialist out-patient	$135 for the first visit, $80 per subsequent visit, $15 per drug item
General out-patient	$50 per visit

Currency: Hong Kong Dollar (1 HK$ = US$0.13 as of January 2019).
Source: Hong Kong Hospital Authority, available at http://www.ha.org.hk/visitor/ha_visitor_index.asp?Parent_ID=10044&Content_ID=10045&Ver=HTML.

In the current fee structure, a general outpatient consultation costs merely HK$50 (1 US$ = 7.85 HK$, 2019) per attendance and the fee for a specialist consultation is HK$135 for the first visit, with a HK$15 per item drug charge. Inpatient care is remarkably cheap with a HK$120 per diem charge. Exemption and wavier mechanisms are available for selected groups of disadvantaged citizens.

The distinguishing feature of Hong Kong's healthcare governance system is the corporatization of its public hospitals. Until early 1990s, the public system had been very centralized; even unimportant financial and operational decisions were made at the Bureau level. This was later identified as the major source of inefficiency and operational inflexibility. The outcome of external review and internal deliberation was to decentralize power from the government bureaucracy to a highly autonomous non-profit corporation called the Hospital Authority (Yip and Hsiao, 2003). The HA is a statutory organization directly accountable to the Food and Health Bureau. After this reform, while individual hospitals continue to receive the bulk of their funding (up to 95 percent on average) from the government, they have become more autonomous in their daily operations, overseen by the HA. Despite the greater managerial autonomy granted to hospitals, the government made clear that privatization was by no means its intention and the commitment to ensure universal access would not change.

The public medical network is organized along seven geographic clusters under the HA's mandate. The clustering was designed to enhance coordination in resource allocation and service delivery. At present, this system has 42 public hospitals and institutions, 48 specialist outpatient clinics and 73 general outpatient clinics, employing 64,000 health workers and providing 27,000 beds. Of public hospitals, 15 are major acute-care hospitals delivering specialized and multi-specialty acute and extended tertiary care. Public hospitals receive over 90 percent of their incomes from government funding via the HA, which thus possesses very strong financial leverage to insist on compliance by public hospitals. There are 11 private hospitals in Hong Kong that serve a much smaller share of the market, catering mainly to the upper and middle segments of society as well as affluent medical tourists from mainland China and elsewhere. They account for around 10 percent of inpatient bed-days (Ramesh, 2004). Recent years have seen government efforts to encourage more utilization of private hospital services.

Public hospitals in Hong Kong are recognized for outstanding levels of performance. Overall patient satisfaction is very high, notwithstanding some growing discontent (He, 2018). The Chinese University of Hong Kong conducted a patient satisfaction survey in 2010, which interviewed about 5,000 patients by telephone. The vast majority of respondents (80 percent) rated the overall care received in public hospitals "excellent/very good" and "good". Patients also rated the performance of public hospital staff very highly. For instance, 87 percent and 88 percent expressed that they "always" had confidence and trust in doctors and nurses respectively. About 88 percent of respondents said that they were always treated with respect and dignity while in hospital (Wong et al., 2012).

Similar to the situation in other Chinese societies, Hong Kong people predominantly choose western allopathic medicine when seeking care (Leung et al., 2005). Yet, traditional Chinese medicine (TCM) continues to play a crucial role in the community. A survey result has shown that approximately 42 percent of Hong Kong residents use TCM as a second or alternative option (WHO and Health Department, 2012). The majority of TCM practitioners in Hong Kong run private practices in their own clinics or Chinese pharmacies. The entire TCM sector had been unregulated, but a strong regulatory framework has been put in place since 1999 (R. Gauld, 2004). In response to rising demands, the government has been making more effort to establish more public TCM clinics and better integrate this sector into the healthcare system as a whole.

5. HEALTH FINANCING

Healthcare in Hong Kong is financed from both public and private sources, each accounting for approximately half of total funding (Figure 2). Total health expenditure rose from HK$69.1 billion in the 2000/01 financial year to HK$157.2 billion in 2016/17, currently accounting for 6.2 percent of GDP

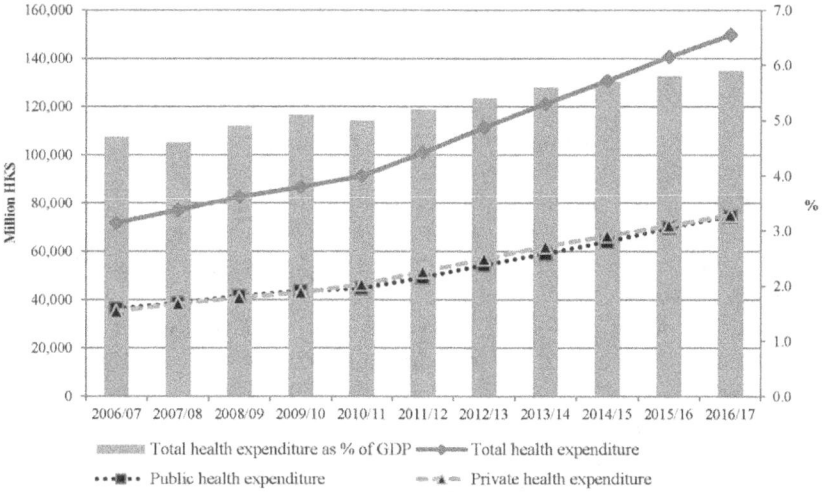

Figure 2. Sources of Health Financing and Total Health Expenditure as Share of GDP, Hong Kong, 2006/07–2016/17

Note: Total healthcare expenditure is calculated in current market prices.
Source: Hong Kong domestic health accounts,
retrieved from https://www.fhb.gov.hk/statistics/download/dha/en/table2_1617.pdf

(Department of Health, 2018). Thanks to the effective cost containment mechanisms, this is still considerably lower than the level seen in other advanced economies. The majority of public funding (more than 95 percent) comes from government tax and non-tax revenues with the rest mainly recovered from frees and charges paid by patients at the point-of-care (Leung et al., 2005). Out-of-pocket payments by households form about 36 percent of total health expenditure. A smaller private contribution to healthcare financing comes from employer-provided group medical benefits and private insurance, accounting for 7.5 percent and 6.4 percent of total healthcare expenditure respectively (Tin et al., 2012).

Health spending made up 14 percent of the total government recurring budget in the 2018/19 financial year (Legislative Council Secretariat 2018). Government healthcare expenditures consist mainly of spending on public and subvented hospitals (about 75 percent of current public expenditures), which provide heavily subsidized services without means testing. Public expenditures are primarily targeted at in-patient care (around 50 percent) with substantially less spent on outpatient care (about 25 percent) (Tin et al., 2012). Private funding constitutes around one-third of total healthcare spending and predominantly derives from out-of-pocket payments incurred at private facilities and nominal fees paid to public facilities. In particular, private payment is the main source of funding for outpatient services as well as pharmaceuticals (Ramesh, 2004).

Social health insurance is the most popular financing method in the developed world, especially in Europe and East Asia (e.g., Japan, South Korea and Taiwan). Its advantage mainly lies in universal risk pooling and equity. Recent decades have seen mainland China and Taiwan moving towards social health insurance. However, owing to historical legacies and political constraints, social health insurance does not exist in Hong Kong (Ramesh, 2012).

6. POLICY CHALLENGES AND REFORMS

Policy challenges confronting Hong Kong's healthcare system mainly arise on two fronts: long-term financial viability and the enormous stress on the public system. The government has taken actions to tackle these challenges. It requires a longer time horizon to see the effects of those actions and thoroughly evaluate them.

First, rapid demographic change and the epidemiological transition to chronic diseases have created tremendous pressure on the tax-based financing regime. As of 2016, 17 percent of Hong Kong citizens were aged 65 or above (Census and Statistics Department, 2017). Rapid aging has been exacerbated by low fertility. The total fertility rate even fell below one baby per woman between 1999 and 2006. The government's projections indicate that the percentage of the elderly will reach 30 percent of the population by the 2030s (Census and Statistics Department, 2017). The effect of an aging population on healthcare spending is significant. According to projections, total health expenditure will double by 2030 and further increase to HK$315 billion in 2033. Its percentage of GDP will climb to more than 9 percent (see Table 3).

The most alarming note is that public health expenditure as a percentage of total government spending would shoot up to almost 30 percent if this trend continues. Note that this prediction is based on the assumption that government revenue grows proportionately. This high and ever-growing fiscal demand is undoubtedly beyond what the Hong Kong government can afford, even leaving aside the "crowding-out effect" of such high health expenditures on education, housing, social security and many other essential social services.

Table 3. Projection of Hong Kong's health expenditure and its share of GDP and government budget

	2015	2020	2025	2030	2033
Total health expenditure	137.2	174.7	219.8	275.9	315.2
Public health expenditure	77.7	100.1	127.5	161.9	186.6
Total health expenditure as share of GDP	6.5%	7.1%	7.8%	8.7%	9.2%
Public health expenditure as share of total government budget	18.3%	20.3%	22.6%	25.4%	27.3%

Note: In constant 2005 prices, HK$ billion.
Source: Projection of Hong Kong's healthcare expenditure, available at http://www.fhb.gov.hk/beStrong/files/consultation/projecthealthexp_eng.pdf.

The SAR Government is certainly not blind to these daunting challenges. Reform efforts to diversify sources of healthcare financing started as early as the colonial period. Several rounds of public consultations proposing medical savings accounts (the Singapore model) or compulsory social health insurance all failed because of tremendous public opposition. It was apparently impossible to enforce compulsory payment on citizens used to highly subsidized care. This attitude was compounded by Hong Kong's liberal society and anti-government sentiments since the handover. Ramesh (2012) suggests that the existence of a liberal legal, economic and political system in a non-democratic context has made the government unable to resist even moderate opposition and make hard but meaningful policy changes. In the end, the government had to abandon any reform proposal that would require a compulsory individual contribution. The final policy proposal announced was the launch of a voluntary private plan, the Voluntary Health Insurance Scheme (VHIS). However, any voluntary insurance plans face the fatal risk of adverse selection and are likely to become unviable in the end. Although the government initially designed a few mechanisms to mitigate the likely negative effects, major concessions were made later due to resistance from the insurance industry (Yin and He 2018). Key commercial insurers are expected to launch their VHIS products between 2019 and 2020.

The public healthcare provision system has also been confronting critical challenges. Low taxes and highly subsidized services give rise to the so-called "buffet syndrome," which was evidenced by Leung et al.'s (2005) finding that the Hong Kong population was over-reliant on public healthcare services. In consequence, public hospitals and outpatient clinics are often overburdened. In the outpatient sector, long wait times as a result of overutilization have been the primary headache plaguing the system. In Hong Kong's public hospitals, access to specialists is only through referral from primary care doctors or other specialists (Wong et al., 2010). Patients still face considerable difficulties in seeing specialists in spite of the gatekeeping mechanisms. Table 4 on the next page sets out the waiting time for first-time appointments with public hospital specialists. It suggests that the overall situation has worsened over time.

Past studies have revealed that long waiting times are a major reason behind patients' non-attendance and their resultant dissatisfaction with the public medical system (Leung et al., 2003; Chan and Beitez, 2006). Hence, wait times are perceived by patients as an important barrier to care, especially by those who are neither rich enough to seek specialist care in private facilities nor covered by staff medical benefits which would allow them to access alternative care in the private sector. Long appointment queues reflect the bottleneck of public hospital efficiency on the one hand, and the weaknesses of the referral system on the other. Janice Johnston (2006) points out that, unfortunately, there are few incentives to improve clinical efficiency or address those aspects of the referral system that are barriers to effective access to care. Similar challenges also face the inpatient sector. Since the inception of the HA, there has been a significant increase in public sector hospitalizations. The total number of inpatient admissions in HA hospitals increased by 130 percent from 1992/93 to 2010/11 (WHO and Department of Health, 2012).

Table 4. Waiting time for first appointment for new specialist outpatient cases in public hospitals (Unit: week)

Specialty	2012/13		2013/14		2014/15	
	Median	99th percentile	Median	99th percentile	Median	99th percentile
Ear, Nose and Throat	18	43	24	59	31	63
Medicine	34	68	39	75	47	83
Gynaecology	17	70	19	76	21	70
Ophthalmology	32	73	40	69	51	66
Paediatrics	15	35	14	31	13	25
Psychiatry	16	70	20	88	22	87
Surgery	30	110	30	99	32	78

Source: Hospital Authority, Cross-cluster Referral as a Measure for Waiting Time Management of Specialist Outpatient Clinics in the Hospital Authority, HAB-P228, September 24, 2015.

In view of the challenges, some have proposed to reform the supply side by enhancing the capacity of the public system by establishing new hospitals, for instance. Unfortunately, this remedy would require a considerable amount of time to show any effect. Others have called for private hospitals to have a stronger presence in Hong Kong, creating pressure for public hospitals to improve performance on the one hand, while absorbing a large number of patients from the overloaded public system on the other. The fact that two new private hospitals are under construction clearly reflects the government's long-term plans for promoting public-private-partnerships (PPP), a key policy orientation arising from the recent public consultations on healthcare reform (Food and Health Bureau, 2008, 2011).

Inspired by the idea of PPP, the SAR Government has launched a series of reforms to alleviate the vast stress on the city's public hospital system. Since the Donald Tsang administration, the government has been experimenting with new initiatives on both the demand side and the supply side. On the supply side, the Hospital Authority has identified several areas in which the private sector can draw off some portion of the heavy outpatient load from the crowded public system. Private practitioners are invited to join the programs and render services. The government heavily subsidizes private providers to maintain the same level of fees that patients pay in the public sector. Patients join the programs on a voluntary basis and enjoy more choices when seeking care. This is intended to mitigate the burden on the overloaded public system by encouraging the utilization of private services.

While most supply-side interventions remain at the pilot stage, demand-side reforms have been scaled up. Hong Kong has been experiencing rapid population aging, with those over age 65 numbering more than one million. This has created enormous pressure on the city's healthcare system. Aggravating the situation is that a large number of the elderly in Hong Kong live below or only slightly above the poverty line, leaving them no choice but to stay within the public healthcare system (Wong et al., 2010). As the flagship PPP program on the demand side, the Elderly Healthcare Voucher Scheme was launched in the 2008–2009 financial year. Distributing cash vouchers to senior citizens 70 years of age or older without means-testing, the Scheme intends to encourage the utilization of private primary care. In the first phase of the pilot, each senior citizen received five vouchers per year totaling HK$250. In 2012, the government doubled the benefit to HK$500 while the next year saw a further increase to HK$1,000. In the Chief Executive's 2014 policy address, the annual allowance was further doubled to HK$2,000 in 2015, and more importantly, the healthcare voucher has become a regular program with the completion of the pilot.

Although well intended, the healthcare voucher scheme seems to have yielded mixed results at best. While the original policy intention was to encourage the elderly to better utilize preventative services instead of curative services, the healthcare-seeking behaviors of the majority have not been changed, with merely 6.5 percent of elders interviewed in a survey using the voucher for preventive care (Yam et al., 2011). Most low-income elderly, who are the heavy users of public healthcare services, have not switched and are unlikely to switch to private services without seeing a significant reduction in prices or an increase in the value of vouchers. As Liu et al. (2013) argue, financial incentives for consumers alone may not be sufficient to promote the use of primary care in the private sector. This suggests that vouchers alone are unable to realize the government's policy of greater use of private primary services (Yam et al., 2011).

7. SUMMARY AND POLICY IMPLICATIONS

This chapter has presented a survey of healthcare policy and reforms in the Hong Kong Special Administrative Region. Clearly, Hong Kong's healthcare system has been performing to a high standard and has provided the population with good services while maintaining equal access to care. However, as a result of longevity, occurrence of chronic diseases and multiple causes of morbidity, the healthcare demands of the older population are growing very quickly. In the meantime, the escalation of costs and reliance on tax-financing are raising serious concerns about affordability. These dual challenges are, of course, not unique to Hong Kong. Policy reforms, however, have been constrained by various factors. The policy decisions made in the end reflect the compromise between reform imperatives and Hong Kong's peculiar sociopolitical environment.

Moving forward, healthcare reforms need to tackle more fundamental aspects of the system. First, the optimal public-private mix must be sought in both financing and provision. The introduction of new private financing mechanisms in Hong Kong is destined to be a formidable task and must be accompanied by skillful political management. While the private sector will play a bigger role in service delivery, essential monitoring and accountability should not be absent. Second, the strengthening of the healthcare system in Hong Kong should be mainly focused on community-based primary care, especially prevention. This is particularly critical in light of rapid population aging. Incentives on both the supply side and the demand side should be aligned to encourage the utilization and adequate provision of preventive services.

REFERENCES

Chan, I. and Beitez, M. A. (2006). Changing patient expectations. In G. M. Leung and J. Bacon-Shone (Eds.), *Hong Kong's Health System: Reflection, Perspectives and Visions* (pp. 81–93). Hong Kong: Hong Kong University Press.

Census and Statistics Department, Hong Kong SAR Government (2017). *Hong Kong Population Projections: 2017–2066*. Available at https://www.statistics.gov.hk/pub/B1120015072017XXXXB0100.pdf.

Cheung, A. B. L. (2000). New interventionism in the making: Interpreting state interventions in Hong Kong after the change of sovereignty. *Journal of Contemporary China* 9(24): 291–308.

Cheung, A. B. L. (2002). Modernizing public healthcare governance in Hong Kong: A case study of professional power in the New Public Management. *Public Management Review* 4(3): 343–365.

Chu, D. K. W. (1994). Economic development and the healthcare system in Hong Kong. *Health Policy* 28: 211–234.

Department of Health, Hong Kong SAR Government (2018). Health Facts of Hong Kong. Available at https://www.dh.gov.hk/english/statistics/statistics_hs/files/Health_Statistics_pamphlet_E.pdf.

Food and Health Bureau, Hong Kong SAR Government (2008). *Your Health, Your Life: Report on First Stage Public Consultation on Healthcare Reform*. Available at http://www.fhb.gov.hk/beStrong/files/consultation/HCR_Report_eng.pdf.

Food and Health Bureau, Hong Kong SAR Government (2011). *My Health, My Choice: Healthcare Reform Second Stage Public Consultation Report*. Available at http://www.myhealthmychoice.gov.hk/pdf/report/full_report_eng.pdf.

Gauld, R. (1998). A survey of the Hong Kong health sector: Past, present and future. *Social Science and Medicine* 47(7): 927–939.

Gauld, R. (2004). Hong Kong. In R. Gauld (Ed.), *Comparative Health Policy in the Asia-Pacific* (pp. 174–199). Maidenhead: Open University Press.

Gauld, D. (2006). A historical review: The colonial legacy. In G. M. Leung and J. Bacon-Shone (Eds.), *Hong Kong's Health System: Reflection, Perspectives and Visions* (pp. 17–26). Hong Kong: Hong Kong University Press.

He, J. A. (2018). Public satisfaction with the health system and popular support for state involvement in an East Asian welfare regime: Health policy legitimacy of Hong Kong. *Social Policy and Administration* 52(3): 750–770.

Hong Kong SAR Government. Hong Kong: The Facts (Population). Available at http://www.gov.hk/en/about/abouthk/factsheets/docs/population.pdf).

Hong Kong SAR Government. Projection on population change. Available at http://gia.info.gov.hk/general/201207/31/P201207310344_0344_98116.pdf.

Johnston, J. (2006). Operations management in the public sector. In G. M. Leung and J. Bacon-Shone (Eds.), *Hong Kong's Health System: Reflection, Perspectives and Visions* (pp. 187–198). Hong Kong: Hong Kong University Press.

Leung, G. M. et al. (2003). Waiting time, doctor-shopping and non-attendance at specialist out-patient clinics: Case control study of 6,495 individuals in Hong Kong. *Medical Care* 41: 1293–1300.

Leung, G. M., et al. (2005). The ecology of healthcare in Hong Kong. *Social Science and Medicine* 61: 577–590.

Leung, G. M. and Bacon-Shone, L. (2006). Organizational, management and quality of care issues. In G. M. Leung and J. Bacon-Shone (Eds.), *Hong Kong's Health System: Reflection, Perspectives and Visions* (pp. 137–186). Hong Kong: Hong Kong University Press.

Legislative Council, Hong Kong SAR Government (2013). Replies to initial written questions raised by Finance Committee Members in examining the Estimates of Expenditure 2014–15. Available at http://www.legco.gov.hk/yr13-14/english/fc/fc/w_q/fhb-h-e.pdf.

Legislative Council Secretariat. *2018/19 Budget, Research Brief.* Available at https://www.legco.gov.hk/research-publications/english/1718rb02-the-2018-2019-budget-20180412-e.pdf.

Liu, E. and Yue, S. Y. (1998, January 22). *Health Care Expenditure and Financing in Hong Kong.* Provisional Legislative Council Secretariat.

Long Finance (2014). *The Global Financial Centres Index 15* Available at http://www.longfinance.net/images/GFCI15_15March2014.pdf.

Su, L. et al. (2012). Willingness to pay for private primary care services in Hong Kong: Are elderly ready to move from the public sector? *Health Policy and Planning* 28: 717–729.

Ramesh, M. (2004). *Social Policy in East and Southeast Asia.* London and New York: Routledge.

Ramesh, M. (2012). Healthcare reform in Hong Kong: The politics of liberal non-democracy. *Pacific Review* 25(4): 455–471.

Tin, K. Y. K. (2012). Hong Kong domestic health spending: Financial years 1989/90 to 2008/09. *Hong Kong Medical Journal* 18(4), supplement: 2–24.

Wong, E. L. Y., et al. (2012). Patient experiences with public hospital care: First benchmark survey in Hong Kong. *Hong Kong Medical Journal* 18(5): 371–380.

Wong, S. Y., et al. (2010). Comparison of primary care experiences among adults in general outpatient clinics and private general practice clinics in Hong Kong. *BMC Public Health* 10(397): 1–11.

WHO and Department of Health, Hong Kong (2012). *Hong Kong (China) Health Service Delivery Profile.*

World Bank (2018). *World Development Indicators.* Retrieved from http://data.worldbank.org/indicator/NY.GDP.PCAP.CD.

Yam, C. H. K., et al. (2011). Can vouchers make a difference to the use of private primary care services by older people?: Experiences from the healthcare reform programme in Hong Kong. *BMC Health Services Research* 11(255): 1–10.

Yeung, R. (2008). *Moving Millions: The Commercial Success and Political Controversies of Hong Kong's Railways*. Hong Kong: Hong Kong University Press.

Yip, W. C. and Hsiao, W. C. (2003). Autonomizing a hospital system: Corporate control by central authorities in Hong Kong. In A. S. Preker and A. Harding (Eds.), *Innovations in Health Service Delivery: The Corporatization of Public Hospitals* (pp. 391–421). Washington, DC: World Bank.

Yin, J.D.C. and He, J. A. (2018). Health insurance reforms in Singapore and Hong Kong: How the two aging Asian tigers respond to health financing challenges. *Health Policy* 122(7): 693-697.

About the Contributors

Chun Chen is an Associate Professor of the School of Public Health and Management at the Wenzhou Medical University. She received her PhD degree in management sciences from the School of Public Health, Fudan University. She was a visiting scholar at Old Dominion University in Norfolk, Virginia, during 2013–2014 and 2017–2018. Dr. Chen specializes in health policy and healthcare reforms, with particular focus on China. Her works have appeared in leading international journals, including *Social Science & Medicine*, *PLOS One*, and *Frontiers of Medicine*.

Weizhen Dong is a Professor of Sociology at the University of Waterloo. She received her PhD degree from the University of Toronto. Her main research interest is social policy, particularly those affecting vulnerable populations' wellbeing such as healthcare, pension, migration, and employment policies. Dr. Dong has published books and papers through different outlets, including the journals *Social Science & Medicine*, *Journal of Applied Social Science*, *BMC Public Health*, *Epidemiology and Community Health*, and *International Journal for Equity in Health*.

Alex Jingwei He is Associate Head and Associate Professor of the Department of Asian and Policy Studies, The Education University of Hong Kong. He received his PhD degree from the Lee Kuan Yew School of Public Policy, National University of Singapore. Dr. He specializes in health policy and social policy reforms, with particular focus on East Asia. He has published extensively in leading international journals, including *Social Science and Medicine*, *The China Quarterly*, *Health Policy and Planning*, *Social Policy and Administration*, *Health Policy*, and *Ageing and Society*. He co-edits the *Journal of Asian Public Policy*.

Qicheng Jiang is a Professor of Health Economics, Dean of the School of Public Health and Director of the Center for Health Policy Research at Anhui Medical University. He received his PhD degree from Anhui Medical University, and specializes in health economics, rural medical insurance system, and public health policy and management. Dr. Jiang is the Deputy Director of the Chinese Preventive Medicine Association, Standing Committee Member of the Institute of Health Management, Chinese Preventive Medicine Association, Standing Committee Member of China Healthcare Service Administration Association, Vice President of Anhui Provincial Rural Health Association, and the Executive Associate Editor-in-Chief for the *Journal of Rural Health Management in China*.

Xin Le is an Assistant Professor at the School of Marxism of Fudan University. Her main research includes social policy and aging issues, such as consumption by the elderly, human resource development of the elderly, and aging-related policies. She received her master's degree from the University of Oslo, and her PhD degree in economics from Fudan University, as well as carrying out postdoctoral research in public management there. Dr. Le has published papers in various journals including *Fudan Journal (Social Sciences Edition)*, *Exploration and Free Views*, *Population Journal* and *Population and Development*.

Xiaowen Lu is a Professor of Sociology and Associate Director of the Institute of Sociology at the Shanghai Academy of Social Sciences. His research interests include social and urban development. He has carried out large-scale research projects and published numerous scholarly works including books and journal papers.

Baozhen Luo is an Associate Professor of Sociology at Western Washington University. She obtained her PhD degree in Sociology from Georgia State University (2009). Her current research examines political economy and social policies related to population aging from a global perspective, with a special focus on China and the US. In addition to publishing scholarly articles, Dr. Luo also takes on the role of being a public intellectual. She currently hosts a column called "Four Dimension Channel" discussing aging policies at www.thepaper.cn based in Shanghai. She has also written for *Foreign Affairs* and served as a commentator for Chinese Central Television.

Zehan Pan is an Assistant Professor of the Institute for Population Research at Fudan University, China. He received his PhD degree in Population, Resources and Environmental Economics from Fudan University in 2015. As a postdoctoral fellow, he worked at the Prentice Institute for Global Population and Economy of the University of Lethbridge from 2015 to 2017. In 2018, Dr. Pan was named "Chen Guang Scholar" by the Shanghai Municipal Education Commission and Shanghai Education Development Foundation. Dr. Pan specializes in migration and regional development. His works have appeared in leading journals of the field, including *Population, Space and Place*, *Cities*, *Chinese Journal of Population Science*, and *Population Research*.

Xiaochun Qiao is a Professor of the Institute of Population Research at Peking University in Beijing. He is also the executive editor-in-chief of the *Journal of Population and Development*, Vice President of the China Population Association, the pioneer member of the International Network of Health Expectancy and Disability Process, and a board member of International Commission of Historical Demography. He received his PhD in Demography at Renmin University of China, and did his post-doctoral research at the Carolina Population Center of the University of North Carolina at Chapel Hill. He was an overseas fellow at the Institute of Developing Economy, Japan External Trade Organization, Japan, and visiting professor in the Department of Sociology at the University of Waterloo in Waterloo, Canada. Dr. Qiao has also served as a council member of the IPPF for Asia and Oceania, and as an advisor to UNFPA and a consultant for China's Sixth Population Census. His research interests focus on population policy, aging, health expectancy, population censuses, population projection, and quantitative methods for social sciences. He has published over 100 articles and more than 10 books in both English and Chinese.

About the Contributors

Lichun Qin is an Associate Professor at the Shanghai Academy of Educational Sciences. She received her PhD degree in Economics from the Shanghai Academy of Social Sciences. Dr. Qin specializes in educational economics and educational policy. Her works have appeared in leading Chinese journals, including *Fudan Education Forum*, *Research in Educational Development*, and *Shanghai Research on Education*.

Li Shen is an Assistant Professor at the Business School, University of Shanghai for Science and Technology. She received her PhD in Economics from Fudan University. She was a visiting scholar at Syracuse University in the United States in 2011 and at the University of Alberta in Canada in 2014. Her research interests mainly focus on health economics and management, entrepreneurship and innovation management. She has published more than 20 research papers in China and internationally, translated two books, and has worked on numerous research projects.

Lidan Wang is an Associate Professor of the School of Health Management at the Anhui Medical University, China. She received her PhD degree in Epidemiology and Health Statistics from the School of Public Health, the Anhui Medical University. She worked at the Queensland University of Technology and at Macquarie University as a visiting fellow in 2013 and 2018 respectively. Dr. Wang specializes in health policy evaluation, with particular reference to rural areas of East Asia. Her works have appeared in leading international journals, including *Health Service Research*, *International Journal for Equity in Health* and *PLOS One*.

Zhennan Wang is an adjunct faculty member at the Whitman School of Management, Syracuse University. She received her PhD in international business from the Schulich School of Business, York University, Toronto, Canada. She has published research articles in the *Journal of International Business Studies*, *Academy of Management Best Paper Proceedings*, and the *Administrative Sciences Association of Canada Best Paper Proceedings*.

Shanfa Yang is a Professor in the Department of Healthcare Management at Anhui Medical University, China. He received his PhD degree in politics from the School of Public Management, Nanjing University of China. Dr. Yang specializes in health policy and politics and social policy reforms, with particular reference to Chinese health policy reform. His works have appeared in leading Chinese journals, including *China Health Economics* and *China Health Administration*. Dr. Yang also serves as the Associate Director of the *Journal of Chinese Rural Health Administration*.

Xin Yang is an Associate Professor of the Institute of Urban and Population Development of the Shanghai Academy of Social Sciences. She holds a PhD in economics. Dr. Yang's research areas include demography, migration, and the social integration of migrants. In the year 2015, she visited the Comparative Program on Health and Society, Munk School of Global Affairs, University of Toronto, as a Visiting Lupina Fellow. Her works have appeared in various outlets.

Heying Jenny Zhan is an Associate Professor at Georgia State University. She received her PhD in sociology at the University of Kansas in 2000. She has been actively involved in long-term care research in China and in research about Chinese and Asian Americans in the United States over the last two decades. She was a Fulbright Research Fellow, twice conducting research in China on long-term care. She was also the key researcher to operationalize the research on recent developments in institutional long-term care in China, funded by an NIA-Fogarty International Research Grant. She teaches sociology and gerontology courses at both the graduate and undergraduate level, dealing with issues of aging, long-term care, and comparative social policies.

Changxing Zhao is an Associate Professor at Xidian University, China. He obtained his PhD in Rural Sociology from the Northwest Agricultural and Forestry University. He was a Visiting Fellow at the Munk School of Global Affairs of the University of Toronto in 2015–2016. Dr. Zhao's research interests include urbanization, social policy and migrants' integration.